Let's Talk About Money

Let's Talk About Money

Low-Conflict Conversations for Couples

Terry Gaspard

BLOOMSBURY ACADEMIC
NEW YORK • LONDON • OXFORD • NEW DELHI • SYDNEY

Bloomsbury Publishing Inc, 1359 Broadway, New York, NY 10018, USA
Bloomsbury Publishing Plc, 50 Bedford Square, London, WC1B 3DP, UK
Bloomsbury Publishing Ireland, 29 Earlsfort Terrace, Dublin 2, D02 AY28, Ireland

BLOOMSBURY, BLOOMSBURY ACADEMIC and the Diana logo are trademarks of Bloomsbury Publishing Plc

First published in the United States of America 2026

Copyright © Terry Gaspard, 2026

Cover image: © iStock.com/pay404
Cover design by Jen Huppert

All rights reserved. No part of this publication may be: i) reproduced or transmitted in any form, electronic or mechanical, including photocopying, recording or by means of any information storage or retrieval system without prior permission in writing from the publishers; or ii) used or reproduced in any way for the training, development or operation of artificial intelligence (AI) technologies, including generative AI technologies. The rights holders expressly reserve this publication from the text and data mining exception as per Article 4(3) of the Digital Single Market Directive (EU) 2019/790.

Bloomsbury Publishing Inc does not have any control over, or responsibility for, any third-party websites referred to or in this book. All internet addresses given in this book were correct at the time of going to press. The author and publisher regret any inconvenience caused if addresses have changed or sites have ceased to exist, but can accept no responsibility for any such changes.

A catalog record for this book is available from the Library of Congress

ISBN: PB: 979-8-8818-0230-1
ePDF: 979-8-8818-6588-7
eBook: 979-8-8818-0231-8

Typeset by Deanta Global Publishing Services, Chennai, India
Printed and bound in the United States of America

For product safety related questions contact productsafety@bloomsbury.com.

To find out more about our authors and books visit www.bloomsbury.com and sign up for our newsletters.

Contents

Author's Note vii

Introduction: Talking About Finances: A Tricky Topic Made Easier for Couples 1

Part I Establishing a Foundation for an "Us Against the Problem" Mindset About Finances 9

1 Understand Your Money History and Discover Your Financial Style 11

2 Have Low-Conflict Conversations About Money and Enhance Intimacy 37

3 Money Management Systems: Joint Versus Separate Accounts 59

Part II Essentials of Financial Health 75

4 Build a Budget 77

5 Get Rid of Bad Debt 95

6 Develop a Savings Plan 111

Part III Troubleshooting the Challenges of Money, Marriage, and Committed Relationships 129

7 Prenuptial and Postnuptial Agreements: The Pros and Cons 131

8 Estate Planning: Providing Safeguards for the Future 151

9 Financial Infidelity: How Keeping Secrets Can Put Your Relationship at Risk 171

10 Remarriage Finances: How to Adopt an "Us Against the Problem" Mindset 187

11 Manage Conflict About Money and Get Back on Track After a Dispute 205

Acknowledgments 223
Notes 224
Bibliography 238
Index 242
About the Author 251

Author's Note

When I decided to write this book, I supplemented my clinical and personal experience by interviewing dozens of individuals and couples whom I approached through my practice and referrals from colleagues. Over a few years, I interviewed one hundred individuals who were either married or in committed romantic relationships. On some occasions, I was able to interview couples who filled out my survey together. The average age was forty-eight, and they reflected a diverse range of ethnicities and backgrounds. The average length of relationships for participants in my study was twenty-two years. The one thing they all had in common was they were all in long-term committed relationships. In order to write a chapter about remarriage and finances, I interviewed thirty remarried individuals. The average age of the remarried people that I interviewed was fifty-two, and the average length of marriage was ten years. They also reflected a diverse range of ethnicities and backgrounds. My total sample consisted of one hundred individuals, and twenty-eight couples interviewed were included in this book.

The couples quoted in the following pages were participants in my study, and the stories told here are profiles and composites based on real people. However, names and identifying information have been changed to protect their privacy. For the participants' protection, details about the locations of the interviews were also altered in some cases. Any likeness to any real person, living or dead, is purely coincidental or unintended.

I also interviewed many financial experts and lawyers who were generous with their time and provided me with rich details about topics such as budgeting, paying off debt, saving money, estate planning, prenuptial agreements, and other money matters. They all signed interview release forms and gave me permission to use their statements in the chapters of this book.

Please note that this book is not intended to replace individual or couples therapy.

Introduction

Talking About Finances: A Tricky Topic Made Easier for Couples

As a couples therapist, I'm constantly reminded that financial issues can take a toll on relationships and that partners often don't have the tools to have low-conflict conversations about money. Long before they realize they're living beyond their means, couples tend to battle about abusing credit cards, conflicting priorities, and different philosophies about spending, saving, retirement planning, and investing their money. When couples argue over money, they tend to blame each other and anger and resentment build.

Talking about money can be tricky—even in long-term relationships or marriages. It can make people feel tense and defensive, so oftentimes partners avoid it. Money is a taboo topic in many households, and often we internalize financial lessons from our families that can make financial conversations fraught. I certainly did.

Since my mother was born during the Depression era, she brought me up with a scarcity mindset, a pattern of thinking focused on not having enough. For instance, when she took her four daughters out for a meal at a coffee shop or diner, we weren't allowed to order beverages and had to share entrees. She drilled into me that spending more than you absolutely need to on food is wasteful and selfish. As a result, I usually order the least costly item on the menu and drink water when I dine in restaurants. Another belief I inherited from my parents is that it's not okay to talk about money.

These beliefs caused problems early in my marriage to my husband, Craig. Because of my scarcity mindset, I was overly cautious about spending money. Sometimes Craig felt I was treating him like a child because I monitored his spending too closely. And while I felt comfortable talking to Craig about most details of my personal life, money wasn't one of them. Since I worried we wouldn't have enough, my anxiety would go sky-high when the topic of our finances came up.

It became clear early on that Craig and I hold different attitudes and beliefs about money that shaped our polar opposite financial styles, or how we approach handling money. Financial style refers to your attitude about money and informs both spending and saving habits. For instance, if you're a saver, you'd be more interested in depositing a check received as a gift in the bank rather than spending it. On the other hand, a spender would have the gift spent before they had a chance to cash it. While I am a saver who feels most secure when our bank balance is high, Craig's a spender who believes we should be able to enjoy an abundant lifestyle of travel, donating to charity, and purchasing nonessential items that bring him pleasure, such as a high-priced bicycle. The scarcity mindset is based on a sense of deficiency and feeling like you need to protect your resources. On the other hand, an abundance mindset is about opportunity and seeing that money is flowing in life, and there's enough to go around for everyone.

Craig's abundance mentality often clashed with my scarcity mindset so badly that it was a frequent cause of stress and disagreements during the first decade of our marriage. Our spender-saver dynamic also created tension because we used to assume the worst of each other and make accusations. When we were first married, I would scan his credit card statements for proof of overspending, and he'd minimize the amounts he spent so he could avoid my disapproval.

At the time, I assumed Craig and I couldn't learn to compromise and that we'd have to settle for perpetual tension about money matters. Unfortunately, these assumptions led to miscommunication, arguments, and eventually silence. For many years, both of us avoided money talks, fearful of a fight.

Avoiding regular discussions about money hurt our relationship as much as our bank accounts. It set the stage for upset feelings and resentment, and we never took the time to develop a budget or map out a financial vision for our future. We also delayed planning for retirement and making investments. It wasn't until we met with professionals who helped us gain insight into the source of our conflicts and how to have transparent, constructive money talks that we were able to work together to achieve our financial goals—and have a happier, more trusting partnership overall. Once we were able to have productive conversations about money, we were able to combine our assets, create joint bank accounts, and make a budget and savings plan to prepare us for the future. Being able to have easier conversations about finances lowered my anxiety about money and allowed us to travel to some of the places on our bucket list without going into debt or setting us back financially.

Unfortunately, the challenges Craig and I faced are common. Couples avoid talking about money for a variety of reasons: Bills are boring, fear of conflict, different priorities when it comes to spending and saving, and a power imbalance between partners. Because people are marrying later in life, they're also more likely to be financially independent with well-established money habits, making them less willing to discuss or commingle funds with a partner.

No matter what the reason you and your partner are having trouble talking about money, I wrote this book to give you the practical, evidence-based tools and confidence to have easier, more productive, and more satisfying money conversations so you can experience all of the many benefits. These include less bickering and tension about spending and saving, and experiencing more joy, happiness, and prosperity.

Communication Is Key

Some couples find it hard to stay calm and avoid getting defensive during conversations about finances, and their negative way of interacting becomes habitual. One engaged couple, Amanda, thirty-five, and Keith, thirty-four, seemed intent on proving a point to each other when they argued in my therapy office. They both came across as critical of one another and highly defensive. Keith also used sarcasm to make fun of Amanda's tendency to be frugal and to nitpick about small purchases. Then Amanda would retaliate by accusing Keith of being a spendthrift. By using a self-righteous approach, they would dig their heels in, and both had a strong need to prove they were "right." And because this couple had difficulty reaching compromises, their money-related disagreements often escalated into full-blown arguments.

Amanda explains,

> Whenever we try to discuss finances, Keith makes fun of me or raises his voice and then walks away. Oftentimes, I criticize his spending habits and I know that it can be tough on him. When I question him about his purchases, he gets defensive and I don't always back down. We've been living together for several years and I don't feel comfortable planning a wedding without more financial security. I admit that I try to keep Keith on a tight leash but he overreacts to my questions about what he spends. He complains that I nag him about money but I don't feel like I have a choice.

What's at the heart of this couple's disagreement about finances, and how can they cultivate a rewarding dialogue? First, they tend to assume that they share common values, and in reality their family history with money, beliefs, and financial styles are very different. They also don't check in with each other enough to see where their values differ and where they're in alignment. It's crucial that they understand and validate each other's feelings and perspectives rather than trying to prove they're "right." If Amanda and Keith's pattern of attack and defensiveness continues over time, it can diminish the love and respect between them. Letting go of the need to be "right" can be empowering for both partners and help them to preserve loving feelings and positive communication.

Most couples discuss finances all the time, as in "Don't forget to pay the cable bill." But they don't have regular money talks that are intentional, meaning with a goal of improving communication about finances. The last thing many couples want to do at the end of the day is discuss their budget or savings plan. If this sounds familiar, read on to learn the tools needed to turn perpetual strain about money into more loving conversations that can leave both you and your partner feeling validated and appreciated.

By making a "Communication Pledge" to schedule regular money talks (described in Chapter 2), you can check in with each other and develop an "us against the problem" mindset when dealing with financial challenges versus "us against each other." This approach will foster better communication and allow you to set financial goals together.

What This Book Offers

Based on over thirty-five years of clinical experience as a couples therapist and 100 in-depth interviews, I know that finances are a source of tension and conflict for many people. In fact, the number one reason why couples come to see me for counseling is financial stress and difficulty communicating and reaching an agreement about problems related to spending, resolving debt, and other money issues. If these are pain points in your relationship, I wrote *Let's Talk About Money* to help you develop the communication skills to create financial intimacy, which is a sense of feeling close, connected, and understood, when it comes to all money matters. In his book *Money Madness*, Spencer Sherman, MBA, says that financial intimacy is vital to emotional intimacy and they're actually two sides of the same coin.[1] He posits that discussing core money transactions with full disclosure is an important element of financial intimacy. Sherman elaborates on why having candid money talks is so important: "You might then reveal secrets, express needs, share vulnerabilities, relate fears, assert desires neither one of you had previously known."

Through accessible, practical strategies proven to work and real-life stories of couples who have successfully navigated issues with money, such as managing debt or financial infidelity, you'll learn how to:

- Identify your beliefs about money, financial style, and money mindset.
- Transform dysfunctional patterns of relating and dial down defensiveness.
- Recover quickly from hurt and miscommunication.
- Be emotionally attuned to your partner to reduce tension and conflict.

- Have regular constructive money talks, develop a budget and savings plan, and pay off bad debt (i.e., credit cards).

Even if you and your partner have opposite financial styles, such as tightwad and spendthrift, you can influence each other and learn to compromise. By gaining insight into the differences in your family background and financial styles, you can validate one another and balance out any extreme tendencies such as incurring credit card debt (you can't pay off) or being too uptight about finances.

This book will also help you better manage conflict about money by adopting a "us against the problem" mindset. This means learning to discuss and validate each other's feelings and subjective experiences. It also means using a gentler approach to making requests, such as, "I feel worried about money because we've had a lot of expenses lately. Do you have time to talk now, or can we plan a time?" Additionally, it's important for you and your partner to accept responsibility for the role you both play when you have conflict. The goal is to come up with a compromise which you can both live with. Using this "win-win" approach to dealing with tension or arguments about money will ensure that you both get some (not all) of your needs met. When you understand your raw spots when it comes to discussing finances and your triggers for upset feelings and defensiveness, you can begin to communicate effectively and adopt a collaborative approach. As a result, you won't let differences in backgrounds, beliefs, financial styles, and perspectives about finances tear you apart and destroy your romantic relationship or marriage.

Your Road Map

Ideally, you should read this book with your partner. However, you can benefit from reading it alone, especially if you begin to implement my recommendations with your partner's support.

Part I helps you build an "us against the problem" mindset rather than an "us against each other" one. You'll begin in Chapter 1 by taking a Money Script Inventory and my Financial Style Quiz to help you understand your money history and discover your financial style. You'll learn about money scripts and how they can impact your interpersonal communication with your partner.[2] If you and your partner have different money scripts and financial styles, I provide strategies for dealing with them effectively. Chapter 2 offers specific steps for having low-conflict conversations with your partner, such as using a "soft and curious tone," ways to avoid defensiveness, and making a "Communication Pledge" to have regular money talks. Finally, Chapter 3 explains how choosing a suitable money management system, such as a "common pot," can help you achieve prosperity and financial intimacy.

In Part II, you'll learn the essentials of financial health which include building a budget, getting rid of debt, and developing a saving plan. Wisdom and advice from several respected financial planners and experts are included throughout. In Chapter 4, a sample budget plan is offered with suggestions for how to prevent money leaks and money laundering. Money leaks are ways that money is pouring out of your account, such as ordering frequent takeout. Money laundering happens when someone uses their debit card for a purchase and gets extra cash to spend as they please but fails to record it or mention it to their partner. Chapter 5 tackles the common issue of abusing credit cards (because of using them like cash) and suggests smart ways to get out from under debt while explaining the differences between good and bad debt. Chapter 6 will show you how to live within your means so you and your partner can save for the "big stuff" such as college educations, vacations, and retirement.

Finally, Part III offers practical ways to troubleshoot the most common financial challenges couples face, including whether to have a prenuptial or postnuptial agreement which is covered in Chapter 7. Both of these agreements protect the assets of one or both partners from the property settlement claims of the other should they split up or one person dies unexpectedly. Chapter 8 explores the sensitive topic of estate planning and explains that it's really about leaving a legacy of love for your children and grandchildren. Based on interviews with estate planning lawyers, I walk you through the steps you need to develop a compassionate estate plan that honors your wishes.

By reading Chapter 9, you'll learn what financial infidelity is, how it can destroy a relationship, and what to do about it. You will learn "The Eight Red Flags of Financial Infidelity" so you can identify them if they appear in your relationship or marriage. Chapter 10 is essential reading for anyone who is remarried and dealing with complex finances involving yours, mine, and ours. Love can be sweeter the second time around, but a remarriage doesn't run on automatic, and having realistic expectations and full disclosure about finances can improve your odds of having a successful relationship. Finally, Chapter 11 explains how conflict isn't avoidable in intimate relationships, but it can be managed effectively. I offer ways to improve your repair skills so you can restore intimacy after regrettable incidents or arguments. For instance, learning how to compromise is an effective way to manage conflict and prevent anger and resentment from escalating and damaging your relationship.

The information in this book springs from many years of struggling to find lower-conflict ways to talk to my husband, Craig, about finances and listening to couples with similar problems. As someone who has come out the other end, I'm happy to say that financial intimacy and relationship success truly go hand in hand. As a lifelong insomniac, I'm no longer losing sleep over financial worries. It's more than likely that I've been up much too late planning my next adventure with Craig.

Let's start you on your journey toward low-conflict money talks and observe how your relationship with your partner and with money thrives with intentional daily practice.

PART I

Establishing a Foundation for an "Us Against the Problem" Mindset About Finances

Chapter 1
Understand Your Money History and Discover Your Financial Style

Money is a sensitive topic for most couples. There is no "right" or "wrong" way to deal with issues such as unequal assets, layoffs from work, and credit card debt. Disagreements about finances are usually not really about money but about your dreams, fears, and insecurities that are often shaped by your history. For instance, growing up in a household where money was tight can impact your beliefs or assumptions about money and your financial style (such as spender or saver). It's crucial that you understand your own beliefs about money and your financial style and how they either match up or contrast with your partners. Avoiding an "us against each other" mindset and adopting an "us against the problem" approach to dealing with financial issues will help you face challenges together rather than blaming each other.

In my case, I was raised in a single-parent family where money was tight, and my mother, born at the beginning of the Great Depression, raised me with a scarcity mindset characterized by a focus on never having enough resources. Unfortunately, I internalized the message that I wasn't deserving of nice clothes because I wore mostly hand-me-downs from my three older sisters. As a result, I often shop at consignment stores and feel guilty when I purchase new clothes. Since I'm worried about not having enough money, I'm also very watchful of the way my husband Craig spends it. Because I inherited a scarcity mindset from my mother, I am frugal, good at saving money, and operate with the belief that we never have enough money, even when there's evidence to dispute my irrational thinking.

On the other hand, Craig's parents never divorced, were affluent, generous with gifts, and money flowed easily in their lives. Since Craig has an abundance mindset, he thinks nothing of eating out at an expensive restaurant, ordering name-brand clothes, and the hottest new electronics online, and generally spending money in a carefree and sometimes inattentive way. He believes that there's enough money for everyone and doesn't worry about it. He also believes that money is a sign of success, while I pay more attention to our financial well-being.

As you can imagine, our mindsets about money, beliefs, and financial styles, which can be shorthanded as a spender-saver dynamic, often collide and have been a source of high conflict in our twenty-seven-year marriage. In this chapter, you will learn the five steps you need to identify and understand both your money script and financial style. And you'll learn the tools to deal more effectively with ways you're incompatible with your partner that are creating stress in your marriage or intimate relationship.

Understand how your history with money impacts your intimate relationship or marriage. Our relationship with money starts in childhood. We all have a story about money which includes misconceptions and outdated beliefs. For instance, my mother told me, "You can't trust others with your money; hold onto it tightly." When our histories, attitudes, values, and beliefs about money clash with our partner's, sparks can fly. If couples don't learn the tools to understand each other's history and communicate effectively in spite of differences, conflict can become perpetual and a source of chronic tension in a relationship.

Many of us were raised by families who told us that talking about money was impolite, or that our personal finances are private and shouldn't be discussed with others. These unhealthy beliefs and misconceptions may cause us to avoid discussing finances or to keep secrets about how much money we spend or the amount of debt we have accumulated. Keeping secrets is a form of financial infidelity which can be defined as consciously or deliberately lying to a romantic partner about financial behavior.[1]

Before you understand your financial style and how it matches up with your partner, and deal effectively with any disparities, you need to comprehend both of your money histories and money beliefs or scripts. Accomplishing these tasks will allow you to lower your anxiety about finances and help you and your partner achieve financial health and harmony. Discussing money with the one you love is worth the effort because doing so will help you collaborate and reduce ongoing tension about finances. According to a 2024 groundbreaking study by Mishra et al., it will also empower you to view financial conflict as solvable rather than perpetual, which increases the likelihood of engaging in financial communication with your partner.[2]

Did you grow up in a family where money was tight, or you never had to worry about spending it? Your childhood substantially impacts your beliefs about money. How you spend it is probably a lot like how your parents did—or an overcorrection of their financial mistakes. Because you and your partner probably grew up with different beliefs about money, you may not always be on the same page. If you understand the source of your differing points of view about finances, you'll be better able to empathize and communicate compassionately.

In order to achieve financial health, it's crucial that you identify your core beliefs and assumptions about money, established during childhood, and discuss with your partner how your beliefs influence your feelings and behavior today. Core beliefs are ones that are essential to your sense of well-being such as owning your own home or saving for retirement. These beliefs are potent and often hidden—deeply internalized fears and anxieties—and they can impact your actions.

Even couples who are compatible in most of their beliefs and values may differ in their beliefs about money. Alyssa, fifty-nine, and Ted, sixty, were childhood sweethearts. They met as teenagers while attending the same summer camp in New England and have been married for over thirty-five years, having raised four successful young adults. They were both raised Catholic in the state of New York and share similar interests, yet they were on the verge of divorce when they first met with me for couples therapy. When I collected data about their family histories, there were significant differences in their upbringing. Alyssa grew up in an affluent family and Ted came from a lower-middle-class family. The difference in their socioeconomic backgrounds didn't seem to be an issue when they were dating and first married but reared its head after they became parents and their responsibilities and expenses increased. Now, they found themselves frequently disagreeing about how to spend money.

During their early years of marriage, their conversations about finances were somewhat harmonious while Ted was in law school and Alyssa was a second-grade teacher. However, soon after their second child was born, Alyssa decided to give up her teaching job and spend time raising her children as her mother had done. Their expenses only increased after their third and fourth children were born. According to Ted, Alyssa never had to limit her spending as a child growing up or later as a student at Columbia University, so she was poorly prepared for living within a budget.

On the other hand, Ted was the last of five children, and he grew up understanding that money was tight and that it was important to save rather than spend. His mother often said, "Money doesn't grow on trees," and his family had a strong work ethic. He graduated from a prestigious Northeast law school and received a full scholarship because he was smart and hard-working. His financial literacy grew while in law school as he read about finances and took online courses. Ted was able to save money to buy an apartment in a prosperous urban town prior to their marriage and considered himself to be fiscally conservative. In spite of that, Alyssa shopped at upscale retail stores and had difficulty living within their means.

The stress that Ted felt being the primary breadwinner led to an increase in conflict between Ted and Alyssa over time. While he supported the notion of Alyssa being a stay-at-home mother, Ted felt overwhelmed with the financial demands of raising four children on one income. Since his mother worked full-time while he was growing up, Ted assumed that Alyssa would return to teaching after their last child was in school. Alyssa, on the other hand, wanted to devote her time to raising her children and volunteer activities at their schools and church. And she assumed that Ted shared her perspective. Meanwhile, Ted felt stressed about finances and would have preferred that Alyssa work part-time. His income as a lawyer was respectable, but living in an affluent suburb and sending all of their children to private elementary and secondary schools hadn't left much of a cushion for college expenses.

Ted reflects, "Alyssa is a terrific mom, but she can't relate to the financial pressure that I feel. She hasn't been able to understand what it's like to be the responsible person in the family, at least with money.

I'm always looking at the big picture and have to figure out how to keep things afloat."

Another hot-button issue in their marriage is that Alyssa has loaned family members money without discussing it with Ted. He has deeply resented this, and they almost separated before seeking my therapy services. When Alyssa agreed to loan a cousin money for a startup internet business, Ted told her, "He's using you. There's a sucker born every day." Ted also felt that Alyssa overspent on household items, dining out, and clothing. In our couples therapy sessions, Alyssa identified a moment growing up when her parents won an award in their community for their charitable donations to a women's shelter, and she understands how that triggers her to loan family members money. In contrast, Ted shared how his parents showed disappointment when he spent his own savings on a ticket to watch his favorite sports team, the New York Yankees, play at Yankee Stadium when he was a teenager. Ted freely admits that they were probably too thrifty, and this message has caused him to be very frugal with money.

Alyssa and Ted's story illustrates how their backgrounds impact their beliefs, values, and attitudes about finances as adults. When Alyssa and Ted were dating and engaged, they focused on their mutual attraction, Catholic faith, and similar tastes in music and friends. But while striving to create a happy life together, they realized that they didn't always see eye to eye on how to spend their money, and this caused a major rift.

The money battles that arose between Alyssa and Ted usually involved the differences in their financial styles and fundamental beliefs about money. Ted is a saver who was told at an early age that you must work hard for every cent you earn and be careful about how you spend it. On the other hand, Alyssa admits to being a spender who used to spend money spontaneously without checking their budget or the balances in their accounts.

During couples therapy sessions, Alyssa and Ted learned how their backgrounds impact their beliefs, feelings, and behavior about money, and they're communicating more openly and honestly. Rather than blaming each other, they now blame the differences in their upbringing and values and have more empathy for each other. With my guidance, this couple has learned how to reframe their beliefs and come up with compromises they could both live with, such as Alyssa teaching part-time at a local school to help boost their retirement account and Ted being more understanding about Alyssa's charitable nature. They argue less and have monthly dates at a restaurant, where they have low-conflict money talks (see Chapter 2).

The issues Alyssa and Ted have dealt with in their marriage are not unusual and demonstrate the potency of beliefs about money stemming from childhood and how they shape our adult mindsets and decisions. They also highlight the stress that some couples experience when they have a large family and one partner chooses to be a stay-at-home parent. For instance, Ted didn't feel that Alyssa gave him enough credit for working long hours as an attorney to support the family, and Alyssa believed that raising children was the most important job in the world.

Fortunately, Alyssa and Ted completed the activity below and gained awareness about their past before they were able to understand and discuss each other's beliefs, values, and financial styles. Completing this activity will increase your awareness and sensitivity to your past and current money mindset (and your partner's) and how they impact your relationship or marriage. The first step in getting out from under the shadow of your past is to gain insight. This might mean talking to one or both of your parents, siblings, or a close friend and asking them about your childhood.

Step One: Couples Activity: Examine Your Family Backgrounds and Gain Awareness About How They Impact Your Money Mindset

Select a private place to complete this exercise. Be sure to have a pen and paper (or electronic device) available to take notes. Answer all of these questions and encourage your partner to do the same. If your partner is unwilling to complete this activity, you can still benefit from completing it yourself. Be sure to sit in a private setting, with few distractions such as a TV or electronic devices. At the end of this chapter, you will be given instructions for discussing both of your answers and asking each other questions. Your discussion will inform both of you and increase your awareness about your family background and how it impacts your money script and financial style, and your communication. *Ask Yourself These Eight Questions:*

1. What cultural, religious, or generational beliefs about money do you bring to your marriage or committed relationship? For instance, if your parents or grandparents were Depression-era babies, they may have passed down values of frugality and worrying about the future.

2. What beliefs about money do you believe were passed down from your family that have caused you difficulty in your marriage or committed relationship?

3. Which of these beliefs has impacted your attitudes about finances on a daily basis?

4. Do you believe that one or both of your parents had a big influence on your feelings or behavior regarding financial decisions? For instance, my mother taught me that "A fool and his money are soon parted," so I feel anxious when I don't have sufficient money in the bank, and I'm very frugal even when I don't have to be.

5. How does your background impact your values about spending, saving, investing, and other financial decisions? For instance, you may have been raised in a family that valued saving and investing for the future and was frugal. On the other hand, your partner may have been raised in a family that valued taking frequent vacations and was more focused on "living in the present" rather than saving for the future.

6. How has your background caused you to thrive or limited you in terms of financial health?

7. What are your attitudes and beliefs about people who are wealthy? For instance, Craig believes that wealth is a sign of abundance, not greed, and he donates generous amounts to charities. In my case, I tend to view wealthy people as materialistic or selfish.

8. Do you believe that your family background contributes to mostly positive or negative ways of relating to money with your partner?

Now that you've examined how your family backgrounds affect your feelings, beliefs, values, and behavior about money, it's time to identify your money script or your core beliefs about money. Keep in mind that your money script often drives your adult financial decisions and can greatly impact communication between you and your partner.

Step Two: Identify Your Money Scripts

Money scripts is the term used by financial psychologists Brad Klontz and Ted Klontz in their Money Script theory to define the underlying assumptions or beliefs about money that are developed during childhood and unconsciously affect us into adulthood, even if they're only partly true.[3] Often, they become a legacy that is passed on from generation to generation within families and cultures. For instance, Alyssa was raised in an affluent family and was taught that it's honorable to help others in need through loans and charitable donations. She developed a money status script which conflicted with her husband Ted's money vigilance script, which is characterized by frugality.

In their book *Mind Over Money*, Brad Klontz and Ted Klontz explain that Money Scripts are core beliefs that are typically unconscious and derive from financial flashpoints—from early life events associated with money.[4] Although these flashpoints are not always traumatic in a traditional sense, they can be intense and emotionally charged. They posit that when we see people react to money in certain ways, we internalize this information, which has a profound impact on us, especially in our most impressionable years. Money scripts are our attempt to make sense of the world, to help us feel safe, and to avoid emotional pain. However, a belief that protected someone as a young child will not necessarily serve them well as an adult. For example, my experience of being told by my mother that I had to wear hand-me-downs from my sisters' wardrobes makes me feel undeserving of nice things in general. As a child, I had low self-esteem because I felt that I never looked as good as my friends. This belief is outdated and makes me feel guilt and shame when I purchase new clothes or personal items.

In their study, published in *The Journal of Financial Therapy*, Bradley Klontz, Sonja L. Britt, and Jennifer Mentzer identified four distinct money scripts.[5] Their research was conducted with a sample of 422 individuals who answered questions about their money-related assumptions and beliefs, and it demonstrated the power of money scripts on financial health.

The four categories of money scripts developed by Klontz, Britt, and Mentzer include money worship, money avoidance, money status, and money vigilance.[6]

1. Money worship. Money worshipers obsess over money and believe that money buys happiness. They may feel chronically dissatisfied because they never have enough money to fulfill their dreams. One of their beliefs might include, "More money will make life better." Money worship scripts develop in part from living in a society that values wealth and equates money with success. Some of the problematic behaviors associated with this category include compulsive hoarding, unreasonable risk-taking, overspending, compulsive buying disorder, pathological gambling, and workaholism.

2. Money avoidance. Money avoiders believe that money is bad, and they typically feel they don't deserve it. They might believe that "money is the root of all evil" and view wealthy people as greedy. This may cause them to believe that it's better to have less money, and this could restrict their sense of abundance. People with money avoidance scripts may be worried about abusing credit cards or overdrafting their checking account; they may self-sabotage their financial success and avoid spending money on reasonable or necessary purchases. This belief might also limit their possibilities of making more money or seeing it flowing in their lives. They may resist budgeting, investing, managing money, or even learning about it. Money avoidance has been found to predict self-defeating money behaviors such as excessive risk aversion, underspending, financial denial, and financial rejection.

3. Money status. People with this script define their self-worth by their net worth. They may buy the best or most expensive

products and overspend in order to project prosperity to others. These scripts can lock individuals into the competitive stance of acquiring more than those around them. The focus is on social acceptance. For them, money is about being liked, accepted, and respected by others. At the core of this belief is shame and a fear of rejection. Some of the problematic money behaviors associated with money status include excessive risk-taking or overspending with the goal of rapid wealth attainment in an attempt to raise one's perceived social status.

4. Money vigilance. People in this category tend to be frugal and believe that you need to work hard to earn money. This may cause them to set goals and earn more money throughout their lives. They tend to be watchful about their finances. For them, money is mostly about security. Money vigilance is associated with generally positive traits like frugality or avoiding debt. On the other hand, while financial security is valuable, a partner's high anxiety and wariness about money can cause serious conflict with an intimate partner if they are too vigilant about finances. It can also limit someone's ability to enjoy relationships and have fun.

The first three scripts are linked to lower net worth, lower income, and high amounts of revolving credit. The fourth script, money vigilance, is associated with being frugal and a belief that you need to work hard and save money, which can contribute to prosperity.[7]

Klontz and Klontz developed a diagnostic tool called the Money Script Inventory to help people identify their money script.[8] During my couples therapy sessions, I encourage couples to take this Inventory and discuss their results. Next, I encourage you and your partner to take the Inventory and score it without criticism or judgment.

Klontz Money Script Inventory—Revised (KMSI-R)

Please take this Inventory to gain awareness about your money script or beliefs about money.[9] Encourage your partner to complete this

Inventory as well. In the blank after each statement below, write the number from the following scale that indicates how strongly you agree or disagree with the statement.

1 = strongly disagree, 2 = disagree, 3 = disagree a little, 4 = agree a little, 5 = agree, 6 = strongly agree.

1. I do not deserve a lot of money when others have less than I do. _____
2. Rich people are greedy. _____
3. People get rich by taking advantage of others. _____
4. I do not deserve money. _____
5. Good people should not care about money. _____
6. It is hard to be rich and be a good person. _____
7. The less money you have, the better life is. _____
8. Money corrupts people. _____
9. Being rich means you no longer fit in with friends and family. _____
10. Things would get better if I had more money. _____
11. More money will make you happier. _____
12. It is hard to be poor and happy. _____
13. You can never have enough money. _____
14. Money is power. _____
15. Money would solve all my problems. _____
16. Money buys freedom. _____
17. Most poor people do not deserve to have money. _____
18. You can have love or money, but not both. _____
19. I will not buy something unless it is new (e.g., car, house). _____
20. Poor people are lazy. _____
21. Money is what gives life meaning. _____
22. Your self-worth equals your net worth. _____

23. If something is not considered the best, it is not worth buying. ____

24. People are only as successful as the amount of money they earn. ____

25. You should not tell others the amount of money you have or make. ____

26. It is wrong to ask others how much money they have or make. ____

27. Money should be saved, not spent. ____

28. It is important to save for a rainy day. ____

29. People should work for their money and not be given financial handouts. ____

30. I would be a nervous wreck if I did not have money saved for an emergency. ____

31. You should always look for the best deal before buying something, even if it takes more time. ____

32. It is extravagant to spend money on oneself. ____

Scoring Procedures

Use the following scoring system to determine how closely you identify with certain money scripts. For each item below, write in the blank space the sum of your answers to the given numbered statements. Then compare these totals to the scale interpretation below.

Nos. 1–9 (Money Avoidance)

Nos. 10–16 (Money Worship)

Nos. 17–24 (Money Status)

Nos. 25–32 (Money Vigilance)

Scale Interpretation

Money Avoidance

> 9–18 = Your response style suggests that you do not have a problem with money avoidance.
>
> 19–27 = Your response style suggests that you exhibit one or more symptoms of money avoidance.
>
> 28–36 = Your response style suggests that you are at risk of developing money avoidance.
>
> 37–54 = Your response style is similar to a person who suffers from money avoidance.

Money Worship

> 7–14 = Your response style suggests that you do not have a problem with money worship.
>
> 15–30 = Your response style suggests that you exhibit one or more symptoms of money worship.
>
> 31–38 = Your response style suggests that you are at risk of developing money worship.
>
> 39–49 = Your response style is similar to a person who suffers from money worship.

Money Status

> 8–16 = Your response style suggests that you do not have a problem with money status beliefs.
>
> 17–24 = Your response style suggests that you exhibit one or more symptoms of money status beliefs.
>
> 25–32 = Your response style suggests that you are at risk of developing money status beliefs.
>
> 33–48 = Your response style is similar to a person who suffers from money status beliefs.

Money Vigilance

- 8–16 = Your response style suggests that you do not have a problem with money vigilance.
- 17–24 = Your response style suggests that you exhibit one or more symptoms of money vigilance.
- 25–32 = Your response style suggests that you are at risk of developing money vigilance.
- 33–48 = Your response style is similar to a person who suffers from money vigilance.

2013 Brad Klontz and Sonya Britt: used with permission

If you prefer to take the Money Script Inventory online, use this link: https://www.bradklontz.com/moneyscriptstest

It's important to identify your money scripts, according to Klontz and Klontz, because the first step in changing money behaviors that are problematic is acknowledging that you have a problem.[10] By examining your beliefs and emotions related to finances, you'll be better able to take ownership of them, become less reactive, and grant yourself permission to change them. If you and your partner have different money scripts, you might have difficulty discussing money-related matters. Also, you might keep secrets for fear of losing status, love, or affection from your partner. Or you may worry about losing the ability to control his or her spending. When couples have discrepancies in their perspectives based on conflicting money scripts, conflict is a likely outcome.

For instance, Lillian, forty, a high school teacher in an urban area, was married for a couple of years to Brian, thirty-five, an electrician, when he admitted that he'd been concealing his high credit card debt of about $35,000. While discussing his debt during our couples therapy sessions, he told Lillian that he'd purchased an expensive car (which he couldn't afford) prior to their wedding. As a result, he often used his credit cards like cash. Since Lillian is a super saver who is frugal and has a vigilance money script, and Brian is a super spender who has a money status script, it makes sense that they'd have conflicts. Lillian admits that she's responsible for some of their arguments because she can be critical of Brian and makes accusations which cause him to shut down and turn away from her.

Lillian shares,

> We've only been married for five years, so we have kinks to work out. But I was shocked when I found out how much debt Brian was hiding from me. He would either go "silent" or walk out of the room when I asked him about his debt. When I finally saw his credit card statements on our desk, I was upset and couldn't hide my feelings. After taking the Money Script Inventory, I realized Brian and I have very different beliefs and this leads to tension. I'm trying hard to have open discussions with Brian about our differences and to show empathy.

It's essential for you and your partner to discuss how you spend your money based on your money scripts after you take the Inventory. While you might value buying designer clothing or items, such as a Vera Bradley suitcase, your partner might be comfortable buying off-brand luggage. You also might overlap on some items, such as agreeing to purchase store-brand groceries because you both feel brand-name products are no better than generic ones in most cases. In spite of your backgrounds, finding values and attitudes about finances you agree upon will bring you more harmony in your relationship. In order to achieve financial health, it's essential that you and your partner be receptive to changing your financial patterns and learn to communicate more effectively with each other.

For example, you can't assume that you share similar values about money even if you consider yourself a loyal, loving partner who is in a long-term marriage or committed relationship. You might want to retire early, and your partner might love his or her job and plan to work into their mid-seventies. Or you might disagree about how much to put down as a down payment for a new car. Sitting down together and discussing your money scripts will empower you to find ways to compromise and set priorities.

For instance, Shane, forty-seven, and Larry, forty-six, married for nine years, were both raised in the Midwest but have very different backgrounds. For many years, they assumed they had similar values about finances and couldn't understand why so many of their conversations about money escalated into arguments. During our first couples therapy session, they told me that they both tended to dig in their heels and become self-righteous when they talked about money-related matters. This "us against each other" mindset left them both feeling dissatisfied with their marriage.

Currently, Shane and Larry are both employed full-time and own their own home in a middle-class neighborhood. Larry is a college counselor, and Shane is a paralegal for a local law firm. Their money conflicts usually involved what they considered to be Larry's overspending on nonessential items and difficulty discussing finances, and Shane's frugal nature since he has a money vigilance script. Raised in a strict fundamentalist Christian family, Larry was taught that it wasn't a good thing (or even a sin) to spend money on himself and that money was a taboo topic. This background caused him to feel uncomfortable talking about finances and to get defensive when Shane asked him about his purchases. Larry tends to overspend, and he has a money worship script. Most of his life, he has operated under the belief that money buys happiness, and this caused him to believe that buying things would make his life better. Shane, on the other hand, is a super saver, with a money vigilance script. He grew up in a family that operated from an abundance mindset because his parents owned a successful restaurant and they had good communication about finances. Shane and Larry's differences often led to arguments when they talked about their financial goals.

During our first couples therapy session, Shane and Larry agreed to work on improving their understanding of each other's perspectives and money scripts and how their differences created a spender-saver dynamic. At first, Shane was accusatory about Larry's overspending patterns, and it's no wonder that Larry became defensive when Shane pointed out that his purchases of nonessential luxury items and loaning money to family members were putting a strain on their budget. Fortunately, they began to blame their family backgrounds rather than each other. When Larry and Shane started having monthly money talks, they experienced less tension and lower conflict.

Over time, Larry was able to curb his overspending patterns, and the couple was able to pay off most of Larry's credit card purchases, a win-win solution. As a result, they began sticking to their budget, living within their means, and saving more money, which led to lower conflict and prosperity. Now, they have a better handle on the money that's coming in and how much is going out monthly, so they can set financial goals and save for the big stuff like vacations and remodeling their home. If one or both of them feel irritated or angry, they've learned to pause and agree to resume their conversation the next day. They know that their different money scripts can lead to high conflict, and their awareness has caused them to be more compassionate and tolerant of each other.

The Money Script Inventory can assist you and your partner in identifying your prevailing money scripts or beliefs.[11] I recommend that each of you take the Inventory and think about ways your money script might either be an asset (i.e., money vigilance) or a liability (i.e., money avoidance script) in your romantic relationship. Before you do this, take time to examine how your money scripts might be creating stress for your relationship and what to do about it.

Step Three: Gain Awareness About How Your Money Script Is Creating Stress in Your Marriage or Relationship

First, identify which money script is the best descriptor of you by taking the inventory. If you believe that your money script is problematic in your marriage, ask yourself these six questions:

1. Is your money script holding you back from having a healthy relationship with your partner or with money?
2. Have you ever felt guilt or shame, or hidden financial information from your partner?
3. What is your biggest worry or financial concern at this time in your marriage or committed relationship?
4. Specifically, how do you think that your money script impacts your communication with your partner?

5. How does your money script influence your attitudes and behavior about spending, saving, and other financial decisions with your partner?
6. Do you believe that you and your partner are capable of financial health and a life of abundance?

The next step in being able to have an "us against the problem" mindset rather than an "us against each other" mentality about finances is taking a closer look at your financial style which is your distinctive way of thinking about and handling money. The goal of taking the Financial Style Quiz is to gain awareness and acceptance of yourself (and your partner) and to adopt a more compassionate approach to your differences.

Step Four: Discover Your Financial Style

Simply put, a person's financial style can be defined as their attitude about spending, saving, and investing money. Everyone approaches money in their own unique way, and your financial style is informed by many factors including your upbringing, past and current financial circumstances, values, and personality. Additionally, your money script influences your financial style. For instance, my money script is money vigilance and that causes me to be a super saver who is frugal and avoids debt. In other words, my money script and financial style are consistent with one another, and this is probably true for most people. There are no "wrong" ways to manage your finances. The key is to understand your strengths and weaknesses and create a plan that helps you build healthy habits that are compatible with your partner. With practice, you'll be able to blend your financial styles and create more harmony in your marriage or committed relationship.

If you're reading this book, there's a good chance that you and your partner have different financial styles. The good news is that you're not alone. According to experts, the most common financial styles are spenders and savers. This designation usually refers to a person's attitude about money. However, a saver doesn't always have a big financial portfolio, and a spender doesn't always go on spending sprees. Because there are degrees of these two financial styles, my quiz categorizes moderate spenders and super spenders, and moderate savers and super savers. For instance, moderate savers can take money out of their savings account for a special gift or vacation and rest easy at night, whereas a super saver will be up late "counting sheep" if they saw their savings balance decline. Likewise, a moderate spender might overspend on occasion and get carried away at a closeout clearance sale or an LL Bean catalog sale, whereas a super spender tends to use their credit card like cash and overspend often.

For instance, my husband Craig and I identified early on in our remarriage that we have a saver-spender dynamic resulting from our different backgrounds. Truth be told, my tendency to be a super saver and to have a money vigilance script still drives Craig crazy at times. And his propensity to see money as status, to be a super spender, and to buy expensive name-brand items can throw me into a tailspin. One of the most frequent arguments in the early stages of our marriage was ignited by Craig accusing me of being a tightwad when I showed disdain for his purchase of a pricey fly-fishing rod (and other gear) which I felt we couldn't afford. In recent years, Craig has been generous when he mentions my frugality and sometimes even tells others that I'm good with money because I'm cautious. He's also become appreciative of my ability to save money. And I do my best to give him more leeway on his spending on nonessential name-brand items so he has more control over purchases. Taking the Financial Style Quiz helped us understand and validate our differences, and it can help you, too.

Understanding the Financial Style Quiz

The questions on the Financial Style Quiz have been designed by me to help you identify your basic style as either a spender (moderate or super) or saver (moderate or super), develop money awareness, improve communication, and achieve financial health.

I recommend that you and your partner each take the Financial Style Quiz. Then read my advice in "Seven Tips for Dealing with Disparities in Money Scripts and Financial Styles for Couples" at the end of this chapter to discuss any differences, address problematic money scripts or financial styles, attempt to gain understanding and compassion, and work toward compromise.[12] Many of the couples in my practice find taking the Money Script Inventory and Financial Styles Quiz (and discussing the results) informative and helpful in enhancing their awareness, understanding, and empathy. It's a good idea to bring your quizzes with you when you're having a conversation about finances to enhance transparency.

The Financial Style Quiz

Please take this quiz in a quiet place, without distractions. Responding honestly to the following statements about your financial values in twenty areas is important to the validity of your results. Please circle the answer that reflects your assumptions about money. In Chapter 4, you'll find a couples activity about how to deal with any differences that might exist in the values you and your partner have about finances.

1. Housing Goals

I am comfortable renting or buying an affordable apartment or home so I have more cash to spend.
  True False

2. Family

An older family member (parent, in-law, etc.) is ill and needs substantial help. I would pay for professional help or assisted living to take care of them. Cost would not be a concern; my only goal would be to get them optimal care, even if I couldn't afford it.
  True False

3. Shopping

I enjoy shopping, and I often spend more than I intend to when I go into a store or shop online. I find shopping hard to control at times. I can't always pay off my credit card charges when my bills are due.
  True False

4. Eating in Restaurants

I get bored eating at home and enjoy going to restaurants frequently, even if I don't have it in my budget for the week and have to use my credit card.
  True False

5. Entertainment

I thrive on going outside of my home for entertainment, even if I have to use my credit card and I'm unsure when I can pay off what I charge.
   True   False

6. Dealing with a Money Gift

If I receive a gift of money for my birthday, graduation, or holiday, I will usually enjoy spending it rather than saving it.
   True   False

7. Credit Cards

I would consider using my credit card or an app like Venmo or PayPal for a purchase, even if I know I would probably not be able to pay it off at the end of the month.
   True   False

8. Accumulating Debt

I believe that debt is a fact of life, and I don't mind having it as long as I can purchase items I want or need.
   True   False

9. Spending Habits

I have trouble controlling my spending and will go over my budget sometimes.
   True   False

10. Budgeting

I don't believe a budget is necessary and rarely record what I spend because it's too tedious.
   True   False

11. Savings

I have not set a goal for saving money and don't often think about it, but it's on my "to-do list."
   True   False

12. Financial Planning

I don't think much about saving, getting rid of debt, making investments, or planning for retirement because I prefer to live "in the present."

True False

13. Spender versus Saver

I don't worry about money and often spend more money than I make. I often buy items that I don't really need or use.

True False

14. Big Purchases

I would purchase a big item (like a car) without sleeping on it if I really wanted it and thought it was a good deal.

True False

15. Full Disclosure

I tell my partner about many of my purchases but don't believe that I have to tell them about everything I purchase.

True False

16. Spending

I live in the present and don't worry much about planning for retirement.

True False

17. Do you consider yourself more of a spender than a saver?

Generally speaking, I enjoy spending more than saving money.

True False

18. I often buy things that I don't need and regret them afterward.

True False

19. I find it hard to say no or pause before I purchase items that I want.

True False

20. I often spend more than I make and worry about my financial health.

True False

Scoring Procedures

*Add five points for all of your False answers and consult the scoring key in the box below.

    80–100 points—You're a super saver who is frugal and values saving for the future.

    60–80 points—You're a moderate saver, but sometimes you spend more than you earn or purchase items on impulse.

    40–60 points—You're a moderate spender but value saving and try not to buy items on impulse.

    0–40 points—You're a super spender who has difficulty controlling your impulses to buy at times, even if you can't afford the item or event. You probably use your credit card or apps such as Venmo or PayPal often to purchase items and don't consider your ability to pay off what you spent.

    Now that you have taken the Money Script Inventory and Financial Styles Quiz, you're ready to discuss ways to deal with differences in your beliefs and attitudes about money with your partner.[13] The following tips will help you achieve your goal of adopting a collaborative, low-conflict approach to dealing with financial challenges.

Step Five: How to Deal with Any Incompatibility in Financial Styles and Money Scripts

Financial problems can cause perpetual tension and high conflict in any romantic relationship. Differences in financial styles and money scripts can cause couples to collide when it comes to managing money. However, you might not discover this incompatibility for many years and blame yourself or your partner when you argue about money. The reason for this delay in awareness is that money is probably the biggest taboo topic in families, and it's common to experience shame when it comes to finances. As a result, you may have avoided talking about your anxieties, fears, and shortcomings with your partner. And you are not alone.

In fact, the latest 2024 Fidelity Investments Couples and Money Study found that only 57 percent of couples make day-to-day decisions about money jointly, and only 57 percent rated their household's financial health as excellent or good.[14] Further, two out of five couples in this study were not aligned about how often they wanted to have money talks. This study surveyed couples and individuals, aged twenty-five and older, who were either married or in committed relationships, and the data was collected from 1,794 couples. This study supports my belief that couples can benefit from regular money talks that are constructive and transparent.

A situation like purchasing a home, funding college tuition, or loaning someone money can bring your differences with your partner to the surface. Gaining awareness about your beliefs about money and your financial style will help you gain insight into the values which you internalized from fiscal lessons learned in your family. This will set the stage for you to have a conversation with your partner and learn about their beliefs and assumptions about money.

Use the following couples activity and tips to help you learn how to deal effectively with any differences that exist between you and your partner's financial styles. Now it's time to examine the relationship dynamics between you and your partner and to consider any incompatibilities you might have and ways to address them. This discussion will take about one hour, and a follow-up session needs to take place in about a week. Read Chapter 2 for details about how to have regular low-conflict money talks.

Couples Activity: Seven Tips for Dealing Effectively with Disparities in Money Scripts and Financial Styles

1. Discuss your values and beliefs about money and your money scripts (based on the Klontz Money Script Inventory[15]) together. Your goal needs to be finding out more about your partner's financial heritage and mindset by identifying your money scripts. In doing so, try to gain insight that will increase your

empathy and understanding of any differences between you. How do each of you see money? Is it a medium of exchange or a measure of success? If you haven't discussed your money histories and childhood messages, do so without judgment or disapproval.

2. Discuss the results of the Financial Style Quiz with your partner. Avoid getting accusatory or defensive. If you feel like you're getting defensive, keep a calm composure and don't forget to breathe deeply. Next, try not to take what your partner says personally; think about their good qualities and use kind words. If you're attending couples therapy sessions, bring your results to at least one of the sessions as a springboard for a transparent conversation.

3. What is your behavior, such as overspending or avoiding talking about money, that comes from your money script and/or financial style, and what are the benefits of changing it to achieve financial health and harmony with your partner?[16]

4. Can you try on a different money script or financial style, such as a money vigilance or saver that would promote financial health?[17] For instance, rather than using shopping as a way to elevate your mood (money worship), can you take a long walk instead and save the money? If so, keep track of your mood and finances for one month to assess any change in either domain.

5. Learn from differences rather than letting them divide you as a couple. While differences may be a challenge to grapple with at times, you can learn a lot from listening and gaining understanding about your partner's financial style and money script. For instance, Lillian learned to relax about Brian buying her a nice gift for her birthday, and Brian learned the value of saving for their future from Lillian's frugal nature and money vigilance script.

6. Discuss your differences in financial styles and money beliefs without blame or criticism. Remember that your differences can be viewed as complementing each other from a "us against the problem" perspective. When you're in conflict, blame a

situation (like too many bills) rather than each other. Be sure to give your partner the benefit of the doubt and work toward a "win-win" solution so both of you get some (not all) of your needs met. Adopting a mindset of abundance (which means that there are enough resources for everyone) will help you and your partner communicate more effectively over the long haul.

7. Show compassion, understanding, and respect for differences. You can demonstrate this by asking good questions, actively listening, validating your partner's perspective, and working toward compromise.

Understanding your beliefs about money and financial style and how they differ from your partner's is an important step in becoming more transparent and vulnerable with your partner about finances. By gaining awareness of how these differences impact your communication, you're on your way to developing a stronger relationship with each other and money. The good news is that you can learn to compromise and balance your money scripts and financial styles so you face financial stress with an "us against the problem" mindset instead of "us against each other." In the next chapter, you will learn the skills to have low-conflict conversations about money so you can become more intimate financial partners and achieve financial health as a couple.

Chapter 2
Have Low-Conflict Conversations About Money and Enhance Intimacy

You've met your soulmate and decided to get married, engaged, or move in together. But while making plans for your happy life together, you soon discover that you have a spender-saver dynamic and that discussing money evokes a variety of complex emotions such as shame, envy, anxiety, panic, and pride. Financial disparities between you and your partner's incomes might also trigger resentment, especially if there are imbalances in the distribution of chores and childcare responsibilities.

Or maybe you've been married a long time, and talking about money transactions is challenging because you have different financial histories and/or financial styles. For instance, when Melanie, forty-eight, and Rob, fifty, discuss money, Rob often gets defensive because he makes reckless decisions about spending that make it difficult for them to pay their bills at times and have caused him to have a bad credit score. As a result, they have not been able to qualify for a lower interest on their mortgage by refinancing it.

This couple has been married for twenty years, and Melanie was raised in a single-parent family where money was tight. She identifies as having a moderate saving financial style with a money vigilance script which causes her to be frugal. On the other hand, Rob was raised in a two-parent middle-class home, and his financial style is that of a super spender. Because his parents often argued about money, Rob frequently feels anxious about the thought of discussing finances with Melanie. He has a money worship script that frequently collides with Melanie's money vigilance script. They have three sons, ages six, ten, and twelve, who are all active in sports. Melanie works as a financial analyst at a bank, and Rob is self-employed as a carpenter.

Even though Melanie and Rob are both employed full-time, they often find that they have more money going out than coming into their bank accounts. And they both have a tendency to blame each other for their financial problems rather than acknowledging that they're equally responsible. As a result, they have a history of arguing excessively about money, and they've become emotionally distant from each other.

Melanie explains,

> When it comes to money, Rob goes on spending sprees and doesn't tell me, so we often overdraw our checking account and have to dip into our savings. Rob has a problem with overspending. Last month, for example, he went shopping with our three sons for school clothes and went crazy buying them stuff they didn't need. Then to make matters worse, he charged several hundred dollars on his credit card and went over his limit and didn't tell me.

During our therapy session, Melanie shared that she set up an emergency fund (for three months of their expenses) when her grandmother left her a small inheritance recently. She also deposited some of the money into college funds for their children. She didn't tell Rob the exact amount she inherited because she doesn't trust him with money. Melanie told me that she's working on building trust with Rob by being transparent during our sessions and their money talks at home. I explained to her that not disclosing the precise amount of her inheritance to Rob is more a matter of privacy rather than keeping a secret because he knows about the inheritance. Additionally, there aren't any negative consequences associated with her keeping the amount private. However, I suggested that she might want to disclose the amount to him as a sign of goodwill. In Chapter 9, you'll learn how to determine the difference between keeping financial information private or keeping secrets, which is considered financial infidelity.

The next time I met with Melanie and Rob in my office, I spoke about the importance of full disclosure when it came to finances (for both of them) so they could build trust and financial intimacy. Melanie agreed to become transparent and disclosed the amount of money in their emergency fund and college funds to Rob, in spite of her fears. During follow-up sessions, we discussed the consequences of Rob's reckless behavior on their finances. Rob stated that he was embarrassed about his irresponsible behavior with money that led to a poor credit score and late fees. He knows he gets defensive because he fears Melanie will give him a lecture and they'll fight. This makes him avoid talking about money with Melanie. By attending regular therapy sessions, Melanie and Rob are working on having lower conflict so they can have more constructive money talks.

The Importance of Full Disclosure About Finances

For a lasting and prosperous relationship, you and your partner need to have easier discussions about money that are candid and transparent. These money talks can lower your tension and help you feel more relaxed about finding ways to achieve your financial goals. You can also attain financial intimacy, which you will learn about later in this chapter. Most of the couples that come to me for therapy complain that financial conflict is putting stress on their relationship. In fact, it's one of the top issues that couples address in sessions. It's not uncommon for couples to have incompatible financial styles or for one partner to be financially literate while the other is not, and this can lead to an imbalance of power and control in relationships. Over time, it can contribute to poor communication, emotional distance, and resentment.

For instance, Melanie and Rob have polar opposite financial styles, and these stark differences set them up for an imbalance in their relationship in terms of power and control. During several couples therapy sessions, Rob brought up how he felt resentful toward Melanie and powerless about making decisions about spending. Melanie's money vigilance and frugality clashed with his spender financial style, and he often felt like a child who had to ask his wife for permission for even small purchases like buying a coffee on the way to work. Rob admitted to Melanie that when he overspent on treats for their children, he did so because it made them feel happy. But he also disclosed that he was feeling very stressed and rebellious because of his lack of control over money. After we discussed the reasons for Rob's money worship script, Melanie and Rob agreed that he could benefit from a monthly budget for nonessentials.

In 2024, researchers Mishra et al. conducted eight studies at both Yale University and Cornell University and investigated how a person's perception of their current financial situation impacts their willingness to discuss money with their partner.[1] They discovered that when people experience high stress about their finances, they're less likely to communicate with their partner about money due to anticipated conflict. They also demonstrated that when couples view their money conflicts as solvable rather than perpetual, they're more likely to engage in financial communication with their partner. Many people worry that having candid conversations about finances will hurt their relationship, but this is actually a thinking mistake. With money problems, the more you avoid talking about it, the worse it gets.

Melanie and Rob's story illustrates how unfinished business from childhood can affect our choices as adults and lead to tension about discussing money.[2] Fortunately, Melanie gained insight into the fact that her scarcity mindset caused her to tighten the reins on Rob and gave her a sense of power that she didn't have during her childhood. On the other hand, Rob realized that watching his parents argue over finances was a financial flashpoint that left him with the assumption that talking about money would lead to high conflict, which he sought to avoid. I explained the concept of money scripts, formulated by Klontz and Klontz, to Melanie and Rob. These authors posit that there are critical "aha" experiences in our family (and other places) that are passed down to us and that we're also impacted by cultural influences, and that money scripts develop unconsciously during childhood and impact us as adults.

In 2020, researchers Shaunti and Jeff Feldhahn studied 1,822 married or cohabitating people for their book *Thriving in Love and Money*.[3] They discovered that 45 percent of their respondents avoid talking about money as often as they need to because it can be awkward, difficult, or stir up negative emotions. In addition, only 23 percent of their sample stated that they talk about money whenever they need to, without any difficulty. Feldhahn's study revealed that not all couples actually fight about money, but most experience tension about it. In fact, 92 percent of the couples they surveyed experienced tension about finances, and surprisingly, 85 percent of those who never fight still experience one or more points of tension. Further, they reported that 44 percent of people in their study experienced actual fighting.

I concur with the Feldhahn's findings that being able to have low-conflict talks about money is one of the most high-leverage things couples can do to thrive in love and money, and that even though finances can cause strife in a marriage or a committed relationship, having constructive money talks can help couples avoid the most damaging, most aggressive tensions in their marriage or committed relationship.[4]

No matter what your economic status is, money is the number one issue couples argue about, according to Dave Ramsey's website, Ramsey Solutions.[5] However, if you make a commitment to have regular money talks and openly discuss finances, you can achieve financial health over time. Adopting a "us against the problem" mindset will allow you and your partner to work toward a shared financial vision for your future. This perspective lessens the likelihood that you will blame each other for financial setbacks or problems that arise with money. Being transparent with your partner and improving communication about money can allow you to have constructive conversations and less stress.

Why Full Disclosure About Finances with a Partner Is Important

- It prevents many arguments about money and lowers tension and stress.
- It can encourage honesty and help couples build trust.
- It helps couples improve communication about finances.
- Couples can achieve financial health and goals such as paying off debt.

According to a recent study by the American Psychological Association, "Stress in America 2023," 50 percent of women and 44 percent of men feel consumed by financial stress.[6] Additionally, 47 percent of women and 42 percent of men said they feel embarrassed talking about their personal money matters with others. Financial stress can take its toll on any couple. For the most part, a lack of constructive communication about money is one of the biggest problems that contribute to financial difficulties for couples, and it can destroy a marriage or relationship.

Have Low-Conflict Money Talks

Learning how to have low-conflict conversations about money is essential if you want to attain financial well-being and lower your stress level. In fact, researchers Garbinsky and Gladstone found that having regular money talks is advantageous because it helps couples spend more responsibly and manage debt more optimally.[7] When most people think about getting married, they don't think about discussing boring topics such as developing a budget plan. Just getting through the financial tasks of paying for a wedding and honeymoon can be taxing enough. It's no wonder that you and your partner felt blindsided if you discovered that you have different financial styles and priorities. Getting comfortable talking about money (with full disclosure) without blaming each other and being defensive will help you reduce tension in your relationship and boost your financial intimacy. Over time, you're building trust in each other. If possible, it's a good idea to do this prior to tying the knot, or soon afterward.

For instance, Caitlyn, thirty-eight, and Ethan, forty, dated for four years prior to moving in together, but they never blended their money or had money talks. In fact, when they paid for meals while dining out and household expenses (such as rent and groceries) prior to marriage, they split costs, had separate checking and savings accounts, and reimbursed each other using Venmo. This money management system worked for them prior to marriage because it reduced conflict, and their expenses were low. It also allowed Caitlyn to keep her shopping addiction a secret because Ethan didn't have access to her bank statements or credit card bills. However, during our interview, it became apparent to me that this money system had become outdated after a decade of marriage and was causing a lot of tension.

Soon after getting married, Caitlyn and Ethan discovered that their spender-saver dynamic made it stressful to discuss finances and to be transparent. Like many couples, they experienced tension when the topic of saving money to buy a house came up, so they often avoided discussing it. Unfortunately, Caitlyn also built up a lot of debt during their ten years of marriage due to her shopping addiction and super spender financial style and money worship script. And since this couple spent more than they earned, they had not been able to save money or discuss finances without triggering each other and becoming defensive. Understandably, Ethan didn't appreciate being in the role of monitoring Caitlyn's spending but felt that he had to in order to meet their financial obligations including household expenses and credit card bills. Since Ethan is a super saver with a money vigilance script, they pay their bills on time, but he feels discouraged about their inability to save enough for a down payment on a condo or small home.

Caitlyn shares:

Whenever we talk about money, I walk on eggshells because Ethan doesn't trust me. I used to have a shopping addiction, and even though I'm better now, he questions every purchase I make, and we argue about even small things like me buying a coffee before work or having lunch with a friend. Ethan worries about our future and having enough to buy a house and retire one day, but I live in the present.

It's clear that Caitlyn and Ethan had an "us against each other" rather than a "us against the problem" approach when it came to talking about money. In the beginning of their relationship, Caitlyn and Ethan were so elated to have discovered each other that they focused more on their similarities than differences. After a while, emotional baggage from their past relationships was causing them to overreact to triggers (such as Caitlyn splurging on online shopping), and they started becoming more accusatory and defensive with each other. They lost sight of the loving feelings that brought them together in the first place. The stress they experienced with trying to buy a home in an inflated housing market in their area put even more strain on their marriage.

Caitlyn elaborates, "We tend to get irrational and dig our heels in when we fight—making things worse. Ethan says, 'You're always right, Caitlyn; you know you're always right.'" Caitlyn paused and continued,

And this would infuriate me even more. So now I say that I don't want to always be right; I want you to understand where I'm coming from. And if that means we can't talk about this right now, I'm going to go in the other room and read until we cool off. When I come back, we can talk.

While interviewing Caitlyn and Ethan, it became apparent that they had vastly different beliefs and values about money and that they had never discussed the source of them. During our sessions, Caitlyn disclosed that she was the middle child in a large middle-class blended family, and she often felt overlooked and left behind in terms of being able to purchase items she needed or desired. This set the stage for a shopping addiction, which she is now in treatment to remedy. As an architect working in a prestigious firm, Caitlyn is also concerned about the image she projects to clients, which has influenced her overspending on clothes in the past.

On the other hand, Ethan is the oldest child raised in a more affluent and fiscally conservative family that focused on acquiring wealth by saving and not overspending. Once Caitlyn and Ethan understood and discussed the differences in their upbringing, they were able to be more patient and compassionate with each other. It made sense to Caitlyn that Ethan was a super saver with a money vigilance script, and Ethan understood the reasons why Caitlyn became a super spender with a money status script. They both agreed that they have a long path ahead, but they're excited about the possibilities that they will face together.

In some cases, couples may find it very difficult to remain calm and receptive during discussions about finances. One engaged couple whom I interviewed, Amanda and Keith, reported that whenever they try to discuss finances, it creates tension between them. Amanda, thirty-five, explained that her fiancé, Keith, thirty-four, an engineer, often walks away when he feels anxious about discussing money. Amanda, a buyer for a large department store, admits that she's partly responsible for their arguments because she gets accusatory when she thinks Keith is overspending on nonessential items. Amanda is a moderate saver, has a money vigilance script, and is frugal. Since Amanda feels that Keith's credit card charges are excessive (his debt is over $20,000), they argue a lot but rarely resolve financial issues. Amanda worries that they won't ever be able to save enough money to purchase a home after they get married since Keith is a super spender with a money worship script. Fortunately, there are some ways to stop feeling so triggered and to become less defensive while having discussions about finances with your partner.

How Defense Mechanisms Impact Financial Harmony in Marriage

To better understand how defensiveness can lead to arguments or misunderstandings about money, let's examine some of the main defense mechanisms that are commonly used by people. Keep in mind that they're typically used to protect us from experiencing anxiety or to cushion us from the painful aspects of life, including thoughts, feelings, or behaviors.

Read about the common defense mechanisms below and ask yourself: How do you use any of the defense mechanisms below to justify your behavior or decisions regarding finances? Also, how are these decisions detrimental to you or your relationship? Lastly, does using one or more of these defense mechanisms play a role in your financial problems, cause you to blame your partner, and/or prevent you from taking responsibility for your own actions? Then, complete the "Couples Activity: Identifying Your Defense Mechanisms" With Your Partner.

Here Are Four Common Defense Mechanisms and How They Impact Finances

1. Denial: When people ignore the reality of a situation to avoid anxiety, they use denial to cope with distressing situations. For instance, Amanda and Keith have frequent arguments about money. Amanda states that Keith refuses to admit that he uses credit cards like cash and that due to his overspending, he spends more than he earns and has acquired too much debt. Amanda proposed a budget to Keith, but he shuts down and refuses to discuss it.
2. Rationalization: People justify difficult or unacceptable feelings for seemingly logical reasons, but they are unconsciously trying

to protect themselves from experiencing anxiety. For instance, some people justify skimming money off their paycheck (and putting it in a separate account).

3. Projection: When people recognize and attribute their unacceptable traits or impulses in someone else to avoid spotting them in themselves. This is a strong form of defensiveness that is self-protective. For example, if Amanda accuses Keith of being a big spender for buying a new motorcycle he can't afford, all the while her credit card debt is excessive.

4. Intellectualization: Removing or isolating feeling from a thought so that the thought can remain conscious without the associated affective cause. For instance, if Keith doesn't feel upset and guilty about his $20,000 in credit card debt (and continues to charge items) even though he thinks acquiring debt is wrong and he doesn't want to hurt Amanda.

Couples Activity: Identifying Your Defense Mechanisms

After reading through the defense mechanisms, attempt to identify the ones you use and share your insights with your spouse. Then ask him or her if they can identify any that they use during tense moments when discussing finances. Keep in mind that you can only truly change yourself, so tread lightly with this activity and attempt to have a constructive dialogue that is non-blaming.

After you have identified the defense mechanisms that you use most often, agree to a way to give each other feedback when you catch each other using them. For instance, when Craig notices that I'm using denial (and feeling stressed about money), he waits awhile and asks me, "Are you okay? Can we finish our discussion later today or tomorrow?" And when I feel that he's using rationalization to explain any of his nonessential purchases, I ask him, "Can we talk about our budget when you have time, maybe over a cup of coffee or dinner?" These questions leave room for flexibility while curbing defensiveness in your partner.

In marriage and committed romantic relationships, one of the biggest hurdles many couples face is how to approach difficult conversations about money without getting defensive, making accusations against his or her partner, or trying to prove a point. Defensiveness leads to an unfortunate pattern of attack and more defensiveness where both partners believe they must prove they're right and must defend their positions. Defensiveness is often a matter of trying to protect yourself from being hurt. Using defensive mechanisms can be helpful temporarily, but prevents you from dealing with reality. The wounds we have from former relationships may surface during arguments, especially about touchy topics such as finances that can cause you to feel intense emotions and to get defensive.

How to Deal with Defensiveness During Money Talks

During tough conversations about money, it's helpful to choose battles wisely and to distinguish between what is and what isn't worth making an issue about. For instance, Ethan feels very triggered by any purchases that Caitlyn makes, and he often jumps to conclusions rather than asking her about them. In some cases, she's buying items for their home that are necessities, such as cleaning products or paper goods. However, when Ethan sees her walk in the front door with bags, he assumes she's been on a spending spree, and he might make a critical comment to her. These comments often elicit a defensive response from Caitlyn, which can lead to an argument.

Many people get defensive when they feel their partner doesn't agree with them or when they point out something they did wrong. For many couples, like Caitlyn and Ethan, bickering about money can feel like chronic warfare that erodes the quality of their relationship. This can make it tough to have money talks in a reasonable or calm way because they use denial or rationalize their own behavior.

When dealing with differences with your partner, the key is to listen attentively, understand each other's perspective, validate one another's feelings, rein in defensiveness, and stop criticizing and blaming each other. When you feel like you're under attack, rather than fighting back, focus on doing a better job at listening to your partner's viewpoint and explaining your views in a loving way.

Self-Protection and Defensiveness

Truth be told, it takes two people to contribute to a miscommunication or dispute. According to psychologist Daniel B. Wile, if a pattern of attack and defensiveness continues over time, it can diminish love and respect between partners.[8] The dynamics of defensiveness and the destructive consequences it can have on a couple's happiness are common when it comes to couples dealing with finances. And while many of us can become defensive from time to time, it's crucial to recognize that a pattern of behavior can become a way of life in a relationship.

Married for over three decades, Alyssa, fifty-nine, and Ted, sixty, who you met in Chapter 1, contacted me for couples therapy due to their ongoing tension and high conflict over money. If Alyssa gets defensive when Ted questions her about loaning money to a family member and she defends her position by saying, "You spend lots of money playing golf," this will only aggravate Ted and cause him to react in an equally defensive manner. Most likely, he will retaliate by justifying or rationalizing his golf expenses. The result is a kind of feedback loop in which they both get defensive, blame each other, and continue to bicker. Instead, it would be more productive for Alyssa to explain why she loaned her cousin $2,000.00 to help fund an internet startup and discuss his repayment plan.

Defensiveness rears its head most obviously when we feel attacked or blamed for what we might view as nonissues or minor infractions, or when we perceive the issue being discussed isn't our fault. However, an equally likely but less apparent trigger of defensiveness is the feeling that our efforts are unappreciated or have gone unrecognized. Keep in mind the high stakes for partners who let defensiveness and its consequences go unchecked. If defensiveness goes unimpeded, it is a common predictor of divorce according to Dr. John Gottman, a leading marriage and relationship expert.[9]

How to Let Go of Being Right and Stop Being Defensive about Money

We've all been there, embroiled in an argument with our partner, caught up in the emotion, and perhaps more crucially, unsure of how something seemingly small escalates. The touchy topic of money often causes couples to try to prove who is right versus who is wrong. This way of relating totally misses the point of moving beyond the spat in a constructive way that avoids future quarrels.

For instance, Amanda and Keith often get caught up in an ongoing cycle of bickering about small money issues that often escalate quickly and cause Keith to retreat. Recently, Amanda noticed that Keith had a $120.00 purchase on his credit card at his favorite bike shop (when she saw his statement on the kitchen table). Without stopping to get more information, Amanda accused Keith of being extravagant, and he counterattacked by blaming her for their financial problems because she went on a vacation with her mother and sister. After calming down later that night, Keith explained that he had refurbished his old bike to get back in shape rather than buying a new one or paying monthly gym fees.

What Amanda and Keith need is a way to stop blaming each other and to let go of being right. Strife in a relationship is given oxygen when partners cling to the idea that one of them is right—which necessarily means that the other is wrong. This dynamic of needing to "win" an argument or conversation breeds resentment and self-righteous indignation that makes growth difficult. In his book, *The New Rules of Marriage*, author and therapist Terrance Real advises that couples ask themselves, "Do I want to be right, or do I want to be married?"[10]

While it's tempting to launch into expressing anger and to get into defense mode when you feel hurt or frustrated, it can alienate your partner and drive a wedge between you. That said, you can accomplish more and improve your communication if you tell your partner how you feel and what you need in a positive way. One of the most effective ways to do this is to use "I" statements to express how you feel and to follow this with a brief explanation about what triggered this emotion and what you need to feel better in the relationship.[11]

To illustrate this strategy, if Amanda says to Keith, "I feel frustrated because we don't have a budget and would appreciate it if you'd draft one with me." This "I" statement might encourage a conversation about money.[12] However, a "You" statement such as, "You never care about saving money or getting ahead in life" is likely to cause Keith to react in a defensive way or to avoid the conversation by walking away.

Next, partners need to break the pattern of defensive fighting and negativity by being quiet or pausing during a disagreement. Instead of continuing to speak when things are tense, do some jumping jacks or share a three-breath hug. Activate your parasympathetic nervous system, calm down, and try to see your mate for who they truly are—your ally, not your enemy, explains relationship expert Cheryl Fraser, PhD.[13] This communication tool is akin to a way in which we feel refreshed in response to a change of scenery. Think of what Dr. Fraser calls "changing your physiology" like a momentary vacation that will hopefully impart of sense of calm and a new, perhaps more empathetic perspective.

Couples also need to consider several other communication strategies that may help break the pattern of defensiveness. For example, stopping and counting to three and taking three deep breaths can work in much the same way that engaging in physical movement does. It slows down a conflict that may be escalating and can restore peace. Another similar tactic is choosing a "code word," suggests Cheryl Fraser.[14] A "code word" such as "peace" allows couples to identify when one or both partners are getting defensive without saying much or rehashing an argument.

During a conversation, if Amanda starts a conversation with Keith with an "I" statement, and she counts to three and takes deep breaths when she's feeling upset, this communication style may reap the result of less defensiveness from him.[15] If partners can bring a sense of mindfulness to their communication and agree on a word or phrase that, when used by one partner or another, is a shorthand for saying "we are getting off track, let's begin again," couples can create for themselves a sort of reset button.

The following are more ways to curb defensiveness during discussions about money before it leads to bitterness and resentment. If one strategy doesn't work, don't give up; simply try another one and see if it will help you and your partner to increase understanding and encourage lower-conflict conversations about finances.

Five Tips to Curb Defensiveness and Have More Constructive Money Talks:

1. Keep a calm composure and don't forget to breathe deeply. While it's natural to raise your voice and get agitated when you feel attacked, lower your voice and focus on staying relaxed when you become aware that tension is escalating. Do

something soothing like doodling or counting to five while you take several belly breaths.

2. Be mindful of your partner's good qualities. Believe the best of your partner's intentions toward you and don't focus on their flaws. Instead of assuming the worst of your partner, get in the habit of assuming he or she really does care about you. Recall fond memories and think about the ways your partner showed love to you in the past.

3. Be sure to express love and use kind words that show support like "I'm on your side," or "I've got your back." Do more listening than talking and validate what your partner is saying. For example, "I get it, you're really upset with me right now."

4. Don't take things personally when you disagree. Imagine that your partner's comments have nothing to do with your character or worth. If you find yourself getting triggered, picture that there aren't any threats, assaults, or insults in your partner's statements. They're just speaking about what upsets them, but it doesn't change your value or worth. If they say something negative like, "You're too sensitive," resist the temptation to respond with a counterattack, such as "You're so mean." Instead, let them know you feel hurt, take some space, and agree to talk when your emotions have simmered down.

5. Don't attack your partner's character, values, or core beliefs. Being in attack or defense mode when discussing money issues can lead to withdrawal, shutdowns, or resentment. Remember that anger is usually a symptom of underlying hurt, fear, and frustration, so stop and reflect on your own emotions. Listen to your partner's side of the story instead of planning your counterargument. Validate their perspective first—then share your viewpoint. When you feel like attacking your partner, ask yourself: What am I trying to accomplish?

In the end, as with so many of the negative behavioral patterns that grow out of a couple's ineffective communication style, defensiveness can cause couples to "dig their heels in" and fight dirty. However, overcoming defensiveness is possible by bringing a sense of awareness and a set of relationship tools to money talks. Remember: We're human, we all make mistakes, and the relationship wins when you both generate a solution within the context of a loving relationship. Commitment to changing the destructive dynamics of defensiveness is a manifestation of a couple's love and will serve to strengthen the bonds that bring you together as a couple and enhance your financial health.

Now that you've learned and practiced the skills needed to dial down defensiveness during money talks, and choosing your relationship over trying to "be right," we'll discuss ways to improve financial intimacy with your partner. Spencer Sherman, MBA, explains that when couples are financially intimate, they share all relevant financial transactions with each other.[16] In *The Cure for Money Madness*, he writes, "Money Talk, therefore, becomes a whole new way to strengthen a couple's intimacy. It's the new foreplay." Boosting your financial intimacy and having easier money talks go hand in hand. Both will help you increase your feelings of trust in your partner and prevent deception and incomplete information from being exchanged. Financial intimacy is an essential element of forming the foundation of a happy, long-lasting partnership.

Low-Conflict Conversations Lead to Financial Intimacy

Communicating love and admiration to your partner is a hallmark of courtship, yet after getting married or moving in together, you might find that positive comments have diminished. This includes telling your partner that you love him or her. These comments start to fade in frequency over time for many couples. You may not express gratitude for your partner aloud because it may not come naturally. Instead, you might make a big deal over trivial issues and miss the big picture. All intimate relationships need to be nurtured, and sharing a money secret is one way to help you feel closer to your partner and improve your financial intimacy.

Couples Activity: Share a Money Secret

One good way to enhance financial closeness with your partner is to share a secret, according to author Spencer Sherman.[17] Tell a story about a time you were bad with money, made a mistake, miscalculated, or any kind of financial error. It's analogous to getting naked with your partner and exposing part of your past that feels forbidden or dark. When Craig and I were first married, I disclosed how I went on a vacation with my children that I couldn't afford (when I was a single parent), and it brought us closer. In fact, he ended up being vulnerable with me and sharing a story about a time he was laid off from a job after college, moved back home, and had to borrow money from his parents.

Sharing a secret with your partner can be transformative if you want to boost financial intimacy.[18] When Ethan and Caitlyn filled out their Financial Styles Quiz in my office, it seemed obvious to me that there were secrets between them that were making it hard to be authentic and vulnerable during our sessions. When I encouraged them to share a secret, Caitlyn hesitated, but after pausing, she opened up about an incident involving her credit card being declined in college that she had never told Ethan.

Caitlyn turns toward Ethan and says,

> I never told you about the time that I was skiing with a group of girlfriends in the Rocky Mountains and we were renting skis and my credit card was declined. Because I didn't have a debit card or cash, I had to wait alone in the lodge for four hours while my friends were having a blast skiing. This was an important day for me because it was the first time I realized the impact my shopping addiction was having on my life. I knew then that I needed to stop and went into therapy shortly after this ski trip.

Fortunately, when Caitlyn shared her secret, it prompted Ethan to share a secret of his own, and he told her about a time after college when he overdrew his checking account because he underestimated the magnitude of paying first and last month's rent (plus a deposit) on a new apartment during a time when his parents held back financial help. Ethan made himself vulnerable by telling Caitlyn that this mistake snowballed and ended up causing him to lose his first choice of an apartment after graduating from college.

In Caitlyn and Ethan's case, sharing secrets had the effect of foreplay before making love because it jump-started a discussion about their lack of intimacy and how good it feels when they are vulnerable with one another. During our second Zoom interview, they moved closer to each other and agreed that part of their "Communication Pledge" was going to be to share secrets more often.

When encouraging couples to share intimate information during couples therapy sessions, I often ask couples to ask each other open-ended questions. My goal is to expand their intimacy and help them to become more familiar with each other's wishes, needs, and desires. This activity can be practiced at home or during a couples therapy session.

Couples Activity: Ask Open-Ended Questions

Another way to increase financial intimacy with your partner during low-conflict conversations and to learn more about each other's preferences and desires is to ask open-ended questions. According to Dr. John Gottman, posing questions that require no more than a *yes* or *no* response can kill a conversation, whereas open-ended questions such as "What did you like about our money talk last night?" require a deeper response that can enhance conversation.[19]

Ultimately, broadly relatable questions serve as a tool for partners becoming more active in taking an emotional interest in and inventory of their mate. And in these trying, unprecedented times, it seems the positive results of such inquiry will provide a counterbalance to the strife, uncertainty, and stress that you're dealing with regarding financial matters.

Couples Activity: Four Open-Ended Questions to Ask Your Partner About Your Financial Communication[20]

1. What's one thing that you think could improve our financial situation?
2. What are two things you like about the way I communicate with you about money?
3. What are two things you would like to see me change about how I communicate with you about money?
4. How would you prefer we spend our money (give more to charity, go on more vacations, save more for retirement, etc.)?

Sometimes couples are so absorbed in their problems that they forget to see their partner as a person. If you answer the above questions and then compare responses (or interview each other), you're on the path to building authentic love and improving the quality of your relationship. Further, the following points can help you lower tension, strengthen your relationship, and create more intimacy.

The strategies below will help you and your partner have low-conflict money talks and achieve financial intimacy.

Eight Tips to Boost Financial Intimacy and Have Low-Conflict Conversations About Money:

1. Make a "Communication Pledge" as a couple to have regular check-ins about finances such as staying on topic, using active listening, and full disclosure. Attempt to have these discussions during times when you won't be distracted by TV, chores, or other conditions. Create ways to have productive and loving money talks monthly or more often if needed. Plan a time to meet with your partner in a private location and take notes so you can keep track of the progress on the goals you've set. Make this a regular habit and pledge to honor it.

2. Start a conversation by sharing your feelings, such as "I feel worried because we've gone over our budget this week. Can I ask you something?" This will encourage your partner's willingness to share and engage in the conversation. State how you feel, why you feel that way, and what you need to feel better in your relationship. Be specific, such as "I feel concerned because we've had a lot of expenses this month. I need for us to go over our bills together, and I'd like to do this once a month when we have a money talk."

3. Agree to change the subject or press the pause button (and decompress) if your conversation becomes too heated or it's not feeling productive. However, resume your money talk within twenty-four hours so resentment doesn't build.

4. Show compassion, understanding, and respect for differences in your values and financial styles and money scripts. You can demonstrate this by asking good questions, actively listening, and expressing empathy. Make sure you understand their message and respond thoughtfully to his or her feelings by offering responses such as "That must have been hard for you when you made a mistake with money."

5. Take fiscal ownership. Fully disclose your financial history, purchases, assets, and debts. This usually means sharing bank and credit card statements. If you focus more on your part of the problem and make a plan to change your behavior, it will encourage your partner to do the same.

6. Freely communicate a money secret to your partner regarding finances. You might say, "I overdrew my checking account and had to pay a fee due to being careless." This kind of sharing will enhance financial intimacy and encourage your partner to disclose important money transactions (with transparency).

7. Ask your partner open-ended questions. For instance, you might say, "I'd love to hear more about how much money you envision saving for vacations and where you want to go."

8. Turn toward your partner when they make a bid for connection, affection, or any other type of communication about finances. Overtures often display themselves in basic but powerful ways such as a smile or a pat on the shoulder. In contrast, turning away might mean you continue to watch TV or look at your phone (and say nothing) when your partner is sharing something important with you. Turning against your partner might be saying something negative like "There you go again, what's the matter now?" In their book *Love Prescription*, John Gottman, PhD, and Julie Swartz Gottman, PhD, write, "What turning toward really does is put money in a couple's emotional bank account."[21] They also explain that turning toward your partner can help you manage conflict.

When one partner communicates effectively, it encourages their partner to do the same. It's also important to be aware of internal and external distractions, including your iPhone notifications and being hungry or tired. While you can't avoid these distractions, you can turn off your phone, shut off the TV, and make eye contact with each other. If hunger or fatigue is an issue, let your partner know you need a snack or nap in order to be fully present!

Married for over twenty-five years, Kendra, sixty-two, and Sam, sixty-four, own a successful real estate business and raised two kids while caring for aging parents. They maintain a partnership in all aspects of their marriage and have achieved financial intimacy. While they had some early struggles when starting their business, they both pointed out, during our interview, that they work well as a team and try to lead a balanced life that includes monthly conversations about money. They strive to make sure their work and home life are harmonious and in line with their values of not spending more than they make, saving money for retirement, and being able to fund travel and time with their two grown children. By making time together a priority, they carve out time to discuss important issues such as unexpected expenses. They also avoid getting accusatory or defensive when talking about finances, whether together or with their financial planner, who is helping them plan their retirement. As a result, they're reaping the rewards of a successful marriage and looking forward to a prosperous retirement.

Communication affects how safe and secure we feel in our relationships as well as our level of intimacy. Since communication and intimacy are connected, take time every day to really listen to your partner and have the courage to ask open-ended questions (rather than making assumptions) to make sure you understand them. Over time, you will find that you will feel closer, argue or bicker less, and feel more satisfied in your relationship with each other and with money.

Kendra puts it like this,

> All of our money and property are together. We rarely argue about finances. We make all decisions together about buying on credit and how we'll pay it off. We discuss places we'd like to go and things we'd like to do. And honestly, our opinions. The one who feels strongly, gets their way. If Sam tells me I should spend more on myself, I listen since I grew up with Depression-era parents who made me conscious of what I/we need versus what I/we want.

By learning to have low-conflict conversations and boosting your financial intimacy, you'll be better prepared to discuss core money transactions, such as saving, giving to charity, paying for your mortgage, and paying off debt. You will also be enhancing financial intimacy by honoring your "Communication Pledge" to make regular money talks a habit. Before we move on to specific topics such as building a budget, getting rid of debt, and creating a savings plan, reading Chapter 3 will help you choose a money management system that works best for you as financial partners.

Chapter 3
Money Management Systems
Joint Versus Separate Accounts

Regardless of the financial status of your household, it's important to understand that financial health is not only about how much money you earn but how you manage what you earn, your savings, and your investments. It includes planning for retirement and your children's future if you start a family. If you desire economic health, it's critical to pay your bills on time, live within your budget, take responsibility for your financial mistakes, and use an effective money management system that matches your goals as a couple.

Kendra, sixty-two, and Sam, sixty-four, whom you met in Chapter 2, have been married for over twenty-five years, and they manage joint accounts and run a successful real estate business together. Their common-pot system, in which they merge all finances, has allowed them to be transparent and helped them navigate the challenges of owning a profitable business together while raising kids and caring for aging parents. What struck me about this couple when we met was their intense love and insistence on full disclosure. They talk about money often and reflect on their financial goals, which they reported is one of the main reasons why they have a strong relationship and have achieved prosperity as a couple.

Kendra reflects,

> It's a partnership. We realize that we're a team and we rise and fall together. Anything of importance is discussed before we act. Our past successes motivate us to keep trusting each other. Combining our resources keeps us honest and stronger as a couple. We don't always agree on how to spend money for our business or home, but we've learned to compromise. When one of us feels strongly about something and has the facts to show good results, their opinion counts more.

According to marriage and relationship experts, Dr. John Gottman and Dr. Julie Swartz Gottman, couples who talk about their hopes and dreams with one another openly are more likely to prioritize time and resources, including finances, and are more likely to create a sense of purpose as a couple and find happiness.[1] For most couples, the beginning of this process is choosing a money management system they're both comfortable with in the present and moving forward into the future.

The Advantages of Merging Finances with Your Partner

One of the first steps for you and your partner to achieve financial health is to decide together if you want to combine assets. Most financial experts agree that setting up joint accounts, like Kendra and Sam have done, is preferred because it enhances transparency and accountability. It can work well for couples because it requires collaboration and ongoing conversations about spending and saving habits. A 2022 study by Gladstone et al. discovered that couples who pooled all of their economic resources (compared to those who keep all or some of their money separate) have greater relationship satisfaction and are less likely to break up.[2] Though joining bank accounts can benefit all couples, the effect is particularly strong for those with scarce financial resources (low household income or who report feeling financially stressed), according to these researchers.

Does marriage or a committed relationship necessitate merging money? Not necessarily, and the good news is that while some couples like Kendra and Sam have been successful in maintaining good communication and financial health with joint accounts, there are other options for you and your partner if your mindset or priorities don't work well with commingling all assets. For instance, having one or more individual accounts might make sense because you value your individuality or because your finances are complex, and you believe combining all of your assets will add stress to your relationship. However, if your partner doesn't want to merge finances, it's a good idea to ask them why and to discuss options, including the positives and negatives of various money management models.

While research demonstrates the benefits of commingling your funds, some financial planners advise that partners have their own individual accounts, in addition to a joint account. For instance, Jeff Motske, CFP, a certified financial planner, writes, "However—and this is a big however—I also think it's important for couples to have their own individual accounts where they can set aside some extra cash just for themselves. It's important to maintain some sense of independence and individuality so long as you remain honest and transparent with your spouse."[3]

How to Choose a Money Management System

A crucial step to improving your understanding and communication about money is deciding how you want to manage it. This involves having organizational systems in place such as balancing a checkbook or using an online money management site like QuickBooks or an app like Rocket Money. Coming up with a system of managing your money that both you and your partner can agree on can be a challenge. This may bring up issues of unequal assets, debts, and differences in your philosophies about spending and saving.

As mentioned earlier, most experts recommend that you share and commingle funds in joint checking and savings accounts (common-pot) if you desire transparency and trust each other. Some couples combine everything and others settle on commingling some of their funds and keeping some separate. Either way, this usually means paying bills out of a joint checking account. Having joint accounts requires that you have a "us against the problem" mindset. Couples like Kendra and Sam manage joint accounts successfully and blend money without high conflict. Their common-pot system has allowed them to be transparent, and they have been faithful about having money talks on a regular basis.

Kendra explains, "We share everything and if one of us overspends or dips too much into our savings, the other person speaks up. We're completely open and honest and that has helped us build a strong, long-term marriage. We are each other's best friend."

On the other hand, some of the couples whom I interviewed or counseled in my practice, who maintain separate checking and savings accounts, reported that they did so because of the complexities associated with remarriage or blended families. Others had issues with mistrust or poor communication. They simply didn't feel confident that their partner would hold the balls in the air if they dropped them, and many have dealt with financial infidelity.

For instance, Deborah and Seth have been dealing with the turmoil that comes with financial infidelity for many years. Deborah, thirty-six, says, "We have separate accounts (checking and savings) because I find it difficult to trust that Seth, thirty-eight, will follow through on things. He has hidden money in the past and kept secrets from me. Communication is a struggle and something we're continuing to learn about. I find it difficult and feel lonely within the relationship." Through our couples therapy sessions, Deborah, a journalist, and Seth, a sales manager for a wine outlet, are learning the value of extending trust to one another through habits such as regular money talks and enhancing financial intimacy.

Keep in mind that you and your partner will benefit from taking the time to select a money management model that's a good fit for both of you. Reading the following section about three options for economic systems will help you assess what will work for you as a couple, and it can be revised as you plan your future together. Remember that your goal needs to be improving your communication about finances and working together as a team, regardless of the system you choose.

The Three Money Management Systems

There are several models that you can use to handle your finances together. Borrowing from researchers on marriage, stepfamilies, and money management systems, I will describe three economic systems commonly used by couples: one-pot (or common-pot), two-pot, and three-pot.

The One-pot System

With the one-pot model, also referred to as a common-pot system, all of a couple's money is combined into one checking and one savings account. This includes both partners' incomes and any alimony or child support. Couples actually commingle their financial resources. All expenses and debts, including rent or mortgage payments and household expenses, are paid out of these joint accounts. Money in these accounts is dispersed according to an individual and family member's needs. In the case of stepfamilies or blended families, there is no distinction between the needs of biological children and stepchildren. The main advantage of this model is that couples can think of their money as belonging to both of them rather than as individuals. If there's a concern with finances, it fosters an "us against the problem" versus "us against each other" mindset.

The Two-pot System

By contrast, in the two-pot system, couples keep their incomes, payments, bills, and debts in two separate checking and savings accounts and pay for all child-rearing and household expenses on a fifty-fifty basis. This is especially relevant if one or both partners have children from a prior marriage. When necessary, couples who use the two-pot system unite economically to meet the needs of the total family, according to family researcher Barbara Fishman.[4] This might mean contributing to a joint checking account for things like paying for a vacation or college tuition for children when these issues arise.

The Three-pot System

Lastly, with the three-pot model, each partner handles personal expenses for themselves and the children they brought to the marriage, and money isn't combined. However, both partners contribute to a third account that's used for the expenses of the entire family (mortgage or rent, food, household repairs, insurance, vacations, etc.). It's really a mixture of the common-pot and two-pot systems, but it emphasizes partners being responsible for their own biological children and not commingling money. Though both partners contribute to this account, the contributions don't have to be equal. The main difference between the two-pot and three-pot systems is that the two-pot system places more of an emphasis on autonomy than the three-pot system. These two models are commonly used in stepfamilies and blended families but can be used by any couple. In Chapter 10, they're described in depth. Couples who use the two-pot or three-pot system often use apps such as PayPal or Venmo to reimburse each other.

In 2020, financial writer Alice Holbrook, conducted a survey in conjunction with The Harris Poll, involving 1,500 US adults who have a significant other.[5] The study revealed that 77 percent of respondents combine money at least partly and that the likelihood of doing so varies by age. Unsurprisingly, 48 percent of Generation Z adults (ages eighteen to twenty-seven) living with a significant other say they don't combine their finances, in comparison with 23 percent of Millennials (ages twenty-eight to forty-three) and 20 percent each of Gen X (forty-four to fifty-nine) and Baby Boomers (ages fifty-six to seventy-four). In other words, 80 percent of Gen X and Baby Boomers do commingle finances. However, "Statistics can't determine what's right for you and your partner," according to Alice Holbrook. Truth be told, only you can decide what's the right fit for you and then adopt a money management system that you can both embrace and actually thrive with.

Most couples who have a common-pot system feel it unifies them as a couple and prevents them from having financial shortages or problems. It eliminates the stress of tracking multiple accounts at various financial institutions. In fact, Kendra and Sam told me that it gives them "one single, simplified point of view when deciding what to spend money on." They give themselves an allowance from their joint checking account every month. Sam also mentioned that it has helped them consolidate points on their credit cards which offer rewards. This allows them to plan their future together and keeps them motivated to save for their retirement.

Sam explains,

> Since we combine assets into one checking account, we've been able to save up our points on our major credit card and we were able to enjoy a trip to Arizona last winter where we hiked the Grand Canyon (in shorts) and got a break from the frigid Northeast weather. If we had separate accounts, this wouldn't have been possible. We're definitely going to take advantage of this in the future, especially after we retire and can travel to some of the places on our bucket list together.

For couples who own a business like Sam and Kendra, the common-pot system simplifies their lives. It also makes sense for couples who have never made the same amount of money. For these couples, figuring out ratios of who should pay what is very complicated, and commingling assets makes it easier for them to have conversations about finances.

In my case, I have discovered that the common-pot method works well because it promotes full disclosure and communication about finances with my husband, Craig. Since I have a money vigilance script, the one-pot system allows me to discuss money with Craig because we both have access to the same checking and savings accounts. If I notice a purchase that seems frivolous or questionable, we've agreed to discuss it openly and I don't assume the worst. Fortunately, we have similar goals about saving for vacations and retirement, and we've met with a certified financial planner (CFP) who has helped us turn some of our assets into sound investments.

Unfortunately, one of the disadvantages of a common-pot system arises when you and your partner are in different places financially. If one partner is carrying a lot of credit card debt, has mismanaged money in the past, or has committed financial infidelity, these undeniable disparities come into focus. For instance, Deborah, who met you earlier, was unwilling to open joint accounts with Seth until he had paid off his debt. That said, most couples do find commingling assets makes it easier to track finances and to have productive money talks with full disclosure.

In recent years, the two-pot system, in which both of you maintain your own accounts for personal spending and savings and occasionally contribute to a joint checking account for shared expenses like a vacation, is becoming more common for couples. This approach can often lead to less friction when it comes to spending on things that affect one of you, like a night out with friends, paying off a student loan, donating to charities, or loaning money to an adult child from a former marriage. The challenges of this two-pot system include creating a plan for thoughtful communication about finances that includes full disclosure and maintains a shared vision for your future.

The two-pot system and three-pot models can also be a practical option for couples who get married, remarried, cohabitate at a later age, and/or have different values about spending. Married for eight years, Lisa, forty-nine, and Carla, forty-five, have struggled to choose a money management system that they agree upon. However, recently they compromised on the two-pot system because they desire personal autonomy and want control of their finances. Both employed full-time, they have similar financial goals, but their values are different. Lisa grew up in an affluent family, and she has an abundance mindset. She's also very focused on sustainability and climate change initiatives. On the other hand, Carla was raised in a lower-middle-class family where money was tight, so she tends to have a scarcity mindset. She supports Lisa's goals, but she doesn't always share her priorities and desire to contribute significant sums of money to non-profits with an environmental mission.

Since Lisa has a super saver financial style and a money vigilance script, she watches what they spend closely and sometimes accuses Carla of being frivolous in her spending and habits. Because Carla is a moderate spender with a money status script, she likes to project affluence to others, so spends a considerable amount of money on clothing, entertainment, and furnishings for their home. Since they've adopted the two-pot system and they each have their own "mad money" to spend on nonessential items, they've felt less tension about finances.

During our interview, Carla reflects,

Lisa and I agree on many things, but we clash sometimes about what to spend our money on after the bills are paid. For example, Lisa donates a lot of money to environmental agencies and recently purchased a hybrid SUV. While I admire her goals, I value updating my attire often and keeping our home looking beautiful. Since we've been using this new money system and have more control over spending, our bills still get paid, but we're arguing less and are more content in our relationship.

Some of the remarried couples that I've counseled and interviewed who wed at an older age and raised children in a blended family have also found that a two-pot or three-pot system works better for them. Generally, the financial considerations of a remarriage are more complicated than those of a first marriage and this can make it a challenge to blend finances. These complications include child support, alimony, college tuition, and weddings (for yours, mine, and ours).

For instance, Barbara, fifty-nine, and Nick, sixty-four, have been remarried for twenty-five years and each brought two children to the marriage. This couple finds success in a three-pot system. This system allows them to have separate checking accounts to pay for incidentals and expenses for their biological children without having to check in with each other about these expenditures. However, their joint checking account allows them to have full disclosure about household and shared expenses.

Another remarried couple, Grace, sixty-five, and Neil, sixty-six, consider their twenty-year marriage harmonious and keep most of their finances separate because it's a second marriage for Neil, and Grace was forty-two when they wed, and she didn't want to blend finances. Neil had two teenagers when they tied the knot, and Grace didn't have children. When this couple married, Grace was a college teacher and ended up retiring after thirty years with a good pension. Neil, a successful architect, has been able to fund both of his grown sons' college tuitions at private colleges, and he has substantial savings. Grace and Neil own a beautiful home in a seaside community, and they both contribute equally to bills and vacations but also have separate accounts. They believe that a two-pot system encourages both cooperation and personal autonomy. Some couples, especially those who marry at a later age like Grace and Neil, prefer having separate accounts. Since both Grace and Neil are super savers (with money vigilance scripts), they have achieved financial health in their long marriage and share household and other expenses that come up.

Grace puts it like this,

> Most of my pension goes into my checking account and I share expenses fifty-fifty with Neil, so I deposit some of it into our household account. But I have a separate account where I deposit the money from a part-time job and some of my pension monthly. This allows me the freedom to plan trips with my extended family and friends without checking with Neil and to preserve my own individuality. Neil is fine with this, and we split expenses for the "big stuff" like the house, remodeling, family vacations, and essential items like groceries. We have a formula for who pays what, and it's close to being equivalent. When we eat in restaurants or go out socially, we are comfortable sharing the cost or taking turns paying.

Grace reflects, "If it's not broken, why fix it?" When we discussed why she and Neil held onto the two-pot system after Neil's two kids launched; she said that they just didn't see the point in changing a system that has worked for them for over two decades.

While the two-pot and three-pot models tend to limit transparency about finances, they can benefit remarried couples who bring children to the marriage and have complex finances involving child support, alimony, or debt from a former marriage, according to researcher Kay Pasley.[6] If you married later in life or have unequal incomes, it might also make sense to adopt one of these systems. While the two and three-pot systems might make money talks more challenging, they might work well for couples who have complex situations or who are coping with financial infidelity and have trust issues. Haley and Conner's story illustrates how you can commingle some assets and have some individual accounts while upholding an "us against the problem" mindset.

Haley, forty-five, and Conner, forty-eight, are a couple who have been in a committed relationship for four years and have complex finances. They became engaged and started living together three years prior to our interview. When I asked them about their long engagement, Haley explained that she was hesitant to get married and blend finances because Conner owns a prosperous business, and she doesn't want him to think that she's taking advantage of him. Unsurprisingly, a situation in which partners have unequal assets can be bothersome to some people. Haley had been divorced in her late twenties and felt guilty because she had limited assets compared to Conner. But prior to moving in with him, Haley worked full-time, earned a good income, and was a saver. After moving in together, she started working for the business that Conner had spent decades building. When we discussed their finances, Conner opened up and expressed concern about offending Haley's sensitivities about her independence because she feels strongly that she needs her own checking account to maintain her autonomy.

Since Conner pushed for a common-pot system where their finances would be joined and Haley resisted, they compromised on a three-pot system. Each person contributes to a checking account for household expenses, like their mortgage payment and utilities, and has a separate checking account for discretionary spending and/or savings. In addition, they both contribute to a joint savings account for household repairs and to fund their vacations. Even though Conner is a saver, Haley has trust issues due to baggage from her first marriage. As a result, she values a separate checking account to spend money as she chooses, including depositing funds into her daughter Kayla's college account.

Haley shares,

> When we met, I fell head over heels for Conner and knew he was the one for me immediately, but it took him a while to come around. We finally got engaged after I threatened to end our relationship if we didn't move forward. Even after we did so, I didn't want to combine finances, and he insisted that we split everything fifty-fifty, including paying the mortgage, utilities, food, etc. So, I told him that I didn't agree with this because he makes more money than I do, and he has two young kids living with us. My sixteen-year-old daughter, Kayla, lives with us full-time, and she has a job on weekends and spends her own money. I also insisted on a prenup before we get married. I want to be sure Kayla is taken care of (if we divorce).

Haley continues, "Because he owns a profitable business, Conner has agreed to contribute more than I do to our joint checking account and savings account (for household repairs). I have my own checking and savings accounts. This seems to be working out, and I'm building trust in Conner. But I have a prenup to fall back on if we break up."

On the other hand, couples who desire high levels of trust, communication, and commitment often choose the common-pot system of commingling all of their assets into one joint checking and savings account. In their book, *Coupleship, Inc.,* authors Debra Kaplan and Rick Kahler explain that the plus side of combining everything is that there is total financial transparency as to income and expenses.[7] They write, "Each partner has full access and opportunity to be fully aware of the money flow. It's easy to track. There are no secrets." If you want to consider merging your money, regardless of your relationship status, the following section will give you the tools you need to succeed.

How to Merge Your Lives and Your Money

If you've decided to take this step and mesh your finances, it may actually be easier than you imagined. When Sam and Kendra got married, they took these four essential steps to set up a joint account:

1. Discuss which bank you want to use for your joint accounts. This involves balancing factors such as interest rates, convenience, and personal preferences. Remember to keep an open mind and listen to your partner's perspective. If one of you feels strongly about the benefits of a certain bank, consider their request, especially if they have data to back it up (such as higher interest rates).

2. Set up a joint checking and savings account. Keep your old accounts open for at least a month so you don't bounce checks. This also allows for any direct deposits and automatic payments to clear. Be sure to inform your bank of this decision and keep in mind that it's a smoother process if you open the new account at the same bank where at least one of

you already has an existing account. If you open up a joint account at a new bank, you'll both need to give them personal information, such as your social security number, date of birth, employment data, and so on.

3. Redirect both of your paychecks into a joint checking account by first informing your employers and giving them your new account number (you may prefer in person for confidentiality). It could take about two weeks for a new direct deposit to show up in your new joint account. Then, you can direct a certain amount of money into a joint savings account each month.

4. Have a discussion with your partner about your budget (see Chapter 4) and what you both agree is a reasonable amount to withdraw from your checking account each month for cash, groceries, eating out or takeout, and nonessential expenses. In addition, it's important to decide how you feel about whether it's okay with both of you to withdraw cash or use your debit or credit card without the other person's permission.

Marriage and committed relationships are made up of thousands of decisions every day—most of them having to do with how to spend money and allocate financial resources. Every couple is unique, and you and your partner need to decide on the money management system that works best for both of you in the present and in the years to come. While having joint accounts may be easier or more convenient, more and more Generation Z and Millennial couples adopt a two- or three-pot approach because they encourage both cooperation and personal autonomy. Many couples, especially those who marry at a later age, prefer having both a joint account and separate accounts which could be considered "mad money" for nonessential items. They may feel this gives them more control over their spending on personal things like buying clothing or going out to lunch with a friend.

Making a "Communication Pledge" to discuss finances once a month will give you and your partner the opportunity to decide how to best manage your money. Developing a viable money management system, revealing any outstanding debts and financial obligations, and arriving at a shared savings goal are all good and well. But the proof (and perhaps the profit) is your ability to regularly check in with each other about your finances. An open, ongoing dialogue will foster long-term happiness and help couples overcome the bumps in the road—and big bills—along the way.

Four Tips for Developing a Sustainable Money Management System for Couples:

1. Listen to what your partner is saying and tune in to the feelings behind their words. Remember conversations about money are sensitive discussions that can trigger intense feelings and fears. Be understanding and show empathy in your words and requests. Be sure to inquire about your partner's dreams and fears and seek ways to manage differences and challenges.

2. Come to an agreement. The best money management model is not set in stone; it's really a matter of what you're comfortable with and can agree upon. The key to success is being able to discuss your options openly and to come to an agreement or compromise that suits your personal and family objectives.

3. Keep the lines of communication open. While the common-pot system lends itself to transparency and less financial infidelity, none of the money management systems described in this chapter are stress-free. Plan to have realistic expectations and regular money talks.

4. Monitor your money management system. It's important for you and your partner to monitor the system you decide to use, evaluate its effectiveness, be transparent, and take ownership of any mistakes that are made. Being able to discuss your money transactions with full disclosure will promote financial health and intimacy.

Regardless of the money management system you set up, you need to be transparent when you discuss finances with your partner. Keeping secrets is not a good way to enhance trust and intimacy, and it can damage your relationship. However, having regularly scheduled money talks to discuss finances with full disclosure will enhance your financial intimacy. It's not always easy to talk about money, so be sure to select a time and a place to talk which is conducive to privacy, and bring statements and a notepad since keeping track of your discussions is very important in achieving your financial goals. In Chapter 4, you will learn about developing a sustainable budget with your partner which will help you achieve prosperity and a relationship that endures the test of time.

PART II
Essentials of Financial Health

Chapter 4
Build a Budget

Having a budget, a spending and savings plan based on income and expenses, in place can help you and your partner achieve prosperity. The ability to become financially resilient and bounce back from adverse financial events, such as losing your job or unexpected expenses (car, home, children, etc.), is directly related to your financial health before the incident. According to CNN Business reporter Kathryn Vasel, "Sticking to a budget can be hard enough if it's just your own spending and savings you're tracking. Add another person to the mix and it gets trickier."[1] Creating a realistic budget—and sticking to it—is a critical step for couples who want to keep track of their expenses and save money.

When I began seeing Shane and Larry (whom you met in Chapter 1) for couples therapy, some of their main complaints were their lack of an updated and accurate budget, overspending, and difficulty discussing finances calmly without shutting down. Shane told me that he considers himself to be frugal and a good saver who is careful in the way he approaches money. On the other hand, Larry described himself as someone who wasn't willing to follow a budget consistently and had difficulty talking about finances without getting agitated, defensive, and justifying his expenditures. In other words, Shane is a super saver with a money vigilance script, and Larry is a super spender with a money worship script. Fortunately, Shane has been able to add Larry to his health insurance plan which has saved this couple over $6,000 a year.

That said, in 2020, only 74 percent of employers offered spousal benefits to same-sex couples, while 26 percent of employers still limited access to thousands of same-sex couples. This is based on a Kaiser

Family Foundation Employer Health Benefits Survey.[2] It's a 31 percent increase from 2016, when 43 percent provided same-sex spousal coverage. Further, a higher percentage of large companies offer same-sex spousal coverage. However, lack of access to spousal benefits can have a negative impact on the financial well-being of LGBTQ+ American couples, increasing their stress levels and contributing to high conflict in their relationships.

In addition, the high cost of healthcare, prescription drugs, and health insurance and the limited availability of affordable health care plans puts stress on millions of couples and families; it's not just limited to same-sex couples. For instance, the choice of a health insurance plan reflects different values, as the cost differential between the basic plan and the "premium" one can be significant and have a major impact on a budget. For example, even though Shane and Larry had health care coverage through Larry's law firm, the "premium plan" that gave them access to the physicians they preferred and had lower out-of-pocket costs was out of reach for them financially due to extremely high deductibles and monthly costs.

During our second therapy session, I explained to Shane and Larry that I believed they were ready to discuss their histories and values around money and that this would prepare them for developing a budget. During our initial interview, they spent time discussing their family background, money scripts, and financial styles, as well as the discrepancies between them. According to Christine Mathieu, a certified wealth coach and certified money coach (CMC), "You need to understand your relationship with money before you work on a budget or you'll keep repeating the same patterns. You also need to understand your hidden money dynamics. If you don't have the right relationship with money, you won't be motivated to live by a budget."[3] According to Mathieu, the most common problem she sees with couples is avoidance. She stated in a recent interview that partners "simply don't talk about money because they're afraid to."

Shane explains, "I believe that our current budget is inadequate and needs to be updated because our finances are complex. We've had to dip into our savings due to Larry's overspending. But whenever I suggest we sit down and talk about money, we argue and never finish the conversation because we have such different ideas about how to spend money. Larry just says he wants to talk about other things, which means he shuts down. This doesn't work well since we rarely discuss finances. I've been trying to remind Larry that we're a team and need to put money into our emergency fund and retirement accounts. We will need to continue to talk about these issues."

Explore Your Money Values Together

Before I worked out a budget plan with Larry and Shane, I brought up the topic of values. Talking about money with your partner brings up many issues, and one of the important ones is the approach you have about spending. It may seem obvious, but we all have different values when it comes to money. For instance, Shane told me he placed great importance on spending money on their home and cars, whereas Larry felt strongly that he valued eating meals out, buying quality clothing, and vacations—if there is any money left over after paying their basic bills. Shane was also more worried than Larry about their future financial health and having enough money for retirement.

Larry laments,

> Most of our disagreements are about how to spend any funds we have left after we pay our monthly bills like the mortgage and utilities. Shane prefers to eat at home, and I love eating in a restaurant at least twice a week. It's so much easier to communicate, and our conversations are more in-depth when we're not distracted by cooking and cleaning up. I get defensive when he calls me frivolous for wanting to eat out so much. He says that I'm not serious about wanting to live within a budget or save money, but I tell him that we just have different priorities.

In their book, *Thriving in Love and Money*, researchers Shanti and Jeff Feldhahn state that 63 percent of the couples they surveyed didn't see the value in what their partner saw as important to spend money on.[4] To make matters worse, most couples don't look for ways to understand and honor the reasons why their partner feels the way they do. Even more striking, their survey revealed that 67 percent of the couples endorsed the view that they privately feel their partner doesn't consider all of the factors involved in finances and that they're biased in their views. In other words, you might believe that your partner just isn't really thinking clearly. Of course, your partner might feel criticized, get defensive, and a clash in values during your money discussions can quickly descend into a battle.

Dr. John Gottman reminds us that criticism and contempt are the two leading causes of divorce, and a common culprit is often our contemptuous attitude about our partner's values about how he or she spends money.[5] Dr. Gottman's solution for this problem is reducing negative comments during conflict and allowing your partner to influence you. Dr. Gottman's long-term study of newlywed couples (mostly heterosexual) highlighted the importance of letting your partner influence you. His study revealed these stunning facts: "Even in the first few months of marriage, men who allow their wives to influence them have happier marriages and are less likely to divorce than men who resist their wives' influence. Statistically speaking, when a man is not willing to share power with his partner, there is an 81 percent chance his marriage will self-destruct." In his research, Dr. Gottman discovered that most women are likely to allow their partners to influence them, whereas men are less likely to succumb to their wives' influence.

Married for ten years, Heather, thirty-seven, and Kevin, thirty-eight, who met with me for couples therapy for six months, had many challenges with conflicting values, backgrounds, money scripts, and financial styles. Both busy professionals, they're raising two children and are expecting their third child soon. Unfortunately, their differences often led to arguments during the early years of their marriage. Since Heather is a super saver with a money vigilance script, and having a nice home and quality family time are a priority for her, she talked to Kevin about these values and was able to influence him. Kevin has been transparent during our couples therapy sessions about his need to display affluence to others—causing him to prioritize purchasing a car every few years.

It was important that Heather and Kevin come up with a compromise and a budget that reflected their different values so that they could purchase a home for their expanding family since Heather was pregnant with their third child. For instance, Kevin was willing to extend the time he drove the same car from four to eight years so that they could spend more on a new home and furnishings to make Heather feel content with their lifestyle. Kevin is a moderate spender with a money status script and is willing to compromise with Heather to bring more harmony to their relationship.

While differences in your values about money may be a touchy topic to discuss, you can gain a better understanding of each other's priorities and begin to honor them if you have an open and honest money talk. You might express the opinion that your partner's purchases are not worth it or not valuable. For instance, Kevin admitted he can be sarcastic and that sometimes he makes fun of Heather's frugal habits. Sarcasm was commonly used in his family growing up, and Heather wasn't raised with this style of communication. I suggested that Kevin express his feelings directly to Heather when he feels upset about her frugality (see Chapter 2), rather than using sarcasm.

For instance, Kevin might say, "I feel frustrated when you monitor all of my spending closely and I don't feel free to make more decisions about what I buy. I'd like to have more input on my purchases."

Likewise, I advised Heather to express her hurt feelings directly to Kevin. Following my suggestion, Heather said, "I feel hurt when you use sarcasm to make a point or to put me down. We won't always agree, but we need to be honest and speak frankly with each other about how we feel and what we need. Our values are very different, and that's why we clash sometimes."

During our therapy sessions, Heather and Kevin used my strategies for creating a budget and were able to come up with one that met both of their needs. And they were consistently following the tips in Chapter 2 to have easier conversations about money so they could communicate better rather than debating who is "right."

Honoring their "Communication Pledge" with each other, they were having regular money talks with full disclosure the last time we met. This turned out to be a date night that they both looked forward to. Kevin owned his part in their financial problems because he tends to overspend and focuses too much on prestige. Heather acknowledged that she can be condescending toward Kevin. At one point, she admitted that she sometimes digs her heels in (in order to prove a point) rather than promoting goodwill with Kevin. Recently, they have also been able to discuss the differences in their values about spending money and have been better able to honor and respect these differences. I explained to this couple that their willingness to explore each other's values about money as well as honor them would hopefully generalize to other aspects of their marriage because they were influencing each other and showing respect.

The process of discussing values about money is especially crucial for engaged couples as they prepare for a life together. Going into marriage with rose-colored glasses can set a couple up for disagreements, disappointment, and resentment. This was true for Amanda and Keith, whom you met in Chapter 2. For instance, Amanda is a moderate saver (with a money vigilance script) who often feels annoyed with Keith, who is a super spender with a money worship script. Keith grew up in a family that believed talking about money was considered impolite, and so he avoids discussing it. He also has a tendency to overspend because he believes buying things will improve his mood and outlook on life. During my two sessions with this couple, they made some headway in understanding their money histories and financial styles, paving the way to work on a budget with a counselor and a CFP in their state. While they have a long way to go on their journey, they're headed in a positive direction toward financial health. You can read about their decision to have a prenuptial agreement in Chapter 7.

It's essential that you and your partner set aside some time to talk about your value differences. The goal is to better understand your partner's perspective by listening attentively, validating, and doing your best to honor their values, even if you don't agree with them. Many couples have a budget, but it's outdated or insufficient because they avoid talking about money or they lack effective communication skills in general.

The following are some suggestions for how to identify your money values and those of your partner, as well as how to respect and navigate the differences you may have. I highly recommend you read this section with your partner prior to building a budget together.

Couples Activity: Four Ways to Discuss and Deal with Money Value Differences

1. Write down the answers to these two questions: What's really important to you? What is the purpose of money in your life? Next, write down at least three core values that you can make a commitment to in the next year. Core values have to do with

what's important for your sense of contentment, such as a gym membership or donating money to your favorite charity. Then, make a date with your partner to discuss your responses. Be sure not to criticize your partner's list and make judgments, focusing on listening with an open mind and heart—as if you're talking to a close friend with whom you aren't emotionally involved.

2. Assume the best of your partner. Rather than jumping to conclusions and assigning negative motives to your partner's wishes, ask each other at least one open-ended question such as "I'm curious about why you believe that remodeling projects in our home are such a great investment." Recognize and validate the logic behind their reasons for valuing things that differ from yours, such as "I know you grew up in a family that valued keeping your home updated; it makes sense that this would be important to you. I will do my best to compromise and honor your values."

3. Accept your partner's influence. Let your partner know that you appreciate and agree with at least one of their ideas about your budget. Implicit in this idea is my firmly held belief that allowing your partner to influence you can lead to more contentment for both of you. Being receptive to input from your partner is a crucial ingredient of a successful intimate relationship. This doesn't mean that you agree with him or her, but you're willing to listen with curiosity and interest, consider their point of view, and validate them. You're showing your partner that their needs are of primary importance to you. It reduces the likelihood that you'll become distant, attacking, or defensive because you're creating a relationship that's satisfying to both of you.

4. Be flexible and willing to reexamine your values. Show each other you're willing to do this by actively taking a closer look at one of your values. Be open to input from your partner. When you are flexible and willing to look at your own values through different lenses, it can soften your approach to a conversation. For instance, Larry told Shane that one of the main reasons he liked to dine in restaurants, rather than cook at home, is

because they had more time to catch up. As a result, Shane compromised on the amount in their budget for dining out weekly.

Now that you've gone over the "Four Ways to Discuss and Deal with Money Value Differences" couples activity, you're ready to get into the specifics and develop a budget that reflects the values you share as a couple. The values you have discussed will influence the line items and the amounts you put in your budget. Follow the ten steps to building and keeping a budget together. The purpose is to earn more money than you spend, have enough money to use on items that represent your essential values, and save money for necessary and nonessential expenses.

Before you make up a detailed budget, you need to take time to decide which money management system is the best one for you as a couple (Chapter 3). Regardless of the plan you choose, be sure to share the details of your finances with full disclosure.

Building a value-based budget can take up to two hours, so make sure you allot this amount of uninterrupted time with few distractions (silence your phones, etc.). Before you begin, make sure you have a notebook (and writing instrument) or laptop or iPad (and perhaps paper and ink in your printer). Don't forget to have a snack and a preferred beverage on hand.

During this conversation, if you feel blindsided or upset by something your partner identifies as a priority, such as visiting his or her parents monthly and needing travel money to another state, do your best to listen before you respond. Avoid making negative or sarcastic comments that could cut off communication. Remember that a budget is a work in progress and can be revised as often as you choose to do so.

Ten Steps to Building a Value-Driven Budget:

1. Gather your financial statements. This will be helpful as you calculate your monthly expenses in step two of this list. It includes bank statements, credit card statements, student loans, and other loan statements, investment accounts, retirement accounts, mortgage or rent statements, and utility and cell phone statements. It also includes direct deposits and debits in your checking accounts (bank statements should

be sufficient). Both partners need to do this to promote full disclosure.

If your statements are online, be sure to have easy access to your apps and the usernames and passwords to your accounts.

2. Calculate your sources of monthly income, assets, and debts or monthly obligations. This includes your paychecks from primary and secondary jobs, bonuses, and so on. If self-employed, deduct about 20 percent for taxes. To build a budget, these are the seven essential financial elements that you and your partner need to each disclose to one another:

   1. Assets: Income, stocks, investments, savings, belongings, an emergency fund, and so on.
   2. Debts: Credit cards, loans, alimony, child support, and so on.
   3. Monthly expenses such as rent, mortgage, utilities, car loans, phones, and cable or Wi-Fi fees.
   4. Obligations and educational expenses: Children, parents, and pledges to charities and institutions.
   5. Insurance: Life insurance (amounts of coverage and who your beneficiaries are), car insurance, and health insurance.
   6. Retirement savings.
   7. Belongings of value such as expensive jewelry or cars and items in a safe deposit box.

   As they change, you can adjust the items on this list or add to them. You might prefer to meet with a lawyer and draw up a formal agreement but most couples will want to do so informally, sign it, and keep a copy in a safe deposit box or locked cabinet.

3. Make a list of daily expenses before you make a list of monthly ones. Finally, multiply weekly expenses by four to arrive at monthly expenses. The purpose of your daily spending record is honestly documenting all of your expenses by tracking them.

Here's a sample daily spending record that Heather and Kevin compiled:

Monday, 5/5/24

1. Coffee $2.75
2. Gas $38.00
3. Lunch out $18.19
4. Lunch money for two children ($5.00 a day)

Tracking and documenting your daily expenses will help you be as accurate as possible because we often forget what we spend money on from day to day. Don't sabotage your efforts to create a value-driven budget with your partner by delaying writing things down or forgetting to do so. I've also seen couples lose their daily expense records, so be sure to store it in a safe place like a file cabinet or keep it on an app or file on your phone. Remember, complete honesty will help you to have an accurate spending record and the data to draft a budget plan. After you have recorded a daily spending record, work on a weekly and then a monthly spending record following step four.

4. Review your record at the end of the first month and then develop a monthly record for three months. Keep track of your spending for three months while you are developing a budget. You might want to use my sample budget from step eight on this list. Both of you need to disclose all of your information to each other. Then, you both need to review the information so you can merge your personal details into one "couple" document that accounts for all of your assets and expenses. This will enable you, as a couple, to create an agreed-upon budget. Discuss the spending that took place without criticism or anger. Label it something like "Heather and Kevin's Spending Record" and be sure to total up the categories of expenditures. Consider eliminating some of your nonessential expenses. Once you and your partner have a clear view of your assets and expenses, you'll be in a better position to come up with a realistic budget and savings plan.

5. Review your spending records without criticism or blame. Speak to your partner as if they're a friend, rather than an intimate partner, and ask questions if you need clarity. For instance, if you notice that your partner spends over $15.00 a week on coffee and snacks, rather than accusing them of being extravagant or thoughtless, simply say, "I'm concerned about your coffee and snack costs because we're trying to save money. I need to devise a plan with you. Can we consider making our own coffee and bringing a snack from home to work? I would be willing to buy more snacks and make coffee." The beauty of this approach is that it's unlikely to end up in an argument because it's not a criticism.

6. Establish an emergency fund. The amount should be enough to pay for at least three to six months of expenses. It is designed to cover unexpected costs such as a job layoff, car accident, or expensive car repair. As you set goals to achieve prosperity as a couple, you're bound to hit some bumps in the road. Has your budget taken unanticipated expenses into account? Ask yourself what you would do if your basement flooded or you needed four new tires and new brakes on your car in the same month. Read Chapter 6 for more details about emergency funds.

7. Review your numbers. Regardless of the type of budget plan you chose, the main idea about developing a budget method is to make sure your money is being spent the way you want and you have money left for savings and retirement. Once you and your partner have a clear view of your assets and expenses, you'll be in a better position to come up with a realistic budget and savings plan.

Ideally, all of your expenses should not exceed 80 percent of your earnings so that you can set aside money for savings.[6] If they do, you might want to consider cutting back on nonessentials that you can live without. In my case, I've often had to cut back on ordering books and holiday gifts for my family and friends. Small expenses add up, and eliminating things like stopping for coffee daily can contribute to a healthy savings plan (see Chapter 6).

8. Make up a budget and both sign it. Review my sample budget (coming soon) to see how you might set up your own. You may want to use an Excel spreadsheet on your computer so that you can calculate your income and expenses. Keep in mind that this is only a guideline and you can customize yours to fit the lifestyle and needs of you and your partner. As your numbers change, you can adjust the items or add to them. You might prefer to meet with a lawyer and draw up a formal agreement but most couples will want to do so informally, sign it, and keep a copy in a safe deposit box or locked cabinet.

Now that you've collected all of your financial data and reviewed the numbers, you're ready to get into the details of building your budget. Keep in mind that your weekly spending record becomes the basis of your monthly spending plan and budget. At this point, you're ready to work on building your monthly budget with the idea that your goals need to be transparency, respect, flexibility, and honesty.

Next, examine my sample budget below to see how you might set up your own. Keep in mind that this is only a guideline and you can customize yours to fit the lifestyle and needs of you and your partner.

Income	Month 1	Month 2	Month 3
Job 1			
Job 2			
Job 3			
Dividends			
Interest			
Retirement income			
Misc.			
Total Income			

Expenses	
Housing	
Utilities	
Food	
Transportation	
Insurance	
Personal	
Phones	
Misc.	
Retirement	
Savings	
Total Expenses	
Profit (Loss)	

9. Stick with your budget. It's no surprise that the tasks that you're undertaking with building a budget and keeping track of spending are not easy regardless of the budget plan you choose. You and/or your partner may be tempted to cheat. At first, this might mean omitting things from your budget (like your daily Starbucks coffee) because you simply forget. And then there might be times when one of you will rebel and say things like, "Why do I have to write down all of the money I spend? It seems so petty."

10. Review your budget plan monthly. This makes sense because things can change rather quickly in any relationship. For instance, one of you might change jobs, retire, or decide to return to college and reduce your work hours. Keep track of

splurges such as that lovely sweater or book about gardening that you couldn't resist, or unexpected expenses such as your teenager needing money for a school field trip. By including columns for an entire year of your budget spreadsheet, you'll have a realistic, long-range view of your budget. Once you've completed your budget, you can compute your expenses and deduct them from your income to determine your net financial standing.

There are many ways to build a budget and your choice of systems may change over time. It takes time and attention to build a value-driven budget that you and your partner can agree upon. However, skipping over creating a budget because it's time consuming or boring is never a good option. Regardless of what method you use, building a budget is necessary to maintain or improve your financial health as individuals and as a couple, and to keep your debt-to-income ratio low.

If making up a budget seems like too big of a task to accomplish without support, contact a couple's counselor or financial planner (or both) to assist you. Or, you might want to consider another option such as the 50/20/30 option proposed by Elizabeth Warren, the senior US senator from Massachusetts, serving since 2013.[7]

The 50/20/30 Budget

In 2006, Elizabeth Warren, then a Harvard law professor, popularized the 50/30/20 budgeting method in her book *All Your Worth: The Ultimate Lifetime Money Plan*.[8] This way of designing a budget is a good option for couples that don't want to do a line-by-line review of their expenses and income. Warren writes, "We start by approaching your money in a whole new way. No complicated lists. No spending diaries. Instead, we help you analyze your spending by dividing it into three simple categories. There's one category for your regular monthly bills, a second category for the money you spend 'just for fun', and a third category for savings." Warren and her daughter, Amelia Warren Tyagi, posit that this method of budgeting will keep your life in balance.

The Three Categories of the Warren's The 50/20/30 Budget Method Are as Follows[9]:

1. 50 percent goes toward essentials such as rent or a mortgage, groceries, utilities, car payments, and other necessary bills.
2. 30 percent goes toward discretionary items or wants such as gym memberships, vacations, and gifts.
3. 20 percent goes toward paying off debt, savings, an emergency fund, or investing for retirement.

Keep in mind that financial experts in 2024 suggest that the budget framework's proportions in Senator Warren's method can be adjusted since rents have soared by 129 percent since 1999, according to Moody's Analytics.[10] They reported that in 2022 the share of the American household income needed to rent an average-priced apartment crossed the rent burdening 30 percent threshold for the first time in Moody's twenty-five years of tracking the US average rent-to-income ratio.

In fact, in 2022 mortgage lender Freddie Mack found that a third of adults aged twenty-five and younger say they don't ever expect to be able to afford their own home.[11] This issue came up often with young couples who participated in my study. For instance, Caitlyn, thirty-eight, and Ethan, forty, who you read about in Chapter 2, experienced a lot of tension about not being able to afford a down payment on a small home. They had been married for ten years when we met and felt discouraged about ever being able to become homeowners due to the inflated housing costs in their area.

According to Michael Finke, professor of wealth management at the American College of Financial Services, if you're a young adult with many years ahead of you before retirement, "60/30/10" is an acceptable distribution of income.[12] This allocation makes provisions for paying more toward a mortgage or rent, groceries, a car payment, and other necessary bills. It also reduces your savings rate by 10 percent. Finke says that as you reach middle age, you will want to consider gradually increasing your savings rate.

Martha C. White, a writer for *Time Magazine*, explains, "A money-management formula introduced nearly 20 years ago by Elizabeth Warren still has relevance, financial planners say—with a few tweaks."[13] She continues, "It sounds good in theory, but in an economy where housing costs alone can easily consume half a paycheck—particularly for young adults earning entry-level income—it can feel difficult, if not flat-out impossible."

For instance, when Caitlyn and Ethan adopted the 60/30/10 budget plan so that they could get out of debt and save money for a new home, they found success. They followed the ten steps in this chapter for three months and discovered that it was easier for them to use the 60/30/10 budget plan since both liked the convenience and ease of this method. Over a period of two years, they were able to save enough money for a down payment on a small home.

Now that you have created a budget and perhaps encountered some potential problem areas in your finances, it's important to closely examine and troubleshoot issues that could undermine your ability to maintain a budget with your partner.

Five Ways to Troubleshoot Issues with Your Budget Plan:

1. Look at money leaks (money that is pouring out of your bank account). Money leaks will make it hard to build trust and will prevent you from achieving financial health. Once you and your partner have compiled your daily, weekly, and monthly spending records, review them together in order to identify money leaks, or areas where money is pouring out of your account. These indicate expenses that could be reduced or eliminated. Unsurprisingly, one of the most common areas is food. This includes groceries, takeout, school lunches, eating at restaurants, grabbing a cup of coffee outside of your home, etc.

    An example of a money leak is eating lunch in restaurants daily. When Heather and Kevin reviewed their daily, weekly, and monthly spending records, Kevin noticed that eating lunch out several days a week cost his family over $160.00 a month. When he was vulnerable and honestly faced this issue, Kevin was willing to cut his lunch expenses in half. The silver lining for Kevin was that he lost the ten pounds he had been trying to shed for several years by not eating restaurant food as often and packing healthy sandwiches and salads in his lunch a few days a week. Leaking money out of your accounts may sound dramatic; however, it's quite common.

2. Look for money laundering. While it might seem surprising that your partner is skimming money out of your accounts for purchases outside of your agreed-upon items, it does happen more often than you would imagine. Often, one person uses their debit card for a purchase and gets extra money in cash to spend as they please, and they don't inform their partner. Another way that people launder money is by making a charge on their credit card when they go out for lunch with friends, collecting cash from them, but never using the cash to pay down the credit card. Money launderers participate in these activities to avoid talking about money or potential conflict. Often they use a defense mechanism like denial or rationalization (see Chapter 2) to justify their behavior.

3. Consider setting aside some "mad money" monthly that both of you can spend any way you wish if you have trouble sticking to a budget. For Shane, it was important to him that Larry honor his wishes to have a household budget (and funds in a separate checking account) that he could spend on household projects without Larry scrutinizing his purchases. This house account was something that they agreed upon, and they added to it monthly. Likewise, Larry's "mad money" account was money he directed to Venmo or PayPal, and it allowed him some discretionary funds for clothing, entertainment, or takeout. In Shanti and Jeff Feldhahn's study, the couples who had "mad money" reported higher levels of happiness compared to those couples who did not have it in place.[14]

4. Make sure you have money to save in your budget. For a more precise idea of how much money you have to budget, remove all the expenses from your earnings and total them up, according to author Nora Graves.[15] In *Budgeting for Couples 101,* she writes, "Ideally, your total expenses should not exceed more than 80 percent of your earnings; this way you will also have the opportunity to set money aside for savings. However, if your outgoings are more than 80 percent, you should consider making some cutbacks."

5. Deal effectively with changes in your lifestyle and plan ahead. Ask yourself if anything has occurred since your last money

talk with your partner that has an impact on your goals, money flow, income, or expenses. For instance, a few weeks ago you may have found out that you need to replace your roof, and this will need to come out of your emergency fund. Be sure to write this item down immediately so you don't forget! Keep in mind, an emergency fund is for unexpected expenses. If you anticipate a large expense in the next month, start planning now by adding it to your budget.

There are many ways to build a budget and your choice of systems may change over time. It takes time and attention to build a value-driven budget that you and your partner can agree upon. However, skipping over creating a budget because it's time consuming or boring is never a good option. Regardless of what method you use, building a budget is necessary to maintain or improve your financial health as individuals and as a couple. Keep an open mind and be prepared to compromise. Your "us against the problem" approach will help reduce tension so you can build a budget you will both love.

Chapter 5
Get Rid of Bad Debt

According to a recent study by Dave Ramsey, couples who fight about debt have roughly $30,000 in consumer debt on average, with 63 percent of all marriages starting off in the red.[1] His study revealed that the larger the couple's debt, the more likely they were to identify finances as a major source of conflict. Further, 41 percent of those surveyed admitted that debt had a negative impact on their relationship and caused arguments, regardless of household income. And those respondents with $50,000 or more in debt were three times more likely than couples with $10,000 in debt to have high-conflict money talks.

In recent years, spending has soared despite inflation and high interest rates, explains Alana Semuels.[2] In fact, US consumers spent a record $19 trillion in January 2024, up 4 percent over the prior year and up 29 percent over January 2020. There are myriad reasons for this surge in spending, including making up for lost time after the Covid-19 pandemic by traveling, eating out, and participating in social events that people avoided while in quarantine. Additionally, after decades of slow salary increases, workers are finally seeing bigger wage hikes, giving them more disposable income.

Many couples in my study discussed the impact that the pandemic had on their spending habits. Cohabitating for three years, Helen, forty-eight, and Mark, fifty-four, have been working through the dynamics of a blended family, with three daughters combined from their previous marriages. During our interview, Helen described the struggles she's had with credit card debt throughout most of her adult life and how she finally confessed to Mark (after they moved in together) that she was buried in debt due to overspending with credit cards. While Helen was getting her debt under control before the pandemic, she developed the habit of purchasing items online and saving her credit card information on different apps once Covid-19 hit. Even though she values honesty and transparency, Helen felt too much shame about her debt problem to open up to Mark when they first moved in together. But after a couple of years, she felt secure enough to fully disclose her high credit card debt.

Helen puts it like this, "Mark is an accountant who makes a good income, and I felt paralyzed at the thought of how wrong our conversation would go when I told him about my credit card debt. The truth is, the longer I waited, the harder it got. Until I sought counseling and help with my debt problem, it just kept growing. Now that I have it under control, I just want to be honest and clear the air. I feel guilty that I have been keeping my credit card debt from Mark all this time. Honestly, things went better than I expected when I confessed, and I wish that I had done it much earlier in our relationship."

Mark reflects, "When Helen first told me about her problem with her credit card debt, I was angry because she kept it from me. I asked her why she couldn't trust me to know about it. I guess she mostly felt embarrassed because I'm an accountant, a saver, and stable financially. Helen has really turned her life around since she started meeting with a therapist and attending Debtors Anonymous. They both explained to her that her debt is what alcohol is to an alcoholic; it makes her life unmanageable. She's taking control of it now by paying off her debt. We can have discussions about money without her getting defensive."

Unfortunately, even though most of us have strong feelings about credit card debt, we don't take the steps that Helen took to pay it off. Sometimes, it's a matter of not knowing what steps to take. Or, it could be that you don't understand the consequences of carrying debt. Either way, an important first step is disclosing to your partner that you have debt, including credit card debt. If you take this courageous action, you will probably feel some relief, as Helen did when she confessed to Mark. Planning a time to talk to your partner and taking a risk will help your relationship move forward in a direction of having transparency and building trust.

The Difference Between Good Debt and Bad Debt

Many people end up in financial trouble by accumulating a lot of debt by paying with credit cards and using them as if paying with credit is the same as paying with cash. To make matters worse, many of these people hide their debt from their partner (see Chapter 9), and financial infidelity can destroy trust and lead to divorce, according to Garbinsky et al.[3] That's why it's essential, when you're taking on debt of any kind, to assess how it will impact your life and the life of your partner, as well as any children you might have.

Is there such a thing as good debt versus bad debt? According to Chelsea Brennan, a contributor to Forbes Advisor (a website offering financial advice), there is a distinction between the two.[4] She acknowledges that "For most people, debt is a part of life" and advises that there are cases when taking on debt can pay dividends in the future, such as taking on a mortgage to purchase a home, student loans to pay for college, or a loan to build or expand a small business. These are common forms of good debt, in spite of risk factors. For instance, a college degree doesn't guarantee a well-paying job after graduation, a new business might fail, and some people take on a bigger mortgage than they can afford. In fact, close to 40 million households in the United States are "house poor," meaning their high mortgage and tax payments make it a challenge to cover other expenses and save for retirement, according to Brennan. But, when approached wisely, mortgages, student loans, and small business loans can be examples of good debt.

With a mortgage, your property will become an asset, will hopefully increase in value, and it can potentially be sold for a profit. You may also be able to refinance your mortgage as a way to reduce your monthly mortgage payment and use the extra money to pay off credit card balances—as long as you don't rack up more debt on your cards after you pay down (or off) the balances on them! Student loans are usually not considered bad debt because they're low interest. In most cases, as a graduate, you can work out a payment plan that works for you. You can even accelerate your payments as your salary increases. Also, if you get a college degree, your earning potential increases over your lifetime compared to those who don't have one. And a small business loan is considered good debt because it's an investment that will potentially pay off in the future.

What exactly is bad debt? It's characterized by spending money in the present that takes away from your future goals. For instance, swiping your plastic to see your favorite musician play in a concert when you're aware that you don't have the funds to pay it off when your credit card bill arrives. Brennan explains, "If the debt won't bring you future income or wealth, but rather funds your current lifestyle, it's bad debt."[5] According to Brennan, the best examples of bad debt are payday loans (under $500.00 due on your next payday with significant fees), auto loans with high interest (cars can depreciate the moment you drive off the lot), and credit card debt. When credit card debt is accumulated for nonessential purchases, like a vacation, it's unquestionably bad debt.

Christopher Yalanis, MBA, CFP, shared an alternative view on debt as a tool and explained to me that good financial planning is the best way to reduce or eliminate debt.[6] He elaborates, "Debt happens when there's a divide between people's desires and their assets' ability to meet these desires. Debt is neither bad or good. It's a tool. Some debt is terrific . . . such as thirty-year mortgages at 2.75 percent interest when cash is earning 5.3 percent."

One common form of debt that is a poor tool for improving financial health—and one of the main reasons couples find themselves in financial difficulty—is credit card debt. Keep in mind that credit card debt is bad debt primarily because of the high interest rate and people's inability to pay it off quickly. According to the Massachusetts Office of Consumer Affairs, a credit card balance of $1,000 will take twelve years to pay off if you pay only the minimum required, which is $25.00 each month at 17 percent interest.[7] By only paying the minimum, you will pay $979.14 in interest to borrow $1,000, nearly doubling the amount you owe. Just do the math; you pay nearly twice as much for everything you buy!

According to Forbes Advisor, in 2023 the average card debt for each American borrower was $6,360 or 10 percent higher than the year before. Forbes Advisors, Becky Pokora and Harlan Vaughn, write, "This shift may be due to inflation or other financial stress and marks a move in the wrong direction. Collectively, this adds up to $50 billion new debt in a single quarter and a total of $1.13 trillion in US credit card debt."[8]

The source of the problem with people not paying off credit card debt, according to Jeff Motske, CFP, is that they pay it off too slowly.[9] This means they're at risk of dying with substantial debt because of this slow repayment method. In his book, *The Couple's Guide to Financial Compatibility*, Motske states that one of the main reasons why Americans have such high credit card debt is that we forget that it's a loan and we use credit cards as if they are cash. In fact, he explains that swiping a credit card may encourage a cavalier attitude toward debt and that there's less stigma about having credit card debt than there was in the past.

Are you someone who looks for immediate gratification? If the answer is yes, keep in mind that swiping a credit card can give you a feeling of instant gratification. Like alcohol, drugs, and other addictions, using a credit card can make you feel euphoric. However, if you pay off the entire amount you charge every month, you won't accrue bad debt. It's easy to track your credit card charges each month by making a quick phone call or logging into your online account or app, and if you pay them off, they won't lead to high finance charges and bad debt.

If you have too much credit card debt and financial stress, there's a strong likelihood that either you and/or your partner are super spenders (see Chapter 1). You're probably spending more than you allotted for in your budget and either deny it or fail to properly account for expenditures. This might not be intentional but the impact on your budget is the same. The result might be that you're spending more than is prearranged for in your budget. Maybe you threw a fantastic birthday party for your mother, partner, or spouse. Or you and your partner are in the habit of going to your favorite restaurant every Friday night—believing you deserve it after a tough week. Whatever the splurge, ask yourself if you're going overboard, even slightly, and the impact this is having on your budget. It's important to be transparent with your partner about any debt that occurs.

Couples Activity: Six Ways to Talk to Your Partner About Debt

1. Schedule a time to discuss your debt. This is a fair way to start the discussion and will set the stage for openness and honesty. It's much better to plan a time to talk when you won't be interrupted than to blast your partner with information about

your debt in the middle of a conversation or when they walk in the door at the end of a workday.

2. Give debt information in a clear and direct way using full disclosure. Your main objective here is to get to the point and avoid vagueness. If you are straightforward, this will promote financial intimacy and economic health. Avoid making excuses or rationalizing your reasons for acquiring debt. Show your partner statements (or apps) from your credit cards and loans, for both good and bad debt.

3. Respect your partner's feelings of anger, frustration, or betrayal if you've been keeping secrets about debt. Hidden debt, like any mistake or lie, will most likely be embarrassing to admit. Understandably, you might want to blame others (like your daughter who requested an expensive prom dress). You might also want to rush this conversation because you're feeling uncomfortable, or to discourage your partner from asking questions. It's important that you take it slow and allow your partner time to process the information you give them.

4. Take responsibility and apologize for financial infidelity or overspending. The definition of financial infidelity is consciously or deliberately lying to a romantic partner about financial behavior.[10] It's a situation where one partner intentionally hides a money-related secret (such as credit card debt) from the other, expecting it would be disapproved of. In some cases, a partner might overspend, but not lie or keep it secret. By owning your error in judgment or regrettable action and offering a sincere apology, you're encouraging trust and healing. Say something like, "I'm very sorry that I hid my debt from you (or overspent). I made a mistake, and it won't happen again. I'll share my debt with you, attempt to pay it off, and be transparent."

5. Present your partner with a debt payoff plan or proposal. After you tell your partner about your debts, they may ask if you've thought about any payoff options. It's wise to research options in advance of your conversation. If you do this, your partner might feel more confidence in your intention to pay

off your debt. If you don't feel you have the skills to develop and implement a debt payoff plan, consider calling a non-profit credit counseling organization or a CFP. Some of these professionals offer free consultations and it's a good idea to invite your partner to join you.

6. Set financial goals with your partner. Make sure your goals are achievable. For instance, one goal might be that you don't use your credit cards for a year unless you travel and absolutely need to use one of them. Or, you will refrain from using your credit cards until the total amount owed (on all of them) is less than $5,000. If and when you use your credit cards, you might promise to pay off what you charge monthly. Invite your partner to monitor your credit card use (when you start using them again) for an agreed-upon amount of time, such as once a month. This invitation will restore trust and goodwill between you and him or her. Another goal might be not to take out any personal or small business loans without discussing it with your partner.

Now that you've been vulnerable with your partner about your debt, focus on keeping your promises and be accountable for your actions moving forward. If you feel discouraged, imagine how amazing it will feel to be free from bad debt and have a clean financial slate. By setting realistic goals and using full disclosure, you'll be more likely to achieve greater intimacy and financial health as an individual and as a couple.

Even if you've not endured financial infidelity, paying off debt can be stressful for couples, and reviewing Chapter 2 on how to have low-conflict conversations about money with your partner offers strategies. If you feel that you have unfinished business that's difficult to discuss calmly, it's also a good idea to reach out to professionals for support. You may want to contact a couples therapist if you believe that your relationship has suffered greatly or you or your partner are struggling to restore trust. It's often a good idea to encourage your partner to attend sessions with a therapist or mediator by making a promise to stop using your credit cards and to get rid of your debt. But before moving ahead, it's important to know more about the reasons why couples acquire bad debt, particularly credit card debt.

How Financial Technology Can Increase Spending

Since the Covid-19 pandemic began in early 2020, there have been additional factors impacting the rise in credit card debt, such as people being more accustomed to using financial technology or apps to pay for things. According to Yuqian XU, a professor at the University of North Carolina's Kenan-Flagler Business School, "Convenience makes it much easier to enjoy the process of shopping, removing the additional difficulties of buying things."[11] Her research shows that the more frictionless the payment method, the more money people spend.

In fact, by 2023, according to a McKinsey survey, 73 percent of consumers had paid for something through a browser on their phone or computer, up from 46 percent in 2019.[12] People are also more comfortable using mobile payment apps like Apple Pay, Google Pay, PayPal, and Venmo. Many couples find it easier to use these apps to purchase items and exchange funds when sharing the cost of items or expenses. This is especially common when they don't commingle money or have separate checking and/or savings accounts.

Further, a Forbes Advisor survey from December 2023 shows that less than 10 percent of Americans primarily use cash to pay for purchases.[13] More than 53 percent of respondents said they used a physical or virtual debit card, and 37 percent used a physical or virtual credit card. Paying with a mobile phone is faster (more frictionless) than using a credit card, and the speed and convenience quicken spending.

When researcher Yuqian XU and her colleagues tracked spending after the Chinese launch of Alipay, a mobile payment method, they discovered that the amounts spent in credit card transactions increased by 9.4 percent and the frequency of transactions by 10.7 percent during the Covid-19 pandemic.[14] Once again, the reasons cited for this increase include convenience and swiftness of payment.

Once consumers start using mobile payments, they become comfortable with making credit card payments on their computers, and they start moving money more digitally. And once they're comfortable spending money digitally, they start spending more money overall, according to financial writer Alana Semuels.[15] The rise of frictionless payments makes it easy to overspend and more difficult for people to live within their means.

That said, if you pay with credit cards, you are likely to spend 12 to 18 percent more than you would with cash. If you were paying with cash, you would probably think more about whether you needed something, as compared to pulling out the plastic. One study by the *Journal of Applied Psychology* discovered that when diners put their credit card on the tray, their average tip is 4.3 percent more than if they pay with cash.[16] Like most people, you probably don't consider whether or not you will have the cash at the end of the month to pay off what you charge. Using credit cards can give you the illusion that you are wealthier than you actually are.

Shopping Addiction

Caitlyn and Ethan, whom you met earlier, have endured Caitlyn's shopping addiction and the financial stress associated with it. In their eight years of marriage, Caitlyn has accumulated significant credit card debt which has put a strain on her relationship with her husband, Ethan. Because they have separate checking and savings accounts, they rarely discuss finances and share expenses like roommates. Since Ethan is a super saver with a money vigilance script, he doesn't like to eat out in restaurants unless they have funds available in one of their checking accounts to cover it. On the other hand, Caitlyn tends to use her credit cards as if they're cash, since she's a super spender with a money worship script. She has a habit of overspending and will often charge clothes online with insufficient funds in her checking account to pay them off.

"We're trying to save for a home since we are currently renting a high-priced apartment, but we can't seem to save for a down payment. Our conversations get heated because Caitlyn lives for the moment and doesn't usually pay off what she charges, so her debt increases fast," says Ethan.

Helen, whom you met earlier, also has a habit of overspending and shared with me that she used to live for the moment for most of her adult life and used her credit cards like cash. Helen's shopping addiction reared its head in college when her grades slipped, and she starting shopping online to boost her spirits by buying too many clothes and spending money on an expensive vacation (that she couldn't afford) with friends during spring break. She wishes that she had sought help twenty years ago so her debt didn't accumulate. Since her parents divorced and she has three siblings, she never felt she could rely on them for financial help. Helen got in the habit of splurging when she needed comfort or felt discouraged rather than using better coping skills such as talking to a therapist, exercising, or using mindfulness.

Helen explains,

> Every time I'd tear up my plastic, it seemed like one of the credit card companies would send me a new card. Whenever I failed a test in college or felt like I failed at something, shopping was my solution. Then it got to the point where I was losing sleep because of my financial worries. I know now that my shopping addiction served a role of filling my unmet needs. My therapist explained to me that since my addiction started soon after my dad moved out and my parents divorced, my self-esteem suffered, and I was trying to fill a void in my life. When Mark came along, I didn't tell him about my credit card debt because I was too afraid to lose him and felt embarrassed.

Every partnership is unique, with its own unique challenges due to each of our past histories, personalities, and financial styles. Coming up with a plan for paying off bad debts that works for your situation is a necessary step. You need to consider seriously that you may be among those who can't manage a credit card, because, like Caitlyn or Helen, you don't use them wisely. If so, do the smart thing: pay them off and perform plastic surgery and cut them up.

Good Reasons to Get Rid of Credit Card Debt

There are many reasons why you need to get rid of credit card debt. First, having financial stress puts your marriage or relationship at risk.

According to a study published by *Family Relations*, which sampled 4,574 couples, disagreements about money were the leading cause of divorce.[17] Talking about finances can be thorny—even when couples have been together for a long time. It can make people feel tense and defensive, so many couples avoid it. Many of us were raised by families who told us that talking about money was impolite or that our personal finances are private and should not be discussed with others. As a result, it's understandable that we don't possess the skills to have effective conversations with our partners about money. As you learned in Chapter 2, being able to have low-conflict discussions about money can improve your relationship. This includes challenging topics such as paying off credit card debt.

Another important reason to get rid of credit card debt is to lower your personal stress. In an in-depth study conducted by the American Psychological Association (n = 3,068), the results showed that three-quarters of Americans are experiencing financial stress at least some of the time, and nearly a quarter of us are experiencing severe financial stress.[18] Financial stress can take its toll on any couple. Almost a third (31 percent) of adults with a partner in this study disclosed that money is a major source of conflict in their relationship and might destroy their marriage. This study suggests that we need to rethink our relationship with money and come up with coping strategies, such as recognizing triggers (ads, promotions, etc.), paying attention to our reactions (use of a mobile app and credit card), and come up with a plan not to overspend.

In a 2023 follow-up study, the American Psychological Association studied stress and found that finances are a top stressor for adults, with 77 percent of the respondents identifying money as a significant stressor.[19] When comparing pre- and post-pandemic survey results, researchers discovered that parents were more likely to say that money (79 percent vs. 71 percent) and the economy (75 percent vs. 71 percent) caused them significant stress—in 2023 compared to 2019.

Lastly, surviving lean times and preparing for the future in a marriage or committed relationship are important reasons to debt-proof according to author Mary Hunt.[20] In her book, *Debt-Proof Your Marriage*, she posits that living from paycheck to paycheck has little to do with your paycheck and even people with six-figure annual incomes are so overextended that they're one paycheck away from being homeless.

Hunt writes, "The truth is it doesn't matter how much money you earn. What counts is what you do with it and how much of it you keep." Even if you have a stable job, do you know with certainty that you will have that job five years from now? Getting rid of credit card debt can provide you and your partner with a safety net in case something unexpected causes either one of you to lose your job due to circumstances beyond your control such as a layoff, accident, or disability.

It's important to come up with a strategy to get rid of debt so that your income is more than your outgo. Mary Hunt describes debt-proof living as a plan for staying out of bad debt and living in a way that makes it a non-issue in your life.[21] It doesn't matter if you earn $50,000 a year or $500,000 a year; unless you have a specific plan, you can fail to stay out of debt. Learning to live within your means will help you to plug the money leaks (the ways that money is pouring out of your account) and hold onto the money that flows through your life so you and your partner can achieve an abundance mindset.

How to Get Rid of Credit Card Debt

There is no single, simple way to eliminate credit card debt. Don't let anyone convince you otherwise.

But, you do need to develop a plan to liquidate your credit cards. For instance, you can begin by not using your cards until your debts are paid off. Then work on paying off the cards that charge the greatest interest and pay as much as you can each month on these, while always making at least the minimum payment on the others. Then, you don't want to incur credit card debt to maintain a lifestyle you really can't afford. It's never been a good idea to try to keep up with the Joneses. Who knows, maybe they have a huge credit card balance!

The two most popular ways to pay off debt are the Debt Snowball and the Debt Avalanche methods. It is important to understand the differences between the two methods in order to make an informed decision. In *Jumpstart Your Marriage and Your Money*, Elle Martinez explains that while each payoff method is similar at first glance, there's a different rationale behind each of them, and understanding that difference will determine your success or failure.[22]

The Debt Snowball method: The Debt Snowball technique involves paying off your debt with the lowest balance first. When the debt with the smallest balance is paid off, you start paying off the next smallest debt and so on until all your debts are paid off. Dave Ramsey speculates that the Debt Snowball technique will work within a one-to-two-year time frame.[23]

Follow the Five Steps to the Debt Snowball Method Developed by Dave Ramsey[24]:

1. List all of your debts including your mortgage, and arrange them from the smallest balance to the largest.
2. Make the minimum payment required on each debt and be careful not to miss due dates.
3. Review your budget to decide how much extra cash you can put toward paying off your debts ahead of schedule. Use this entire amount to pay down the debt with the smallest balance.
4. When the debt with the smallest balance is paid off, roll over the monthly payment amount to your next smallest debt.
5. Repeat this process until all of your debts are paid off!

The good news is that this method is practical and easy to follow because you are paying off one debt at a time. Dave Ramsey and other experts believe that the Debt Snowball method is very motivating and works well for most people who have debt because they see the positive results.[25] Now let's learn about another popular method often used to pay off credit card debt.

The Debt Avalanche method: If you and your partner resent paying a cent more to your lenders than is absolutely necessary, you will want to consider the Debt Avalanche method, suggests author Elle Martinez.[26] With this method, determining the order to pay off your debt is based on the interest rate associated with the debt rather than the balance. You pay off the debt with the highest interest rate rather than the one with the highest balance. Once the debt with the highest interest rate has been eliminated, move on to the debt with the next highest interest rate and so on. This approach is more mathematical than the Debt Snowball method, but it may not be as immediately gratifying to some people. However, other couples will find it rewarding to spend less money on debt repayment by focusing on high interest rates. For example, they appreciate that this method recommends slashing high interest credit cards first.

While there are some similarities between these two methods of paying off debts, there are important differences. Be sure to discuss both methods with your partner and consider exploring other strategies by seeking out a financial advisor or reading books. Regardless of the plan you choose, be sure to automate your payments and pay your payments early enough so you don't get stuck with a late fee.

When Caitlyn and Ethan made a decision to get rid of credit card debt, they chose the Debt Snowball method, and it worked for them. They were motivated by seeing some of their debts being paid off quickly, and they were successful in paying off most of their debt in two years. Caitlyn cut up her plastic cards and made a pledge to herself and Ethan not to feed her shopping addiction monster any longer. When I asked her how she did this, she explained:

> I would not allow myself to charge clothes (online or in person), and I opened an account at an upscale consignment store. I gave myself a budget of $50.00 a month to spend there, whether I sold anything or not. If I made money from my items that sold, I also allowed myself to spend this plus the $50.00. Some months, I'd forget to go, and that credit would be rolled over to the next month.

Melanie and Rob, on the other hand, choose the Debt Avalanche method, which involves tackling their debt based on interest rate rather than balance. This method appealed to Melanie since she is a saver who appreciates a mathematical approach to getting rid of credit card debt. She convinced Rob that this would be the most effective method, and he agreed. They celebrated paying off Rob's credit cards by staying at a lovely seaside resort for three nights, where they enjoyed the beach, delightful seafood restaurants, and sightseeing together.

Six Smart Ways to Get Out of Bad Debt for Couples:

1. Make a commitment to pay off your bad debt as a couple. The most important thing to keep in mind is that communication

is essential to paying off debt. Without it, your partnership isn't sustainable, and your debt will continue to accumulate. Remember to make a "Communication Pledge" to have regular money talks at least once a month. As you learned in Chapter 2, having regular money talks is beneficial for couples because it helps them manage debt more effectively and avoid overspending (Garbinsky & Gladstone, 2019[27]).

2. Consider the time that you want to pay your credit card debt off and the method. Talk to your partner about your short- and long-term goals and discuss your individual and couple objectives. This includes the method you will use to pay off debt, such as the options described in this chapter.

3. Try to anticipate any obstacles such as upcoming college expenses, weddings, or vacation plans. You're not going to anticipate all upcoming expenses, but do your best to play fortune-teller with your partner in a realistic manner. For instance, if you're not sure of the average costs of a four-year college education for one of your children, go online and research this topic.

4. Put all of your debts on the table. Make a list of your bad debts, big and small, and devise a plan based on your payments and the method you choose to pay them off (consider the ones in this chapter). Study the options of credit card transfer and debt consolidation. Also, consider whether any debt, such as a car loan, will take away from your financial goals as a couple. In other words, will it be worth the inherent risks of taking out a high-interest loan?

5. Be totally honest and transparent about your debts and your goals. Don't let feelings of shame or guilt become a game changer. Consider the big picture and remember that paying off debt and improving your credit score are your number one priorities. Be sure to discuss any sacrifices you will have to make, such as giving up a monthly massage or eating at restaurants often.

6. Contact a CFP for assistance. Knowing when to reach out for support is important and is a sign of strength. If you feel your

financial worries and/or debts are impacting your ability to work effectively, or your relationship with your partner, you may want to contact a CFP. The role of a CFP is to give personalized guidance and help you determine if you're on track to meet your financial goals and to develop a plan that reflects your values. You don't have to be wealthy to work with a CFP, and they can assist you in saving money, reducing your debt, and investing wisely.

Before you choose a method to pay off credit card debt, schedule a time to talk to your partner thoughtfully and be prepared to discuss how you acquired your debt and any emotions you both have about this process. Keep in mind that conversations about money are really about more than finances; they usually involve our past histories, financial styles, and money scripts (see Chapter 1). Also, it might take a few low-conflict conversations to decide on a plan for paying off debt that works for both of you. Changing financial habits is the only way to get rid of bad debt, and you and your partner will want to discuss the plan that best meets your lifestyle. Remind each other that the best approach is "us against the problem" so that you can begin the important process of becoming financially healthy as a couple.

Chapter 6
Develop a Savings Plan

A sound financial plan includes having enough money in savings to withstand an emergency and plan for retirement. If couples live frugally, stop living beyond their means, and stop spending more than they earn, they can build a financial safety net. These assets can help them recover from unexpected setbacks and restart their lives as well as live comfortably as they age. According to a recent Forbes Advisor report, 28 percent of Americans have savings below $1,000.[1] Breaking this down by age, 32 percent of Gen Zers, 31 percent of Millennials, 27 percent of Gen Xers, and 20 percent of Baby Boomers have savings below $1,000. This report indicates many Americans are not financially resilient and could not withstand a major money challenge such as a job layoff.

    Brittany, forty-five, and John, forty-four, arrived at my office for a couples therapy session a few years ago feeling discouraged about their future. They both expressed concern about their increase in debt and financial tension in their relationship. It seemed like everything they tried failed, and they didn't know how to create change. As a result of climbing out of a huge financial loss on their house when it was foreclosed due to not paying their mortgage (for several months), Brittany and John were on the brink of bankruptcy. They experienced the total loss of their savings and emergency fund due to John's financial infidelity. As a result, they met with me for couples therapy and with a CFP. During their therapy sessions, they reassessed their spending, developed a savings plan, and bounced back to financial health after a couple of years of tightening their belts and using full disclosure.

Brittany shares,

> We went through a tough period when there were so many things going on, and John was keeping secrets about his overspending. When we met with Terry for therapy, we realized that there were some things we could control—and one was our spending on nonessential items and being open with each other. So, we took a close look at our budget and made some adjustments. John also stopped keeping secrets and no longer spends money recklessly without discussing it with me. We feel bad that our son, Justin, had to eventually take out student loans, but he accepts it and will be OK.

The good news? Brittany and John took care of their reckless spending and began saving for their future after a financial crisis. While Brittany and John's story may seem a bit dramatic, the lessons they learned are relevant for all couples when one or both partners have a financial style of spender, are risk takers and see money as status. In fact, John's credit score was very poor, putting them at a disadvantage when it came to borrowing money for essential items such as cars or college tuition for their son. What this couple learned in couples therapy with me is about the value of cutting out extraneous expenses, such as unnecessary travel and eating at expensive restaurants, so that they could divert money into their savings. Since both John and Brittany are super spenders who have money status scripts, they worked hard in therapy at being transparent and honoring their "Communication Pledge" to have low-conflict money talks monthly to stay on track financially.

The bottom line is: spending less is the best way to save money. Thinking about saving in this way may mean adjusting your lifestyle. Habits such as going to Starbucks every morning or buying discretionary items online (and not paying them off) must be eliminated. Small purchases add up and should be the first to go when you're looking for ways to boost your savings. These small spending shifts can bring big rewards over time. In terms of paying your bills, switching to autopay can also save you 5 to 10 percent a month with some companies, and you'll avoid getting hit with a late fee.

For instance, when Brittany identified that she was a super spender from taking my Financial Styles Quiz, she said that she used to dine out often, made daily stops at Starbucks, and that she was guilty of overspending on unnecessary items such as frequently buying video games for her son, Justin. While John is generally honest, he admitted to me and Brittany (during a couples therapy session) that he kept secrets about using his credit card like cash, having a bad credit score, and using up their savings and emergency fund. When I explained to John that keeping secrets is really financial infidelity, he was surprised but contrite and willing to make a commitment to change his behavior.

Many couples who are not at risk for overspending on nonessentials also need guidance on how to save on necessities. For instance, Kendra and Sam, whom you met previously, are super savers, but they have a lot of expenses such as helping their young adult children launch and helping to pay off their student loans. When they went through their budget, they realized that even though they're not extravagant, they could cut back on groceries, gifts, holidays, and vacations in order to save for their retirement. Kendra and Sam also hope to sell their real estate business in a few years and plan to move closer to Kendra's aging parents when they retire.

Kendra reflects,

We want the same things in life, and we're both frugal because of our upbringing. Sam says that I should spend more on myself, but growing up with Depression-era parents has made me more conscious of what I/we need versus what I/we want. We've made a few plans to travel but usually put them off when it means saving less for retirement and avoiding debt. Even when Sam tries to persuade me to book a cruise, I find a way to talk him out of it, and I usually win.

When Sam and Kendra talked to me about some of their frugal habits, they focused on being flexible and going grocery shopping together at some newer discount chains. They also use apps such as flashfood.com to save money on items that are near their sell-by date. This couple shared that they were not too proud to use money-saving apps and go to discount grocery stores. Their "us against the problem" mindset helps to keep them motivated and on track to save money for their retirement, which will mean relocating and living on a fixed income.

One good rule of thumb when you're trying to save money for your future is to pay all of your essential bills first. Then, the rest of the money that's left over is divided four ways: an emergency fund, 401K, stock portfolio, and a fun envelope (usually put toward a common goal or vacation or other "big stuff"). With good communication and planning, Kendra and Sam were able to establish an emergency fund a few years ago, so they've been able to deal with repairs to their home, car repairs, and any other unexpected situations or expenses that come up. They've also been able to save for their retirement with good financial planning.

What Is an Emergency Fund and How Much Do You Need?

Possessing good financial health includes having a large savings account, which can be used solely for emergencies. Keep in mind that none of us expects an emergency to happen, such as a job layoff, a blown car engine, a leaky roof that needs replacement, or a medical emergency (with high copays). Using debt, such as credit cards, to fund emergencies is never a good idea because of high interest rates.

According to Dave Ramsey, a fully funded emergency fund covers three to six months of expenses.[2] He recommends that you start an emergency fund when you've paid off your debts, except for your mortgage, and that you can begin with $1,000. When deciding on the exact amount, Ramsey suggests that you think about how much money you'd need if you lost your income for three to six months. He advises that you use three to six months of expenses instead of income because the fund is to cover expenses, not replace income. It's a good idea to look at the budget you created in Chapter 4 as a guideline. While the amount varies for all couples, the average emergency fund that's fully funded will range from $10,000 to $25,000, explains Ramsey. He also recommends that this fund be liquid and easy to access. For instance, a money market account with no penalties and debit card or check writing privileges.

Brittany and John, who you met earlier, set up an emergency fund during the early years of their marriage. They were very grateful to be able to draw from this during their financial crisis a year later. Once their finances were restored and they eliminated bad debt, they were eager to deposit $20,000 in their emergency fund, the amount they'd need to pay bills for three months. Since their CFP suggested that they have easy access to this fund, they deposited it in a money market account, which gives them a debit card to use in the case of an emergency.

John puts it like this, "We've had many unexpected things happen during our marriage, from extensive car repairs to job layoffs. Brittany and I know the benefits of having an emergency fund firsthand, and we hope we never have to use it again."

Another essential aspect of saving money is saving for retirement. Following the retirement planning tips below will help you to take action and jumpstart your plan.

How Much of Your Income Should You Save for Retirement?

While everyone's vision of their golden years varies, many people struggle to save enough to adequately fund their retirement. A 2022 Northwestern Mutual study found that US adults estimate they'll need $1.25 million, on average, to retire comfortably.[3] In order to get there, you will have to save $520.00 per month for forty years, earning a 7 percent annual rate of return.

While retirement is the most important goal people will fund in the course of their lives, we delay planning for it. In an article written for Buy Side, contributor Tanza Loudenback writes, "Retirement is the most expensive goal many Americans will fund in their lifetime. But everyone's picture of their golden years is different—and costs vary."[4] Loudenback recommends the following tips for retirement planning:

Five Retirement Planning Tips Recommended by Tanza Loudenback[5]:

1. Look at your time horizon. How many years do you have to save for retirement? Those who start early have a big advantage. If you start putting money away in your thirties, you will have double the amount for retirement as someone who started saving in their forties. You will read more about this advantage later in the chapter.

2. Life expectancy. How long do you need your nest egg to last? Although life expectancy rates vary throughout history, you will need to factor in your family history to make a good prediction.

3. How much will you need to live on annually to maintain your lifestyle? The standard guideline is 70 to 80 percent of your preretirement income. Keep in mind that you might want to add in expenses for travel and leisure activities to your budget—both of which require cash flow.

4. Additional sources of income. This includes social security and other income sources such as inheritance. Data shows that social security benefits for someone retiring at age sixty-five replace about 40 percent of their prior earnings.

5. Consult a CFP if you want to crunch the numbers and have access to sophisticated software to help you understand specific retirement account types and which stocks or mutual funds fit best for your portfolio, as well as to help you minimize taxes while you enjoy your retirement years.

Dave Ramsey defines retirement as reaching your golden years with dignity and getting to the point in life where your money works harder than you do.[6] He explains that you can't attain this level of success in life without a plan. Ramsey suggests that many people are in denial about saving for retirement, and getting serious about retirement planning means investing 15 percent of your income in retirement. His rule is simple: invest 15 percent of before-tax gross income annually toward retirement. You might ask, why not more? Ramsey explains that you need some of your income that's left for college savings (if you have children) and to pay off your home early. He posits that saving less will not be in your best interest. Ramsey also advises that your potential social security benefits shouldn't be factored into your calculations because you can't count on the government for your dignity at retirement. He writes, "You'll need cash to put food on the table when you retire."

While saving money for emergencies and your sunset years are important goals, it's important for you and your partner to look at your budget closely (see Chapter 4) and save money on daily and weekly expenses such as groceries, gas, entertainment, and travel. I'm not suggesting that you forget about putting away money for an emergency fund, retirement, and the "big stuff" such as graduations, weddings, and purchasing a new or used automobile. But let's start with the essential and practical topic of saving money on groceries.

How to Save Money on Groceries

While it may seem trivial, you can save a considerable amount of money on groceries by planning ahead and using strategies such as comparison shopping. By this, I mean actually price-checking items that you use often and visiting some of the newer discount stores to get the best value. It's easy to get stuck in a rut when it comes to grocery shopping. But smart shoppers mix it up a bit and let go of pride and preconceived notions about discount stores being low quality.

Twelve Tips to Help Grocery Shoppers Save Money:

1. Be smart about sections in a store. Many items such as cheese, spices, bread, crackers, and chips are sold in more than one section of a store. Be sure to compare prices for the best deals.

2. Purchase grocery items at a discount. Beth Braverman, David Schiff, and Amanda Gengler, writers for the AARP website, suggest the flashfood app, which offers deals for up to a 50 percent discount.[7] You can pay for the items on your app and then pick them up at a designated area in the store. If interested, check out flashfood.com.

3. Maintain two grocery lists. The first list is for essential items such as milk and bread, and the second one can be a running list of items such as cleaning supplies that can usually wait. By keeping this running list, shoppers can keep their eyes on sales and make sure they don't purchase too many nonessential items weekly. In other words, they can space them out throughout the month so the costs are evenly distributed throughout the year.

4. Look for new store brands to buy. As I mentioned before, try to avoid getting stuck in a rut and look for new items that are not name brands but can still be high quality. This is usually

true for items such as cleaning supplies, coffee, some juices, and canned food such as tomatoes, beans, and corn. House-brand products are almost always cheaper than name-brand ones, and new items are put on the shelves on a regular basis.

5. Download your grocery store's app. Your loyalty card has probably gone digital, and most grocery stores have deals only available on their apps. If you "clip" them within the app, they will automatically be applied to your card.

6. Use coupons when ordering online. The typical shopper can save over $25.00 a month by doing this, and it's a quicker process than only takes a few minutes if you plan ahead.

7. Shop at different grocery stores. New discount grocery stores open up all the time. Don't be afraid to check them out for the best deals. Grocery stores and discount chains often sell quality items at discounted prices. Be sure to limit yourself to two shopping trips a week and be mindful of your budget for groceries while you reduce your carbon footprint.

8. Use cards that offer rewards for purchasing groceries. Using the right credit card can save you money. Search the internet for a credit card that can give you 5 percent off for purchasing groceries.

9. Have a shelf in your refrigerator designated for items that need to be eaten first. This includes leftovers, perishables, a small serving of pasta, cubes of cheese, or produce that is on its way out.

10. Use self-checkout at grocery stores. Couples that do this pay more attention to how much they spend than those who rely on a cashier to check them out. It may take a little more time, but it's a great money-saving step.

11. Consider starting a garden in your yard or on your deck or terrace, or join a community garden. Growing vegetables that can be canned such as tomatoes, carrots, and cucumbers have many benefits such as improved nutrition, better flavor, and lower cost. In the dead of winter, why not enjoy a fresh

pasta dinner with marinara sauce made from vegetables grown in your own garden?

12. Plant edible perennials. Many herbs and spices that can add zest to your dishes, such as garlic, oregano, and rosemary, can be grown in pots and will grow back every year. Using your own instead of store-bought ones will save you money.

Now for some thoughts about online shopping, which has benefits but also risks. It has become very popular in the last few decades, and shoppers must use a credit card or mobile payment app like Venmo or PayPal to purchase items. This practice is good from a time management perspective, and it can curb impulse buying, but it also encourages people to use credit cards like cash. As a result, it can increase bad debt for shoppers who are addicted to shopping or have a spender financial style. On the other hand, mobile apps like Venmo or PayPal can be linked to your bank account and used like a debit card.

When it comes to credit cards, it's always a good idea for you to pay off the amount you owe monthly to avoid accruing interest. It's important for online shoppers to be mindful of not running up charges on their credit cards that they can't pay off when their bill is due. If you can do this and pay off your credit card charges monthly, online shopping can save you money (on gasoline and time) and limit purchases.

Living together for two years, Caroline, twenty-seven, and Nathan, twenty-eight, both pay off their credit card charges monthly and are conservative in their use of digital purchases. They share all expenses while taking into consideration that Caroline has a higher salary as an engineer than Nathan does as a librarian. During their interview, Caroline and Nathan spoke about the fact that they have separate checking and savings accounts, and they're both trying to save money, with the goal of eventually buying a home. In order to do this, they have been price checking at different grocery stores and eating out less in restaurants.

Caroline and Nathan also go grocery shopping and plan meals together, taking turns cooking healthy vegan meals. Recently, they've been limiting ordering takeout and they've been trying to eat fewer meals out, averaging about two meals in restaurants a week, including one lunch, one dinner, and an occasional brunch at their favorite vegan restaurant. Since they reside in a temperate climate, they're able to grow most of their vegetables year-round, which saves them money and satisfies their goal to lead a healthy, sustainable life.

Caroline reflects, "We never used to shop for groceries together, but decided it was a wise idea since we both cook and want to look for bargains. Nathan is really good at checking for new stores that offer vegan products, and we've started a small garden so that we can eat most of our vegetables (in season) from it. We've recently started canning sauces, salsa, jams, jellies, and storing dried herbs that we keep in our pantry. We've also been making our own pasta and bread. They're not only delicious, but growing some of our own food makes us feel happy because we're saving money."

How to Save on Gasoline and Other Driving-Related Expenses

While saving money on gas and other driving-related expenses may seem inconsequential, it involves a major shift in perspective. It comes down to looking at how much you drive vehicles (and the kind of cars you drive) and reducing your carbon footprint. There are three different types of electric assist vehicles: hybrid, plugin hybrid electric (PHEV), and electric vehicles. Many hybrid and electric car shoppers are purchasing slightly used vehicles that are three to six years old. Most experts agree that driving less, using public transportation, and driving hybrid or electric cars is a good practice to save energy and money at the same time.

Consolidating errands in order to drive less, save on gasoline, and save time is a good idea. Ask yourself, do I really need to run to the market or pharmacy for nonessential items today or can it wait until my weekly shopping trip? It may take a little extra time to plan where and when you will shop to consolidate your errands, but it's well worth the investment in planning time.

Over the past two decades, Lisa and Carla, whom you met earlier, have looked for ways to save gasoline since Lisa drives a lot for her job in the insurance industry. In addition to driving a hybrid vehicle, Lisa often consolidates her errands so that she's only running them a couple of days a week. She's also enjoying saving gas (and not contributing to climate change) by driving her slightly used hybrid vehicle. In fact, Lisa purchased it at a discount because it had 30,000 miles on it and was two years old when she bought it from a dealership.

Lisa shares,

> When I first told Carla that I was interested in purchasing a slightly used hybrid vehicle, she shut me down because we usually buy new cars, and she was suspicious of driving a hybrid, thinking it might run out of gas and wouldn't have much space for traveling with luggage. But when we car shopped together, compared prices, and she drove a hybrid SUV with lots of storage and amazing mileage, she was sold. Two years later, we are very pleased with my purchase.

Many people have found success cutting back on gas and expenses at stores by scheduling their errands on the same day and eliminating excessive trips to stores where they might be tempted to buy unnecessary items because they are appealing to the eyes or senses. For instance, it's hard for me to resist the aroma that emanates from the bakery items at the grocery store. Overall, it's a good idea to reduce trips to the market to once or twice a week and to cut down on gas by consolidating errands and driving a smaller car or a hybrid or electric vehicle. Shaving off a few dollars here and there can do wonders for your monthly budget so you can increase your savings plan.

Another useful savings tip for drivers is to learn to brake less and coast more. Every time you brake, you waste gas you just used to get to your current speed. And the more you coast, the higher your gas mileage will be. Get in the habit of accelerating gently, coasting to stop signs, and using your brakes less. An added benefit will be safer driving, lower insurance rates, and perhaps fewer accidents, suggest Beth Braverman, David Schiff, and Amanda Gengler, writers for the AARP website.[8]

How to Save on Travel and Entertainment

Traveling off season is a good money-saving strategy. Since the Covid-19 pandemic, travel costs, including airline fares and resort fees, have skyrocketed. Airline fees, for example, have increased by 4.1 percent or more in the past year according to the Consumer Price Index.[9] However, renting a condo in April instead of June can save you $100.00 a night, and you can avoid the crowds.

Avoid renting a car when you travel. Car rental prices have soared beyond the inflation rate over the last few years. Consider traveling to places that have public transportation such as trains, subways, and buses. These cities include Boston; New York; Washington, DC; and Chicago, where you will also find some discounted hotel fees if you search online. If you and your partner stay at a resort, avoid paying a resort fee which can run you up to $25.00 a day by choosing one that doesn't charge a fee.

For instance, when Brittany and John were planning a vacation, they searched for a low-cost option where they could enjoy time with their son Justin, avoid paying airline fares, and use public transportation. Since Justin had never visited Washington, DC, they checked hotel rates because they could drive from their home in one day and visit the museums at the National Mall without paying an admission rate. Fortunately, they found a medium-priced hotel (in a suite large enough for all of them) located outside of DC in Fairfax, VA. In fact, they enjoyed taking the subway into the National Mall daily (for $2.00 to $5.00 for a one-hour ride) where they visited the Smithsonian Institution, the Lincoln Memorial, and various sculptures, statues, and museums. Brittany and John also found many moderately priced restaurants in the DC metro area to dine at.

Get It for Free

Many cities offer low-cost or free admission to museums or national parks for children, seniors, and families. These include children's museums, various art museums, aquariums, and zoos across America. Check in with your local library and find the wide variety of discounted coupons to wildlife refuges and nature centers as well. On a handful of days each year, the national parks which usually charge admission offer free admission for everyone.

In terms of entertainment, you might consider an outdoor activity such as hiking at a national park or wildlife refuge. There's usually a small or nominal fee to enter. Plus, going for a hike is great exercise, and it can feel exhilarating. Hiking trails can vary from 2 to 3 miles for a beginner's hike, to 4 to 6 miles for a moderate hike, or an advanced hike of 7 or more miles for seasoned hikers. Be sure to check the elevation before you head out to the trail. Keep in mind that the terrain and weather can impact your choice of clothing and shoes, so be sure to check weather conditions and pack a trail guide. Bring plenty of water and snacks to prevent dehydration and hunger pangs, because this can result in irritable hikers.

There are many other ways to enjoy low-cost or free entertainment. Some couples like to watch movies at home with a home-cooked meal or pizza takeout. It can be fun to play games and even invite friends over friends for a card or game night. Other low-cost forms of entertainment include visiting a local farm or brewery that might have an option for an inexpensive food truck or bringing a picnic to a nearby park on a nice weather day.

Saving for the "Big Stuff"

Saving money for big purchases such as a home, car, or college tuition takes planning and commitment. Most likely, you will also need loans for these big items, but a substantial down payment will lower your monthly payments dramatically. Looking at a 20 percent minimum down payment on purchases such as a new car is a good strategy. You and your partner might want to automate your savings so you don't have to worry about calculating it monthly. This is especially important when you're saving for retirement or an emergency fund so these funds don't get depleted or forgotten.

Saving for the "big stuff" often means saving for a new vehicle. Brittany and John are looking to save money for a new hybrid vehicle. Because John has a long commute, and he wants to save money on gas, saving money for a down payment on a hybrid car is a great idea. Brittany and John, both super spenders, have made great strides toward this savings goal by using full disclosure and looking for ways to curtail their spending on nonessentials.

Saving Money Is Good for You and Your Marriage or Relationship

Saving money is often an overlooked category in a budget, and it can improve your marriage or committed relationship if you have regular, low-conflict money talks that are productive. When you live within your means and save money for your future, it can provide a safety net to fall back on. The truth is that there are simple strategies that you can employ to save money and jumpstart your financial health, as well as to improve your marriage.

Having ongoing conversations with your partner about a savings plan and ways to cut back on discretionary items is a wise idea. This is a crucial step to achieving the goal of boosting your savings. Select three or four items that can be eliminated from spending, such as a daily trip to Starbucks or a monthly shopping trip to the mall. As you begin to get rid of financial baggage in your life, your new minimalist perspective will help you to take pride in the items you own and limit spending on nonessential items. You might also begin to feel grateful for small things such as a fresh, home-brewed cup of coffee or a newly purchased outfit or jewelry from a consignment store.

Married twenty-six years, Kelly, fifty, and Alan, fifty-one, met me for an interview at their cozy seaside home and described how they used to live paycheck to paycheck before they decided to work toward a savings and investing plan. Having monthly money talks and being on the same page with finances has allowed them to have some financial breathing space. Both college teachers at the same university, they make it a point to go over their budget monthly over coffee on campus. This is essential to their communication about money since they have three children who will be going off to college in the next five years.

Kelly and Alan are both moderate savers who have money vigilance scripts, and they use a common-pot money management system with a joint checking and savings account. They closely track what they spend each month. The rest of the money left over is divided four ways: an emergency fund, retirement accounts, investments, and a "Mad" money account (usually put toward nonessentials that are not included in their budget).

Kelly elaborates,

Alan and I practice full disclosure about finances and we go over our bills and our budget often. We sit down once a month, pay bills online, and then record all transactions in a binder on a handwritten spreadsheet. Our financial decisions are made collaboratively. We both decided early on in our marriage that we would rather sleep well at night than "keep up with the Joneses."

Alan responds, "We've agreed to max out our 401(k)s, buy some stocks each month, and keep our living expenses low so hopefully we can retire by around age sixty-two. Each time we received raises over the years, instead of going out and buying the newest house or car, we started paying off debt and investing."

It seems clear that Kelly and Alan embody the "us against the problem" mindset when it comes to finances. They both described what Kelly referred to as a stable base of support that allows her to feel calm and happy in her marriage. While they had some financial struggles during the first two decades of their marriage and were slow getting started, they both realize that time is of the essence if they're going to attain their goal of financing college for their children and being able to retire early. Boosting their savings plan is one sure-fire way to do this as well as making good investments. For information on making investments, it's a good idea to contact a CFP who can help you and your partner map out a plan so you can fulfill your vision for your future as a couple.

10 Suggestions to Boost Your Savings for Couples:

1. Avoid treating yourself with guilty pleasures. Rather than using shopping to elevate your mood, go for a long walk with a friend or join a low-cost gym. If you believe that you're a compulsive buyer or have a shopping addiction, seeking treatment is essential to boosting your savings plan. If you're used to indulging in habits such as purchasing nonessential items either online or in person, ask yourself if the item is something you need versus what you want. For instance, do you really need two pairs of leather boots that you rarely wear?

2. Establish an emergency fund. Set aside an emergency fund of at least three to six months so you have something to fall back

on in the case of unexpected expenses such as expensive car or home repairs, or a job layoff. If you don't set aside money for an emergency fund, all of the progress you've made with savings is at risk. The vast majority of adults (89 percent) surveyed by Bankrate in 2024 say they would need at least three months of expenses in an emergency fund to cover a job loss or emergency.[10] Despite that, only 44 percent of Americans actually have this amount saved.

3. Save at least 15 percent of your combined income.[11] Some advisors recommend that you save 20 percent. While this may seem like too much to ask, you will reap the psychological and financial benefits of this decision. Speaking to a financial planner about how to invest this savings is a smart idea.

4. Start a retirement fund. Most jobs have a 401(k) plan for employees. If you are self-employed or don't have one at your workplace, consult a CFP. There is no way couples can enjoy their golden years if they're underfunded and don't plan ahead. Christopher Yalanis, MBA, CFP, explains, "Time is an investor's best friend. Doing well isn't about timing the market. It's about time in the market. Longer is better. It's been said, and attributed to Einstein, that the world's most powerful (man-made) concept is the compounding of interest."[12] He advises that people start planning for retirement as young as possible. He explains, "The more time you miss, the more opportunities you lose. The biggest problem people have funding retirement is that they don't plan early enough."

5. Shop at consignment stores. It's a good habit to recycle the clothes and other items you and your family don't wear (or use) but hang onto anyway. Most cities or towns have consignment stores which screen their items and sell high-quality merchandise including clothes, toys, household items, and furniture. It's easy to open an account at a consignment store, and you can spend the money you earn monthly on items you need or want rather than spending more on a new item of clothing.

6. Consider using cash for purchases. In our digital world, using cash is still a good alternative that can help you keep track

of purchases, so you can spend less and save more. This is especially true during the holiday season. People are often in shock when their credit card bills arrive in January because it's easy to forget about the extra gifts they bought during last-minute shopping at the mall or online. Some people use an "Envelope budget" when shopping for holiday gifts and only use the cash they have budgeted from the envelope.

7. Become a frugal food shopper. By using some of the strategies offered in this chapter, you can save a considerable amount on groceries. Be sure to price-check the staples on your list at different stores for several weeks. Record prices as you shop or use an app like Google Notes. If you transfer your data onto a spreadsheet, you'll be able to compare prices at different stores to assess the best bargains without sacrificing quality. Also, take advantage of weekly sales.

8. Evaluate your cell phone plan. Cell phones have become a necessity of life, but their costs have increased dramatically over the last several years. Go online or visit stores to compare prices. Consider a family plan for two or more family members that will cut costs.

9. Give homemade gifts. It's true that you might not want to give homemade banana bread to your supervisor, but it could be the perfect gift for a close friend or neighbor. Baked goods, crafts, and homemade ornaments make a perfect gift for many people on your gift list.

10. Consolidating errands. As you learned earlier, this will help you spend less on gas and nonessential items. It may take some getting used to, but with practice, it will become easier.

Spending Less Is the Best Way to Save Money

What I have learned from doing the research on this chapter is that spending less, while a challenge, is the best way to save money. The most important lesson that couples like Kendra and Sam taught me is the value of living within your means, working as a team to cut spending, and being aware of what they refer to as what I/we need versus what I/we want, which allows them to save money. I also learned the critical importance of starting to plan for retirement early from Christopher Yalanis, MBA, CFP.[13] Yalanis explains, "Time is on the side of the investor. Growth on growth. What is called 'compounding' growth is a tremendous way to leverage one's assets. So, start early!"

That said, the most fitting way to end this chapter is with a quote from the oldest and one of the wisest couples I interviewed. I asked them to tell me about how they were able to achieve prosperity and such a happy long-term marriage.

Sam reflects,

> When Kendra and I married, we both had high ideals about how we wanted to have this great life together. The truth is that it's mostly worked out. We made a commitment to be "in it together" and not give up on each other, through thick and thin. When one of us overspends, the other keeps them in line. We are best friends as well as lovers.

Kendra responds, "Recently, we decided that we've made enough wise decisions in our twenty years of marriage to enjoy a trip to Key West for our anniversary. By living within our budget most of the time and not overspending much, our vacation budget was intact, and we enjoyed ourselves immensely."

Your journey to becoming financially healthy and happy like Kendra and Sam starts with changing your scarcity mindset about money to an abundance mentality. You have learned to have low-conflict discussions about finances with your partner, create a money management system, build a budget, get rid of bad debt, and save for the "big stuff," like a new vehicle. The next section of this book will help you with troubleshooting many of the challenges of finances, such as prenups, estate planning, financial infidelity, and getting back on track after a conflict or dispute. By reading these chapters, you and your partner are preparing to survive challenges together as you build a rock-solid foundation of love, trust, and financial intimacy.

PART III

Troubleshooting the Challenges of Money, Marriage, and Committed Relationships

Chapter 7
Prenuptial and Postnuptial Agreements
The Pros and Cons

Marriage is a meaningful and romantic experience where two people come together, but it is also, practically speaking, a legal agreement. No one should enter marriage casually, and though it might ruin the mood to discuss finances, both parties can benefit from going into it with their eyes wide open. There are many instances where a couple may want to consider a prenuptial agreement, which is a contract between two people engaged to be married in which they agree that certain assets will not be considered marital property in case of divorce. A prenup protects the assets and property rights of one spouse, or both spouses, should they split up or one partner dies unexpectedly.[1]

Despite the fact that a prenuptial agreement is drafted before marriage, you can still sign one after tying the knot. This is called a postnuptial agreement, and you will learn more about this later in the chapter. Since many couples are getting married later in life and may have more assets, and/or have been divorced, many people don't want the courts to decide what would happen in the event of a divorce or untimely death. Prenups are a written contract created by two people prior to marriage, listing all the assets and debts of both people and specifying what each person's rights will be after marriage. They can lessen the likelihood of disputes during a divorce and protect children from a prior marriage. Unlike prenups, postnups are usually drafted by married couples who are struggling in their relationship, but they're not quite ready to get a divorce. They often feel there's a potential for divorce, but they haven't yet given up on their marriage.

Reasons to Choose a Prenuptial Agreement

According to lawyer and divorce coach Karen Covy, a prenup is simply a legally binding contract that stipulates what happens when a marriage ends (either in divorce or in the death of one partner).[2] She explains, "And as with any contract, nothing is set in stone, and the particular circumstances of a couple's union can be incorporated into a prenup in a way that best serves them. In other words, prenups are not one-size-fits-all." Covy continues, "People from all walks of life can benefit from one, if mutually agreed upon by both partners in a spirit of love."

During our interview, Covy pointed out that the majority of prenups are concerned with finances (especially if couples have unequal assets).[3] However, she made it clear that any number of factors, choices, and expectations can be baked into a contract, from how frequently partners have sex to how often a spouse is responsible for cooking, cleaning, or taking care of household chores. She elaborates, "Not that including any of those kinds of requirements in a prenup is a good idea. It's not!" Covy continues, "It's also common for parents to want to protect their children from a prior marriage by clearly stating in a prenup that certain property is non-marital. In addition, most parents don't want their death to break up the family, and a prenuptial agreement can lessen the likelihood of disputes between adult children." In fact, Covy explained that in some cases grown-up children, over age fifty, will encourage their parents to get a prenup to protect the interests of their parents and themselves in the event of a divorce or untimely death. Oftentimes, the partner who initiates a prenuptial agreement owns a successful business, has children, and/or has more assets to protect.

For example, when Maura, forty-eight, a small business owner, met Kenneth, fifty-eight, a mechanic, she fell head over heels for this handsome bachelor. However, she had lingering doubts about whether he was trustworthy and would protect her children if she died. Because Maura had recently inherited money from her deceased parents' estate and had significant savings and assets, she felt vulnerable. Maura was hesitant to move ahead with their engagement without a prenuptial agreement. She wanted to protect the interests of her two grown daughters, Lilli and Shelby, and her employees. On the other hand, Kenneth had a spotty work history and had very little in the way of savings or investments, and no children of his own. During our interview, it was apparent that they both had trust issues.

Maura explains,

> I love Kenneth and I thought he felt the same way, but he went ballistic when I asked him for a prenup to protect my assets for myself and my children if we divorced. My daughters were estranged from their biological father after my divorce ten years ago, so I'm all they have. They're both in high school, so need a way to finance their college and living expenses in a few years. Kenneth accused me of not trusting him when I asked for a prenup. I guess there is truth to this, but I can't move forward without feeling financially safe. I have two daughters from my first marriage to consider if things don't work out with Kenneth or I die before he does. Since he doesn't have kids, he has less to lose if our marriage doesn't pan out. I wish he didn't take it the wrong way and feel threatened.

Remarried for three years, Tara, sixty-five, and James, sixty-seven, have a different take on prenups. They own their own home in an affluent suburb and are both comfortably retired. When James proposed to Tara four years ago, he didn't foresee her need for a prenup in advance. However, once they became engaged, Tara asked for a prenup to protect the assets from her first marriage and her substantial retirement income stemming from her job as a nurse practitioner. In Tara's case, she also wanted to protect the interests of her younger sister, Samantha, who has special needs, in the event that they divorce or she dies before James. In James's case, he was accepting of her desire for a prenup, and he didn't feel threatened by it. James, a retired engineer, had a good retirement income and assets due to smart investments.

It was important to him and his legacy that his twenty-year-old son, Alexander, inherit a considerable amount from his estate, and he was more than happy to honor Tara's request for a prenup. Rather than see it as threatening and getting defensive, James saw a prenup as a rational idea that could give them both security and peace of mind.

In the case of Tara and James, they were definitely on the same page when it came to writing up a prenup, and each of them wanted to do their best to honor each other's wishes. As professionals, they both had high incomes prior to retirement. During our couples therapy session, when Tara announced unexpectedly that she wanted a prenup, James chose not to take it personally. Since he had already been divorced and James had a grown son, he knew how fragile relationships can be and how sensitive Alexander was to feeling overlooked by a stepmom. In fact, after he told Alexander that he was proposing to Tara, they discussed his will and how his estate would be divided between him and his stepmother if James died before she did. During this conversation, they spoke honestly, with full disclosure, and James became aware that Alexander was prone to feeling left out and possibly resentful.

James shares,

> I love Tara and respect the fact that she worked hard in the medical field for over thirty years. She also has a sister with Down syndrome, and wants to protect her interests in case she passes away before I do. This makes sense to me because her parents are both deceased and they didn't leave much inheritance. I also want to protect the interests of my son who is still in college. So, we both hired our own lawyer, wrote up the terms of the prenup, and sat down with our lawyers separately to ask questions. Then we met with Terry to hash out the details. This made our marriage stronger because we saw our prenup as potentially benefiting a lot of people—mostly Tara's sister who has special needs and my son from my first marriage. It really helped us clear the air and feel more secure.

Keep in mind that every person is unique, and if your partner asks for a prenup, it's important to give them the benefit of the doubt and not to assume that they don't trust you or have other objectionable motives. It's wise to give yourself time to get used to the idea of a prenup, do research, and ask questions. In many cases, both people have something to gain by signing a prenuptial agreement. Discussing a prenup forces couples to talk about their financial goals, their attitudes about money, their spending and savings habits, and any debt they have acquired. Most of all, don't assume the worst of your partner if they ask you for a prenup. Having these conversations before marriage can set the stage for a healthier and stronger marriage. Many couples, especially if remarried, avoid discussing finances, and yet have anxiety about a possible divorce since they've already experienced a breakup. As a result, they might worry about protecting their assets and those of other family members. For these individuals, a prenup can spell out certain rights, helping them to move forward with their plans to marry or remarry, reducing their fear of the unknown.

According to the American Academy of Matrimonial Lawyers, 51 percent of the lawyers surveyed reported an increase in the number of millennials seeking prenuptial agreements in the past three years, and 62 percent of divorce attorneys cited an increase in the total number of prenup requests.[4] For millennials, reasons often relate to their age and circumstances. Some common motivations include marrying at a later age, having more assets to protect, and they may also be expecting an inheritance. This chapter will explain what a prenuptial agreement is, what it can and cannot do, and the advantages and disadvantages of entering into one for both partners. Since I'm not a lawyer, I consulted legal sources to obtain information about prenups and postnups. Further, I believe a counselor or mediator can help couples compromise when one partner desires a prenup and the other one doesn't. Every relationship is different, and lawyers who specialize in family law and couples therapists can help partners navigate through the tricky process of prenuptial agreements.

When I interviewed Attorney Karen Covy about the recent increase in prenups, she stated,[5]

> In spite of the fact that a prenup is about as romantic as a root canal, more and more people are getting them. People are living longer, and many people want to protect their assets such as a business. In other cases, adult children might be encouraging their parents to get a prenup when they marry a second (or third) time.

When I asked Covy what prenups typically cover, she gave me a long list, and here are the top ten items[6]:

1. What will happen to the assets you and your spouse had before you got married in the event of your death or divorce.
2. Whether you or your partner is responsible for paying debts that you had before you got married.
3. What will be considered "separate" property and what will be considered "marital" or community property?
4. Whether you or your spouse will be eligible to receive alimony/spousal support if you divorce.
5. Whether the money you and your spouse earn or acquire during your marriage automatically becomes marital money or not.
6. Whether the money you or your spouse inherit during your marriage will become marital money.
7. If your premarital assets grow in value (like a business), will that progress be considered non-marital?
8. Who pays for attorney fees if you get divorced?
9. How each of you will provide for children from prior relationships if you die or divorce.
10. How each of you will handle finances during your marriage and whether putting your spouse's name on premarital assets turns them into marital property.

In a recent podcast interview about prenuptial agreements, Family Attorney Katy Mickelson, says that a prenup is

> Entering into a contract before marriage. It's only going to be effective upon marriage. There are certain things that can be contracted for in a prenuptial agreement and most of them are going to be related to finances. Specifically related to the classification of property, and additionally how we define that property during the course of the marriage, be it marital or non-marital (also referred to as separate property).[7]

Mickelson continues, "A prenup is somewhat taking the guesswork and pre-planning out of divorce which no one wants, but it's like an insurance plan. You are essentially solidifying certain rights for the future. A prenup deals with assets, but it also deals with issues regarding support, such as maintenance, also known as alimony."

A Prenuptial Agreement Should Be Fair and Voluntary

It's important to consider that courts will invalidate a prenup if they believe that it's unfair toward one party or otherwise unconscionable or involuntary. For instance, if the prenup imposes undue financial hardship on one partner, unfairly limits child custody for one spouse, or imposes marital conditions regarding a spouse's appearance, sexual acts, or other private behaviors, it might be deemed invalid by a court, according to Jennifer Bell, a legal writer for Schwartz, Fox, and Saltzman, LLC, a Philadelphia-based law firm.[8] In addition, duress or lack of capacity of one spouse can invalidate a prenup, explains Bell. She writes, "If one spouse can show that they had undue pressure to sign a prenup, whether that pressure be a physical, emotional, or financial threat, the court will invalidate the prenup." For many couples, such as James and Tara, mutual respect and fairness are at the heart of a voluntary prenup that reflects their goodwill toward one another.

When James and Tara agreed to draft a prenup, they each met with an attorney separately to draw up the conditions of it so they could discuss the details in person. Since they didn't have significant trust issues, this process was pretty straightforward. However, their lawyers advised them to be transparent with each other throughout the process of finalizing the prenups. In most cases, prenups are upheld, but a judge could nullify a prenup if they suspect dishonesty or believe one partner is being treated unfairly. After their individual agreements were drafted by their lawyers, Tara contacted my office to set up a couple's therapy session to go over their drafts in order to encourage full disclosure. Cautious by nature, Tara wanted to be sure that she and James were going forward with a prenup without rose-colored glasses. This couple also wanted to ensure that they would be able to have low-conflict conversations and a fair agreement.

During our first couples therapy session, James was very vocal about his legacy and wish to have his son, Alexander, inherit half of his estate in the event he died before Tara. He also expressed a desire to leave at least half of his estate to Tara. Fortunately, both Tara and James shared the same desire to compromise, and they each drew up a prenup that honored their wishes to divide their property and assets equally among themselves and their loved ones. Specifically, James's prenup designated that 50 percent of his estate be left to Alexander and 50 percent to Tara in the event that he died before she did. Since Tara appreciated James's devotion, honesty, and generosity, she agreed to split her estate equally between her sister, Samantha, and her loving husband, James, if she died before he did. In the event that they divorced, they agreed that they would not be given assets from each other, and this was spelled out in the prenup. Over a period of three months with regular therapy sessions, Tara and James were able to discuss their perspectives and come to an amicable agreement.

The Advantages of Having a Prenup

People who own a successful business or have substantial assets that they wish to protect for their family members or loved ones often ask their partners for a prenup. They hope to protect their business and/or other assets from property settlement claims that could arise from divorce. In other cases, someone who feels betrayed by a former partner may want to protect their assets and their children in the case of divorce or death.

When I interviewed Haley, who you met in Chapter 3, she was happy to share her reasons for a prenup. She told me that she was forty-one years old when she met Conner, who was forty-four at the time, and that they've been in a committed relationship for four years and engaged for the past two years. She also stated that Conner's two young daughters, Bethany and Taylor, and her teenage daughter, Kayla, all lived with them full-time. A successful entrepreneur who owned a mid-size landscaping business, Conner was comfortable financially with high assets. However, he wanted to make sure his assets were taken care of since his ex-wife had limited financial means and couldn't contribute to the fiscal welfare of their two daughters. In the event that he and Haley divorced or he died before Haley, Conner wanted to be sure that his daughters were all set financially and didn't have to rely on Haley to support them. Likewise, Haley wanted to protect herself since they had built the landscaping business together from the ground up, and she worked as the general manager with a relatively low salary and hasn't owned shares in Conner's business so far.

Haley shares,

> Conner is my soulmate and I have tremendous love and respect for him. But we share some expenses and keep some of our finances separate. I have Conner and his two young daughters listed in my will, along with my daughter Kayla, and I will make sure everyone is taken care of when I die. But due to the fact that I've been divorced and suffered a loss financially, I felt that a prenup (to protect my assets) was a good idea. Conner was fine with this. We communicate fairly well and have an open, honest relationship when it comes to money. We didn't feel that having a prenup meant that we don't trust each other, but our situation is complex.

As you can see from reading the real-life stories of these three couples, deciding to embark upon a prenup is a complex and lengthy journey. It is not a process that should be rushed or taken lightly. However, if approached thoughtfully and in the spirit of goodwill and extending trust to your partner, faith and optimism can prevail. The following section will break down the advantages and disadvantages of prenuptial agreements for you and your partner.

One major advantage of a prenup is that some assets can be considered outside the marital property, so one spouse can preserve them for their business partner or partners, children or grandchildren, offspring from a previous marriage, or whomever they wish if one spouse dies.[9] A prenuptial agreement can also streamline the process and lessen tension if a couple divorces because you can establish in advance what is and is not marital property. This can serve to reduce legal fees and be more efficient. However, keep in mind that prenuptial agreements are not always enforceable in all states. Some states are more skeptical, and there may be a concern about what led up to the agreement. State laws regarding prenups vary from state to state and the agreement must conform with state law and be properly signed by both parties. This is one of many reasons why it's a good idea to consult an attorney before you move ahead with a prenuptial or postnuptial agreement.

Amanda, thirty-five, and Keith, thirty-four, agreed to a prenup when they got engaged two years ago. Even though they didn't have children, Amanda inherited an expensive home from her father, who died suddenly in his late seventies. Since her mother died when she was in college and she was the only heir to her father's estate (and he was wealthy), her inheritance was substantial. Because she and Keith had a prenup prior to marriage and the process was fairly cordial, it was low-cost. Since they had only been living together for a year in Amanda's home when her father died, it made sense to Keith that this home and other assets left by Amanda's father not be considered as joint property in the divorce process.

Amanda and Keith's story illustrates how a prenup is a very good idea for couples with unequal assets and how it doesn't always lead to high conflict. It can actually make a divorce smoother, less costly, and less adversarial. No one gets married with the intent of getting divorced, but when they do, having a prenup that preserves each partner's premarital assets can lessen the stress of a divorce and the legal proceedings that accompany it. It can also give both partners more control of their assets. For instance, in the United States, only nine states have community property laws. Therefore, the courts have discretion over the division of assets after a divorce if a couple doesn't agree or doesn't have a prenup.

The Disadvantages of Having a Prenup

The simple act of asking a partner for a prenup may create distrust in your relationship. There's nothing less romantic than contemplating your eventual divorce or death. The process alone may cause some people to terminate an engagement. Some of the reasons why people initiate a prenup are because they have more assets than their partner, they own a successful business, or they have an inheritance that they want to protect.

If you initiate a prenup, you need to keep in mind that your partner may feel hurt that you want to protect your assets or not share them. They might also feel that they want to keep their personal life and finances private and/or avoid paying a lawyer to prepare a prenup. In Kenneth's case, he decided to marry Maura (and get a prenup), but it created many trust issues that led to tension and disagreements. Prenups can add stress to a couple's interactions because some people feel threatened or uneasy with the process. As a result, it can take time to resolve trust issues and improve communication between partners. For this reason, it's important to proceed slowly and consider positive ways to introduce the idea of a prenup to your partner.

The Best Way to Initiate a Prenup Conversation

If you initiate a prenup, negotiate in a loving way, and keep your partner's best interests at heart. Be sure to start the conversation when you and your partner are not rushed. Ask your partner in advance if they have time to discuss an important issue. When the conversation takes place, be prepared to listen and show understanding for their point of view. If you're the partner being asked to consider a prenup, do your best to keep an open mind, ask questions, and strongly consider their request and any advantages of it. If you need time to think before you give your mate an answer, let them know that you need a period of reflection, and that you might even want to consult a lawyer before giving him or her a definite answer to their request for a prenup (or a postnuptial agreement). Most importantly, don't panic and don't take it personally!

Prepare to answer your partner's questions without defensiveness. In most cases, if you're the person asking for the prenup, you can expect that your partner may feel blindsided and need time to digest the idea.

If this is the scenario, do your best not to get defensive when he or she has questions. It's a good idea to remain responsive rather than reactive to questions or feedback from your partner. Take things slowly and talk it over thoroughly. And consider meeting with a couples therapist or mediator if one or both of you are struggling to come to terms with the concept of a prenup. One thing is certain, it's important to respect each other's perspective and to listen more than you talk to your partner.

During our couples therapy sessions, Kenneth spent a considerable amount of time voicing his negative feelings about a prenup and feeling it was a sign that Maura had trust issues that were not warranted. Over the course of several sessions, I encouraged this couple to use a soft and curious tone to ask and answer questions. By using a "softened start up," it helped to minimize their defensive responses. In their book, *The Love Prescription*, John Gottman, PhD, and Julie Swartz Gottman, PhD, write,

> How you start a conversation matters. No matter how legitimate your need, if you begin with a harsh startup, (a criticism, or a "you always," or "you never" statement), you're putting yourself (and your partner!) at huge disadvantage: not only will neither of you get what you want or need, but you may do damage to the relationship—especially if the harsh start up becomes a habit.[10]

On the other hand, using a "softened start up" encourages good communication and keeps conflict low.[11] How does this work in a conversation? First, you start with how you feel (sad, worried, etc.), why you feel that way, and then state your request. When Maura was able to use a "softened start up" during our session to request a prenup, Kenneth was able to dial down his defensiveness, listen to her request in a calm and attentive way, and he eventually agreed to it.

Maura puts it like this,

> I love you, but have some worries about the future. I know I'm insecure because I feel that my ex-husband took advantage of my kindness during our divorce, and I settled for too little. So, I want to go into our marriage feeling trusting and secure in the event that it doesn't work out or I die unexpectedly. I also want to protect my kids

because they depend on me and don't have a father to lean on for financial support.

Once Maura was able to use this "softened start up" approach with honesty and transparency, Kenneth stopped taking her request personally and became convinced that her concerns were legitimate.[12] Maura carefully explained that she would make sure that Kenneth would have a share of her assets if she died before him, but this would not be the case in the event of divorce. Kenneth agreed to this logic and they were both ready to draft a prenup with their attorneys, which they would bring to our counseling sessions to discuss before the final drafts were prepared.

What to Do If You Want a Prenup and Your Partner Is Resistant

While it's not the most romantic subject to discuss, you must sit down and tell your partner the reason or reasons you want to enter a prenuptial agreement. Explain that your rationale has nothing to do with how you value your partner or your expectations about the success of the marriage. Instead, you can clarify that your need for a prenup arises from the need to protect yourself by shielding your business or certain assets from potential property settlement claims. If your discussion seems to bring up fear, mistrust, anger, or resentment in either you or your partner, it's wise to seek out a couples therapist or mediator. Remember that both prenup and postnup agreements need to be made voluntarily.

Framing the discussion around what you seek to do to protect your business partners, children from previous relationships, or a family member who may need continuing care, helps keep emotions in check. Write down exactly what you want to keep out of marital property and determine a true current value so their partner can make an informed decision. Be sure to have an attorney help you prepare the prenup. Courts might nullify a prenup if it isn't prepared by an attorney who specializes in family law. Many states require that both partners have their own attorneys.

Couples Activity: What to Do If Your Partner Wants a Prenup

1. First, know that prenups are common, and if your partner wants one, you should know the reasons and try not to feel threatened, according to legal writer, Jennifer Bell.[13] Ask each other at least two open-ended questions, as this will encourage communication. For instance, why do you want a prenup? Or, in what ways do you think having one will improve or harm our relationship?

2. Discuss specific ways you protect both of your assets with dignity. Understand that any prenup is a two-way street. You may have assets you want to include in the prenup even if you didn't initiate it or have concerns.

3. Remember that full disclosure promotes financial intimacy, so don't hold back when sharing your fears, concerns, or questions.

4. Work toward a "win-win" approach. Discuss how you can support each other in the process of getting a prenup, including meeting together to discuss the terms. If you hit a rough patch, agree to seek couples therapy to work through issues.

When Haley and Conner met with me to discuss their prenup drafts, they were ready to listen and compromise. Since I worked with both of them on using "I" statements and a "softened start up," they came prepared to turn toward each other and didn't see it as an opportunity to prove a point or to be self-righteous.[14] As a result, the defensiveness that I have seen with some couples was not present between Haley and Conner.

Many couples considering a prenup don't have the basic knowledge to make a decision. As a result, it's important for me as a therapist to have a list of facts to present. Knowledge can be very empowering and can set the stage for a more cordial tone when we discuss whether a prenup is a good fit for them and their situation. The following is a list of common questions that I share with couples.

Common Questions About Prenuptial Agreements

Many couples who are considering getting engaged or married have questions and these should be addressed by a legal professional. Here are some of the common questions asked by couples about prenups. Read through the list below to determine any that are relevant for you.

1. What's a good definition of a prenup?

    According to Attorney Karen Covy, it's a contract entered into by two people who plan to wed.[15] It determines their rights regarding property and financial support should the marriage end in divorce or an untimely death. Some prenups provide for each party to keep all of their assets earned before and after their marriage. Some prenups allow partners to keep the assets they acquired before they married, but to share those acquired afterward. Other prenups spell out the financial arrangements in the event of divorce (cash or property).

2. Do I need a prenup?

    It depends. An older couple with children or grandchildren may want to allocate funds to them in the event of death or divorce. A younger individual who is wealthy, owns a business, and/or has the potential for substantial inheritance may want to protect against property settlement claims.[16] However, not all couples need a prenup. If you're young, don't have many assets, don't own property, or if you don't own a business, and you don't have children, you may not feel a need for a prenuptial agreement.

3. My finance asked me for a prenup. Does that mean he or she doesn't trust me?

    Not always. There are many other reasons a person considering marriage would request a prenup. They might want to provide for children from a prior marriage, protect a family member with special needs, or protect assets from a business in the event of a death or divorce.[17] Sometimes, people simply want a sense of security, especially in cases where there is a stepparent or a family member who is helping to raise a child. Most people who have been married previously acknowledge that marriage is fragile at times and that it's a good idea to discuss the possibility of divorce in the future rather than to be blindsided.

4. Are prenups only for wealthy people?

   It depends. People at all socioeconomic levels might want to consider a prenup. Agreeing to a prenup can greatly reduce legal fees in the event of a divorce. If certain issues such as alimony, property, and attorney fees have already been resolved, it can save time and money in the event of a split. However, if someone has modest means, they may want to consider the cost of drafting a prenup.[18]

5. If my partner and I both have children, can a prenup determine custody or child support?

   No. A prenuptial agreement doesn't decide a parent's obligation to support their children or delegate custody during a divorce.[19]

6. My partner and I both have children from prior marriages.[20] Can we decide which children receive our assets through a prenup?

   Yes. An individual may want a certain portion (or the entirety) of their assets to go to a child or grandchild and not to a new spouse or a step-relative. A prenuptial agreement can ensure that your offspring will receive your assets and make it clear to your prospective spouse that you want to delegate assets to your biological relatives.

7. Must both people enter into a prenup voluntarily and also disclose all of their assets?[21]

   Yes However, you should also consider the fairness of terms before signing the prenuptial agreement and show the document to both of your lawyers.

8. If my partner and I both want a prenup, can we use the same lawyer?

No. Both of you need to have your own independent legal advice, especially if there is disparity in your incomes or assets, advises Karen Covy.[22] She says, "An independent counsel for the partner with weaker assets is always a good idea because they can negotiate on their behalf and explain the terms of the agreement."

9. If you want a prenup, what do you do next?

Karen Covy[23] explains that the first step isn't to get a lawyer. She explains, "A prenup is an agreement between two people in a relationship. It is about money. Money is a very sensitive topic. Money means different things to different people. What's more, people's relationship with money can be very different." Covy recommends that you start by talking about the big financial stuff, then get into the details. She also suggests that if you want to have a constructive money conversation, you may want to work with a relationship therapist who can help you dig into the emotions that are beneath how you feel about money. At this point, being transparent with your partner and disclosing your desire for a prenup is a good idea. Then gather your financial information (assets, liabilities, amount and sources of income, etc.). Full disclosure of assets is required to make sure the prenup is legally binding in the years to come.

10. Why do I need to hire an attorney?

Hiring an attorney is the best way to understand your rights and help you prepare a prenup. This will ensure that you're informed about the decision you're making in entering into a prenup, according to legal writer Jennifer Bell.[24] A lawyer will give you the guidelines and format you will need to draft a prenup. After the first draft of the prenup has been written, both people should take a copy to read over with their own lawyer. This gives both of you a chance to ask questions and request edits. Both partners can then negotiate for better or fairer terms. Hopefully, your lawyers will work together to craft an agreement that is acceptable to both you and your partner.

Many couples wait too long and underestimate the time it takes for lawyers to write up a prenup.

There Are Good Reasons for a Postnuptial Agreement

A postnuptial agreement is a similar concept to a prenup, but parties can enter into a contract after they marry, according to Family Attorney Katy Mickelson.[25] However, she explains that there are a couple of things to know about postnuptial agreements. Prenups are going to be governed by statutes, and there's a uniform prenup agreement act that lawyers conform to. But with postnups, there are no statutes or things that are allowed if litigation occurs. Mickelson says, "With a postnup there has to be a financial consideration, things people are bargaining for. This is not the case with a prenup. What kinds of things make for a bargaining agreement? Some kinds of support and setting up an account for this."

While prenuptial agreements are more common than postnuptial agreements, there are some good reasons why couples are increasingly considering making a postnup. When done correctly, they can benefit both partners. Oftentimes, couples who draft a postnup are facing major challenges in their marriage and considering divorce, but they have not thrown in the towel yet. However, they see a postnuptial agreement as solidifying their rights and bringing them a sense of security if their marriage fails.

On the other hand, if your marriage is strong, you might want to discuss the advantages of assessing all of your separate and shared assets and speak to a lawyer who specializes in family law about the advantages of a postnuptial agreement. This is especially true for remarried couples who have been divorced and have children from a former marriage and/or have complex finances like a successful business or a child or relative with special needs to protect.

Four Reasons to Consider a Prenuptial or Postnuptial Agreement:

1. Harmony: Even if your relationship or marriage is overall successful, you might struggle with financial differences, and this can put pressure on your communication. For instance, if

one partner has gambling debts, but otherwise your marriage and finances are fine, you can stipulate that you don't share these gambling debts. Writer Tim Grant, reporting for the Working Woman Report, says, "Postnuptials also can be handy when couples argue about gambling, credit card debt and other problems.[26] Separating the finances might reduce the number of fights."

2. A safety net: If you have concerns about whether your marriage will last, this fear might have a negative impact on your interactions with your spouse. However, if you prepare a prenup or postnup agreement that safeguards your assets, business, and children (from a former marriage), you might be able to relax knowing you've got a way out financially.[27]

3. Promotes full disclosure: Since prenups and postnups require full disclosure of assets and debts, this process might help you trust your partner because it requires honesty. Financial infidelity is a common problem in relationships and marriage, and having a postnuptial agreement might reduce the likelihood of this becoming an issue.[28] Learning how to talk about finances is a critical way for couples to protect their relationship and strengthen it. Often, problems like financial infidelity are a symptom of deeper issues that lay hidden for years. Financial infidelity can be defined as consciously or deliberately lying to a romantic partner about financial behavior. It's a situation when one partner intentionally hides a money-related secret from the other, expecting that it would be disapproved of (read Chapter 9).

4. Peace of mind: Talking about money can be tricky—even when you've had a long and happy marriage. It can make you and your partner feel tense and defensive, so you might avoid it. The person who has fewer assets may feel threatened or attacked by being asked to prepare a prenup or postnuptial agreement. But if you both agree, it can help spell out and cushion your financial future and that of your children. For instance, you might experience peace of mind knowing that your children will be financially stable in the event of divorce or an untimely death, according to attorneys Dan Prather and

his law partners at Prather, Ebner, and Wilson.[29] They believe that this is especially true for remarried couples who bring children from a previous marriage into a stepfamily and that a contract can assure you that the interests of those children are secured.

Making a decision to get a prenup or a postnuptial agreement isn't an easy one, and it can raise questions about trust and intentions. Family Law Attorney Katy Mickelson clarifies,

> Discussing a postnup or prenup with your partner can make you feel uncomfortable. Both partners must disclose assets, liabilities and income by a certain date. If there is purposeful withholding, there is a problem. It doesn't have to be penny for penny, but there is due diligence. It's incredibly important to be honest and open and to give adequate disclosure. If you withhold information, it may come back to haunt you.[30]

In most cases, having accurate information and being transparent can help to promote an open and honest discussion with your partner, and drafting a prenup or postnup may help facilitate this process. However, they're both voluntary and cannot be created if there is any kind of duress. Many people ask me if a couple should consider counseling before finalizing a prenup. My response is that I advise couples to seek couples therapy (or mediation) to keep the tone of their conversations positive and low-conflict if they have concerns about maintaining a respectful dialogue. A trained therapist can offer you suggestions for communicating your feelings, thoughts, and motives for a prenup or postnup so that you feel listened to, valued, and more confident as an individual and as a couple.

Chapter 8
Estate Planning
Providing Safeguards for the Future

One of the most emotionally taxing topics that I discuss with couples is estate planning. Most people think that estate planning is about death planning. It's actually about planning for the unexpected.[1] The intention is to help people pass on a legacy of love by clarifying where their assets will go after death and their wishes if they become incapacitated or disabled while alive. We're not immortal, and no one knows the last day they will be alive; yet, less than half of all people have an estate plan.

While we usually draw up a birth plan when we're expecting a child, our delusions and denial about death and serious accidents or injuries often cause us to avoid preparing an estate plan. For instance, Janet, sixty-four, a retired school counselor, met with me to discuss her anxiety and fears about not having an estate plan in place. Married for over thirty years, Janet's desire to draft an estate plan was sparked recently by her own father's initiatives to start the process due to his failing health. But when she approached her husband Tom, sixty-five, with the idea of meeting with an estate planning lawyer, she was met with resistance.

Janet explains,

> I wanted to do an estate plan four years ago, but my husband resisted it. I was thinking about going to see a lawyer on my own, but that felt disloyal. My husband Tom is sixty-five years old, but

he's still working and has his head in the sand when it comes to our future. We have three kids, and even though they're grown and have good jobs, I still have fears about whether we'll spend our last dollar or leave them anything. We also don't have a will or living trust, and I don't want them to end up in probate court [the court that oversees the distribution of a deceased person's assets according to their will or other legal documents or state law], arguing about who gets what from our estate. I feel very stressed about not preparing for the future, but don't know what to do to put a fire under Tom.

After meeting with Janet and Tom together, it became clear that Tom was in denial about death and that Janet's fears were warranted. The good news is that Tom was willing to discuss a plan for their future because of some recent events in their family. Since Janet's father turned eighty-six, he was just starting to do estate planning, and it felt overwhelming to him. Tom expressed a desire to take action fairly soon so he wouldn't follow in his father-in-law's footsteps. He also articulated his love for his children during our session and a desire to leave a legacy so that their lives could be easier than his was as a young adult.

When Tom described his childhood growing up in a poor family, without many assets or property, he expressed fear that his three grown children might not have enough money to purchase homes, due to the rising costs of property in their community. Since Janet's mother died when she was in college, her father moved in with them, and they have a close and loving extended family. During our interview, Tom and Janet both stated that they were proud of their relationship with Janet's father, since he resides in an in-law apartment on their property, and they eat meals together. Janet shared her wish that they'd be able to continue this tradition with their children as they age.

Tom reflects,

Janet is right and I need to apologize to her for putting off making an estate plan. I'm a contractor and I worry that if I'm in an accident on one of my work sites and I get badly injured, we wouldn't have a good plan for Janet. She could be on her own and I love her too much to do that to her and our kids. I have worked hard for all we have and I want our kids to do well after we die. I didn't have this advantage, and I don't want my kids to struggle like I had to while they're getting established.

By our second meeting, Janet and Tom had begun the estate planning process and felt that they were on their way to providing a legacy of love for their three children. Their lawyer explained to them that estate planning doesn't always ensure that your wishes are being honored but that it protects your assets and how they will be distributed after you die or become incapacitated.

What Is Estate Planning All About?

Estate planning is an important way to provide safeguards for your loved ones in the event of death, disability, or incapacity, according to Attorney David Bazar.[2] He continues, "Without a solid plan in place, estates might go through probate court, which can take a lot of time, and families might incur unnecessary legal fees and taxes. While people often think they have to be rich to have an estate plan, it's for anyone who cares where their assets go after they die and wants to make sure someone they love and trust can make decisions for them."

Most people don't want the government or courts to make these crucial decisions for them. However, many people don't get serious about estate planning until after they have a medical emergency or after they have kids, explains Jeff Motske, CFP.[3] He continues, "There's nothing like a heart attack to spur one into action! Then again, we tend to become more emotional during a health scare and may not always make the best decisions."

Many people believe estate planning is a taboo topic, and 41 percent of individuals between the ages of eighteen and thirty-four, and 34 percent of people between the ages of thirty-five and fifty-four, have never discussed estate planning with anyone. In fact, 52 percent of people surveyed by Cambridge Trust didn't know where their parents stored estate planning documents, and only 46 percent[4] of executors surveyed were aware of their parent's will.

While estate planning can be scary and intimidating to the average person, it can be started at any age. Creating an estate plan can reassure you and your partner that the people you love and trust can make decisions for you and honor your wishes when unexpected events occur.

Good Estate Plans Provide for the Following Four Provisions According to David Bazar, Estate Planning Attorney[6]*:*

1. They protect your assets and how they're distributed when you die or if you become incapacitated. You will be able to make choices about who you leave your assets to in the way that you want to do it.
2. They minimize taxes, court costs, and attorney fees for your beneficiaries so that they won't feel burdened.
3. They make sure that someone you love and trust can make decisions for you when you die or if you become incapacitated.
4. They ensure that a court doesn't have to appoint a guardian or conservator which can be a difficult process emotionally and expensive.

Tara, sixty-five, and James, sixty-seven, whom you met in Chapter 7, struggled over the best time to do estate planning, but they agreed to start the process during their couples therapy with me. Married for three years, they own their own home in an affluent suburb and are both comfortably retired. When James turned sixty-five, he began thinking about an estate plan to protect his assets for his son Alexander.

Likewise, once they became engaged, Tara and James drafted a prenuptial agreement which you read about in Chapter 7. After they had been married for a couple of years, Tara asked for an estate plan to protect the assets from her first marriage and her high-income job as a nurse practitioner for thirty years. In Tara's case, she also wanted to protect the interests of her younger sister, Samantha, who has special needs, in the event that they divorce or she dies before James. In James and Tara's case, they were in agreement to draft an estate plan as a way to pass on a loving legacy to Alexander and Samantha in the event that one of them dies or becomes incapacitated. They both agreed to stop procrastinating, and they made an appointment with an estate planning attorney to discuss their options. Our therapy sessions gave them the opportunity to have low-conflict discussions and to draft an estate plan that they could both feel pleased with.

It was important to James that his legacy be passed down to Alexander, so he could inherit a substantial amount from his estate. He was more than happy to honor Tara's request that he divide his assets equally between her and Alexander if he dies before she does. Likewise, Tara agreed to divide her assets equally between James and her sister Samantha. Rather than using denial about the inevitability of death, James and Tara viewed estate planning as a rational idea that could give them both security and peace of mind about their gifts of love to Samantha and Alexander.

Fortunately, James and Tara were definitely on the same page when it came to creating an estate plan, and each of them wanted to do their best to honor each other's wishes. As well-established professionals, they both had high incomes prior to retirement. During our couples therapy session, James announced unexpectedly that he had concerns about leaving all of his assets to Tara or making her the trustee who would be in charge of the trust (if he died or became incapacitated before she did). He had read an article in the *AARP Magazine* that advised remarried couples not to assume that if they leave everything to their spouse, he or she will kindly bequeath what's left to their child.[6] Fortunately, Tara chose not to take James's comments personally. Since she had already been divorced and James had a grown son, she realized how fragile relationships can be and how sensitive Alexander was to feeling overlooked by his stepmom.

As a result, after James told Alexander that he was proposing to Tara, James and Tara discussed his will and how his estate would be divided fifty-fifty between her and Alexander if he died before she did. During this conversation, they spoke honestly, with full disclosure, and Tara became aware that Alexander was prone to feeling left out and possibly resentful. Since she wanted to preserve a good relationship with her stepson, she was motivated to move ahead with their estate plan. As a couple, they decided to make James's younger sister, Claire, the trustee and executor of his estate. Tara became comfortable with this plan after discussing it in a therapy session. After all, she didn't want to do any damage to her relationship with Alexander, and she has a good relationship with Claire.

The Process of Estate Planning

Keep in mind that estate planning is a process that requires effective communication and a willingness to push past denial and focus on the welfare of a person's loved ones in the case of death, disability, or incapacity, reminds Attorney Bazar.[7] Refer to Chapter 2 in this book for suggestions on how to have low-conflict conversations about money when talking to your partner about starting an estate plan. Many of the couples that I interviewed or counseled were able to successfully set up an estate plan with sensitivity and care about the legacy that they were going to pass on to their loved ones.

Hire an Attorney Who Specializes in Estate Planning

Working with an attorney who specializes in estate planning can help you understand your options and identify the approach that is right for you and your family. A lawyer can also help you understand the potential tax implications of your estate plan. Each state is different, so be sure to work with a lawyer who is knowledgeable in the estate and inheritance taxes specific to your state.

The death of someone who is close to you is one of the most stressful things you can go through in life, and sorting through the emotional turmoil is difficult enough without dealing with a complicated or missing will. Oral wills and holographic wills (they're handwritten and signed by a testator, but don't require witnesses or notarization) are rarely recognized by courts, so it's important to make sure you're getting the assistance of a lawyer who is an expert in estate planning.[8]

In fact, a competent estate planning attorney can help you with many aspects of estate and trust law. Amy Pittman, an estate planning attorney, elaborates, "He or she also might offer to aid you with estate administration, which is the maintenance and distribution of your assets after your death.[9] They can go over the terms of the will or trust you prepared with them and explain all of the available options to your beneficiaries after you die." This can be very helpful for couples who have resistance to approaching this topic.

Do be prepared to share a lot of personal and financial information with your lawyer. According to David Bazar, this includes details about the people on your family tree, such as close family members and your relationship with them[10]. This would also include whether you have a child or sibling with special needs or a disability. Bazar posits, "There are two things that go into an estate plan, people and property. The property doesn't mess up the plan, but the people can."

A good estate planner will also want to gather information about your finances, such as a list of assets and investments and whether or not you are working with a financial planner, explains Bazar.[11] He or she will want to learn about your goals and concerns and why you're interested in beginning the estate planning process.

During my interview with Nicholas A. Lambros, an estate planning lawyer, he shared his in-depth step-by-step estate planning process, which includes asking clients to fill out an intake questionnaire and priority quiz.[12] After this initial step, Lambros meets with his client(s) and has a comprehensive session to go over their questionnaire. His clients find this session beneficial, and it can ease any stress or anxiety they have about embarking on the estate planning process.

Know the Key Documents of an Estate Plan

There Are Four Legal Documents You Should Be Aware of as You Begin Estate Planning:

1. Living trust or revocable trust. Not everyone will decide to create a living trust, but it's a common estate planning document you should be aware of and consider as an option. A living trust is a legal document in which your assets are placed in a trust during your lifetime, and assets are transferred to your beneficiaries when you die. It's changeable and can provide more control than a will. According to Attorney Christy Bieber, a grantor, or person who creates a revocable trust, can name themselves as a trustee but should also select a successor or trustee(s), who takes charge after their death or in case of incapacity.[13] The grantor also has power over who will be designated as beneficiaries.

    With a living trust, the terms, trustee(s), and beneficiaries can be changed or amended at any time, suggests Attorney Bieber, it makes sure that your children or beneficiaries have access to your financial records and accounts (bank and credit card) in the event of a medical crisis.[14] However, during your lifetime, you can use or spend your assets as you desire. The assets in the trust are transferred to beneficiaries after you die and distributed by a "successor trustee" whom you appoint. The trustee determines how assets will be distributed when the owner dies. However, they must do so following the guidelines laid out when the trust was formed, including giving funds to the designated beneficiaries. A living trust can help families bypass probate court and can be set up to reduce paying estate taxes, court costs, and attorney fees when their family member dies. There are other types of trusts, and the irrevocable and testamentary trusts will be covered later in this chapter.

2. A will is a legal document that spells out what happens after a person dies. The person who is drawing up the will decides who gets property and possessions after they're deceased. It outlines who they want to get their money, property, and personal possessions such as a car or artwork. This can also include deciding who will be the guardian for any children who are under the age of eighteen, and choosing beneficiaries and executors for an estate. People under the age of twenty-five don't need to plan for the division of their estate unless they have a life partner or young children, suggests Attorney Amy Pittman, but everyone else needs one.[15] This includes people who decide to create a living trust. Pittman recommends that people who have a living trust prepare a specific type of will, referred to as a pour-over will, which will catch any property inadvertently left out of the trust and include it in a distribution.

3. A healthcare directive details what will happen to a person who becomes incapacitated or disabled or is not of sound mind. This honors the individual's decisions about their wishes for care at the end of their life and only goes into effect if they can't communicate their preferences. According to Lambros, a medical power of attorney, HIPAA waivers, and living wills are legal instruments that can help make sure that your wishes regarding medical treatment are carried out and they're part of a healthcare directive.[16] A medical power of attorney is an instrument through which you can appoint a person to

make medical decisions on your behalf in the event of your temporary or permanent incapacity. The designated power-holder is directed to make decisions based on your previously expressed wishes, or in the absence of a clear expression, to act in your best interests based on what they know about you. A HIPAA release allows family members to access your health care records and a living will is a statement that allows someone to specify with clarity his or her wishes regarding life-sustaining medical treatment. It describes what sort of physical condition is intended to trigger the document's provisions and lists the types of treatments the person wishes to avoid.

4. A durable power of attorney is a legal document that designates an agent who will make financial and legal decisions on a person's behalf in the event they are temporarily or permanently incapacitated, based on previously expressed wishes or their best judgment of the person's best interest. Lambros explains that examples of financial and legal decisions include designating a specific person to manage your business or property in your estate.[17]

Lambros also advises his clients to document end-of-life wishes with a final disposition which states a person's wishes to be either buried or cremated, their funeral details, and cemetery information.[18] In addition, a letter of last instruction for things such as personal property distribution is highly recommended by estate planning attorneys. In the years that I've been a couples therapist, I've witnessed dissent and animosity among family members when their parent fails to draft a letter of last instruction. It can lead to strife and resentment if adult children feel entitled to the personal belongings of their parent or family heirlooms and their siblings or relatives don't agree.

For instance, Kendra, age sixty-two, and Sam, age sixty-four, whom you met earlier, experienced turmoil in their family when Kendra's mother died suddenly and had not updated her will or written a letter of last instruction. Kendra was blindsided by the resentment expressed by her two sisters when they found out that she took an heirloom, a collection of antique dishware and glasses, that had been passed down in her family for many generations. Since Kendra's mother told her that she wanted her to inherit these items, she assumed that it would be acceptable to her sisters to take them when she discovered them in her deceased mother's kitchen.

However, this wasn't the case. As a result, Kendra returned the heirloom and had bitter feelings toward her sisters, who disagreed about who would inherit many of their mother's belongings.

It took Kendra and her sisters a few years to resolve their resentment and to divide up their mother's belongings and heirlooms. This story illustrates the value of taking the time and money to draft a letter of last instruction to promote goodwill among family members after a loved one dies.

Kendra reflects, "I love my sisters and frankly didn't anticipate such hard feelings when my husband Sam and I decided to take the antique dishes and glassware from my mom's home. It was very unsettling to see the reaction of my younger sister, who perceived me as being selfish and controlling for not running this action by her. Then she convinced my other sister to jump on the bandwagon, and they pretty much all ganged up on me. I hope no one else has to go through this when their parent dies and they're unprepared."

Decide on a Will-Centered Plan or a Trust-Centered Plan

One of the essential aspects of estate planning preparation that will help you avoid or lessen communication problems in your family is deciding on what type of plan is a good fit for you and your partner. Attorney Lambros explained that a priority in the estate planning process is assisting the client(s) in choosing either a will-centered plan or a trust-centered plan.[19] An estate planning attorney can guide you based on your age, health, and financial situation.

Attorney Michelle Kaminsky writes, "People with fewer assets, a modest estate, or just a relatively simple estate distribution plan don't need a living trust, which incidentally, generally has more upfront costs than writing a will—and that may also be a consideration in deciding whether you need to include a living trust in your estate plan."[20]

Lambros explains,

> A will is a legal document that sets out your wishes for distribution of assets upon your death. In the will, you designate an executor to

carry out your instructions instructions and to administer the estate. The only way that a will takes effect is by petitioning the applicable probate court to approve the will and appoint the executor. Probate court is expensive, delays distribution of assets, and is public. The only assets that go to probate court are assets that do not designate beneficiaries or are not titled in the name of a trust.[21]

According to Attorney Kaminsky, the provisions of a will only go into effect after your death.[22] She explains that a will does go into probate and makes it a document of public record. Kaminsky continues, "Those who have complex familial situations (such as children from more than one relationship), a family business, a lot of assets, or property in more than one state might consider using a living trust to set out a clear estate plan."

People who have assets such as owning property, savings, and investments may benefit from a trust-centered plan. Many people who contact estate planners seek this out, clarifies Bazar, and some of their goals include avoiding probate court and paying high taxes, as well as designating someone you trust to make decisions for you if you're unexpectedly incapacitated.[23]

For instance, Lucy, age sixty, and Tanner, age sixty-two, are a remarried couple who wisely chose to start drafting an estate plan which included a living trust soon after they married and blended their two families. They own their own home and have savings and investments, in addition to living in a blended family with complex financial issues. Their estate planning attorney explained to them that a living trust had several benefits that appealed to them, including helping their beneficiaries avoid probate. In fact, their attorney informed them that probate could take upward of a couple of years and eat up much of the value of their estate.

Legal writer Tiffany Lam-Balfour explains, "Living trusts are effective once signed and funded while you're still alive, and they usually aren't subject to probate, so they're less likely to be contested after you die."[24]

Lambros elaborates,

> Revocable trust assets pass to the beneficiaries you name in the trust document and are not controlled by your will. This cuts out the costs and delays that can arise as part of the probate process.

Unlike probate, the identity of beneficiaries and instructions for distributing estate property are not part of the public record. This allows you to maintain your privacy. An added benefit to creating living trust documents is that you have the ability to condition the distributions to your beneficiaries upon a myriad of terms that you select, including structuring distributions for minor beneficiaries so they receive a certain percentage at certain ages, allowing the entire distribution to be spread out over time rather than paid out in one large lump sum. Also, a living trust provides the ability to allow the trustee discretion to distribute, or not distribute, to beneficiaries given their circumstances including if a beneficiary is facing addiction issues, having marital issues, creditor issues, facing a lawsuit, or any of a plethora of situations that may subject the transfer to the beneficiary to being taken by a third party or the funds being mismanaged or wasted.[25]

Another advantage of a trust plan, advises Attorney Lambros is that it reduces estate tax exposure.[26] Lambros says,

> The trust plan can also be designed to reduce or eliminate estate taxes when the trustor dies, depending on the size of the estate at the time of the trustor's death. However, if there's no estate tax based on the amount of the assets, it may not be worth the expense of creating a trust plan (if there are no other reasons to do so).

The following quote from Lambros[27] highlighted the benefits of a trust-centered plan: "Visualize a big empty box that holds a trust. I help clients move assets into the trust. Whatever is in the trust helps people avoid probate court and avoid delays. Clients can put in restrictions, and it reduces inheritance taxes."

Remember, clients with a living trust should still have a will, known as a pour-over will. Attorney Lambros explains,

> Even if you have a trust, a pour-over will is a good idea because it will catch any property inadvertently left out of the trust and include it in a distribution. This will save the property from being subject to state intestacy laws, which come into effect when someone dies without a will. These laws provide distribution based on familial relationships — which may not match what you would have preferred to happen with

your estate. A pour-over will act as a safety net that catches assets and "pours" them into the trust. It serves to tie up your legal loose ends and ensures that your legal wishes are carried out.[28]

Lambros continues, "A pour-over will is an essential estate planning tool when creating a living trust. It pertains to funding the trust by transferring funds. Some people die leaving assets that haven't been transferred, and an estate planner will help you make the best decision for you and your family regarding estate planning."

When deciding whether you need to include a living trust in your estate plan, Kaminsky advises keeping in mind that a living trust generally costs more money to establish up front than writing a will.[29]

Kaminsky also suggests that preparing a will while you're deciding whether to get a living trust may be a good idea because it will give you peace of mind to know that your affairs will be handled according to your wishes after you die.[30]

Once you've decided on a trust-centered plan, another aspect to consider is which of the two types to establish.

Trusts	Will
• Can be expensive to set up • Avoids probate process • Reduces estate tax • Provides long-term management of assets	• Good for those with a modest estate and few assets • Takes effect after death and probate • After probate, it is a document of public record

Revocable	Irrevocable
• Flexible and fluid; can be changed or revoked at any time	• Cannot be amended or revoked, except under limited circumstances

The Two Types of Trusts

Revocable Trust (Also Known as a Living Trust)

A revocable trust is the most common type of trust chosen by people, explains legal writer Tiffany Lam-Balfour.[31] The benefits of the revocable trust are that it's changeable and can provide more control than a will, according to Lam-Balfour. It protects you in the case of incapacity. It also provides privacy because probate proceedings are public record. It's created when a person is mentally capable of agreeing to the document. When the person dies or becomes incapable of handling their financial affairs, the trustee takes over. Lam-Balfour explains, "The trust document lists assets the grantor wishes to include in the trust. It also names a trustee, as well as heirs or beneficiaries who will receive assets after the grantor dies."

What are some of the drawbacks of a revocable trust? It can be complex and cost more money than a will to set up, according to Lam-Balfour.[32] It takes time to transfer assets to it. The revocable trust might be subject to estate taxes during your lifetime. It can't be used to set up guardianship for minor children (a will does). The revocable trust also doesn't shield the grantor's assets from creditors, which is the case with an irrevocable trust.

Irrevocable Trust

Irrevocable trusts make up only about 20 percent of living trusts, and they're usually recommended for people over age sixty-five who may be concerned about going into a nursing home.[33] The state won't be able to seize their assets. Five years from starting the process of the irrevocable trust, the state can't touch their assets, according to Lambros. However, he only recommends creating this type of trust if the client does not need access to their assets, such as proceeds from the sale of property. A downside of an irrevocable trust is that you can't use your assets from the time you create one.

Lam-Balfour explains some possible mixed blessings, "An irrevocable living trust removes control of the assets and thus can reduce the tax liability to the beneficiaries."[34]

It's a good idea for you and your partner to discuss the pros and cons of both revocable and irrevocable trusts and to keep in mind that he or she might have a different perspective. By using active listening, validating each other's viewpoints, and using compromise, you'll be more likely to avoid an "us against each other" approach when selecting an estate plan.

Beyond Formal Estate Planning

Another option for people who want to ensure that they're passing on a legacy of love to their heirs is to gift them, or to gift them money while you're still alive, according to Jeff Motske, CFP.[35] In fact, you can gift loved ones up to $14,000 to one person while you're alive without paying gift tax on it. By taking advantage of this generous option, you'll see your estate shrink, and as a result, your heirs will lower the amount of estate taxes they will have to pay in the future. Along these lines, some grandparents enjoy gifting their grandchildren money for college tuition or expenses. They're rewarded by appreciative children and grandchildren who can avoid excessive college loans.

For instance, when Janet and Tom were creating their estate plan, they decided to gift each of their three children the maximum amount of $14,000 so they could get a good start on life. As you might recall, Tom was worried about his children being at a disadvantage financially due to the high cost of living and property in the region where they lived. When their attorney brought up the option of gifting his children, he was happy and wanted to take action so that he would be able to contribute to their well-being and he wouldn't have to burden them by paying taxes on it.

Tom puts it like this,

> When our attorney explained the gifting option for our children, it made my day because I want to make their lives easier than mine was as a young person. Even though I procrastinated setting up an appointment with an estate planner, it has opened up a lot of possibilities. These are things that Janet and I didn't know existed that can provide protections for my entire family in the years to come. I only wish we had developed a plan sooner.

What About Guardianship Issues?

If you have a child under the age of eighteen, it's a good idea to plan for their care. For instance, you would want to consider drafting a testamentary trust, a specific type of trust often created for minor children, which designates a trustee who would manage the property in your estate and distribute funds to beneficiaries after you die or become incapacitated. It's drafted in accordance with the instructions in the last will and testament and can't be recognized until a person dies, explains Attorney Bazar.[36]

In addition, you would want to address guardianship issues head-on by naming a guardian for minors under the age of eighteen. This does not need to be the same person who is the trustee of the testamentary trust. In fact, these roles are often played by two different people. In some cases, you might have an adult child who would be best suited as a guardian to her younger sibling and another adult child who is good with finances and would be well-equipped to become the trustee. According to Bazar, your plan needs to be tailored to your needs, strengths, and unique qualities of family members.[37]

Another option for parents who don't want to develop a testamentary trust is that they can add provisions to a living trust. According to Lambros,

> I also recommend adding continuing trust provisions in a revocable trust to protect the assets for a child until the child attains a certain age if the parents are deceased. You can set it up so the child gets the proceeds spread out over many years, such as age twenty-five, thirty, and so on. You can also designate money for educational purposes.[38]

Attorney Lambros clarified more about minor children's guardianship issues.[39] He stated, "If a child is under age eighteen, parents should ask someone 'Would you be willing to be my child's guardian?'" He elaborates, "Guardianship allows the guardian to make certain decisions for the child, such as education, religion, association, medical care, and residence, among others. Usually, a guardian is nominated in a will."

Five Things That Can Go Wrong with Estate Planning

In spite of good intentions, there are many things that can go wrong with estate planning, according to legal experts.[40] It's a good idea to become aware of these five things and to educate yourself before entering the process.

1. A lack of communication between the parent(s), children, and other beneficiaries. Communicate your wishes as much as possible and as clearly as possible in your estate planning documents to avoid conflict. Lambros explains that 90 percent of the arguments adult children have after their parent(s) die involve personal property, not assets.[41] Adult children often argue about things like personal possessions (jewelry, artwork, collectibles) and say things like, "Mom wanted me to have her pearls or diamond ring, etc." If it's not written into the trust or will, it can create sibling conflict. A trust or will should include a letter of last instruction which lists personal property and who inherits it. Also, executors can still sell personal property and split the proceeds.

2. Neglecting to address health care issues such as end-of-life care. Who is responsible for taking care of you when you need assistance?

3. Neglecting to leave a final disposition plan. It should detail their last wishes and needs to include all personal and financial accounts (from credit cards and shopping accounts to social media), including all login and password information, and whether they want to be cremated or buried (and where they want to be buried).

4. Minor children guardianship issues are not addressed. Jeff Motske, CFP, cautions parents of children under the age of eighteen to designate a guardian.[42] He writes, "Let's start with your duty as a parent. You bring these children into the world, these little beings who rely upon you to nurture them, teach them, and be there for them at all times."

5. Failure to update documents when there are reasons to do so, such as marriage, divorce, children birth, illnesses, and so on.

While estate planning can be emotionally taxing for couples, the silver lining is that it can leave them with a sense of accomplishment and pride because they're preparing for the future. The couples whom I interviewed who had developed an estate plan expressed feelings of contentment because they were able to employ some control over important decisions. However, the conversations that are involved in estate planning are not always smooth; it can be a painstaking process for some couples to agree on an estate plan.

Married for twenty-five years, Grace, sixty-five, and Neil, sixty-six, whom you met earlier, put off estate planning for a decade due to working full-time, raising Neil's two children, and his unwillingness to discuss the topic. Since Neil had difficulty facing the inevitability of aging and death, he was resistant to talking to Grace about an estate plan. When she brought up the topic, he usually changed the subject or became easily annoyed with her. One thing they often disagreed on was whether to create a will or a trust. Since Neil is a super saver with a money vigilance script, he felt strongly that he didn't want to waste money on a trust when a will would cost less and be easier to draft. When I interviewed Grace, she explained the process of convincing Neil of the benefits of a living trust. Grace is also a super saver with a money vigilance script, but she researched estate plans and believed that a living trust was a better fit for their complicated stepfamily because it's more flexible and fluid than a will.

Grace explains,

> I understood Neil's reluctance to talk about serious illness and death. He also didn't want me to feel slighted by his wish to leave his two sons' part of our estate. But since I love them and helped raise them, I convinced Neil that we could come up with a fair estate plan. I read about the gifting option and my sister Kathleen agreed to be the trustee of our estate plan. Since Neil gets along with her, he was comfortable with this option.

Fortunately, once Grace was able to persuade Neil of the importance of making an estate plan, they set up an appointment with a lawyer, and they felt that the process went fairly smoothly. They both decided on a trust-centered plan due to the fact that Grace helped to raise her two stepchildren and wanted to be sure that their interests were protected if their father, Neil, died before she did or became incapacitated. They also decided to gift Neil's two sons $10,000 each so they would be in a better position to purchase property, and they'd be able to enjoy a legacy of generosity left by their father and stepmother.

A couple who you met earlier, Lucy, sixty, and Tanner, sixty-two, have been married for over a decade and have had an estate plan in place for many years. A remarried couple, they have blended four children in a stepfamily, and Lucy's youngest daughter is fifteen and still in high school. This couple has many legal documents, including a living trust, a health care directive, and a durable power of attorney. They explained to me that they want to be sure that their assets are divided equally between their four children if they both die together. Tanner is a successful businessman, and Lucy sometimes accompanies him on trips which involve extensive travel. Lucy also explained that even though three of her children are adults, she and Tanner want to make sure that they're all left with a heritage of abundance and that they will have a guardian for Stacy, Lucy's youngest child.

Lucy puts it like this, "We want to avoid having our children (and stepchildren) having to go to probate court and paying unnecessary legal fees and taxes. We took the time to do estate planning and feel very proud of ourselves for taking the time and protecting the future of our family."

Five Troubleshooting Tips for Smoother Estate Planning for Couples:

1. Be sure to select an estate planning attorney together by getting a referral from a friend or your family lawyer. Discuss the selection process with your partner and schedule a time and location to meet that's convenient for both of your schedules.

2. Take notes during your meetings with an estate planning attorney and go over them together after the session so that you can ask informed questions at your next meeting. If neither of you enjoys taking notes, rotate this task.

3. Establish common goals that you and your partner can agree on. Remember to discuss any feelings you share on estate

planning issues and identify your "core needs." For instance, if your partner has strong feelings about how to divide up your assets in your will or living trust, listen actively without making evaluative or negative comments. When your partner identifies an inflexible area of a need, ask for more clarification about why it's important to him or her and discuss their feelings, beliefs, and values on this issue.

4. Listen to your partner's contributions and validate their perspective during the estate planning process. Instead of focusing on your own agenda and the points you want to get across, ask your partner what they feel is important to include in your estate plan and their thoughts on all of the various decisions you'll be making. When you respond to their comments, validate their perspective. Work toward compromise whenever possible so that you both feel your ideas are being considered and respected.

5. State your needs clearly and calmly while you're talking about the estate planning process. While it's natural to get agitated when you're discussing a sensitive topic, adopt a cordial attitude. If your conversation is getting heated, press the pause button and suggest a twenty-minute break to your partner before continuing the conversation.

By developing a solid estate plan with your partner, you're giving a gift to your children and other family members. Estate planning is really about putting your affairs in good order and planning for the unforeseen (whether alive or deceased) in order to make things easier for your loved ones during an already tough time. You're also giving yourself peace of mind that your affairs will be handled according to your wishes after you're gone. Give yourself and your partner a pat on the back and celebrate with a special meal after completing the valuable and substantial process of estate planning.

Chapter 9

Financial Infidelity

How Keeping Secrets Can Put Your Relationship at Risk

Financial infidelity is defined as consciously or deliberately lying to a romantic partner about financial behavior. It's not occasionally forgetting to record a check or debit card transaction. There are two components to it. It's a situation when one partner intentionally hides a money-related secret from the other, expecting that it would be disapproved of. Second, they intentionally fail to disclose this information to their partner. According to the National Endowment for Financial Education (NEFE), two in five Americans have committed financial infidelity against their partner.[1]

For instance, Lillian, forty, and Brian, thirty-five, whom you met in Chapter 1, came to me for couples therapy because Lillian has Financial Post Traumatic Stress Disorder due to Brian's financial infidelity.[2] Lillian's Financial PTSD developed two years into their five-year marriage because of Brian's overspending and credit card debt, her being laid off from a teaching position, and their lack of an emergency fund. They literally could not pay their mortgage or utilities for over three months. During that time, Lillian developed extreme anxiety, sleeplessness, negative thoughts, and flashbacks about not being able to pay their bills and child support to Brian's ex-wife (for his two children). Lillian has a money vigilance script and she's a super saver. As a result, she has a tendency to be careful with money and experienced severe distress over their financial situation. You will learn more about Financial PTSD later in this chapter.

Ideally, romantic relationships and marriage are built on trust. This isn't the case for Deborah and Seth, whom you met earlier. They have separate checking and savings accounts because Deborah mistrusts Seth with money. She simply doesn't have confidence that he has her best interests at heart because he skimmed money off of his paycheck, which he put into a separate account without telling her. Seth rationalized his behavior because he used the money to fund a startup business. Meanwhile, many of this couple's basic bills went unpaid and the consequences were severe, including their credit scores plummeting.

In the course of their six-year marriage, Deborah, a journalist, has been laid off twice from magazines. Even though she's a super saver and has a money vigilance script, she feels anxiety about money and the future of her marriage. Since Deborah grew up with a father who was reckless with money and made bad investments, she worries that she's reenacting the old struggles she grew up with. Seth is a sales manager for a wine outlet, and he has a habit of overspending (using credit cards like cash) on unnecessary items. He's a super spender with a money status script, which means he tries to project affluence to others. Seth also dines in restaurants and attends social events without checking the balances in his checking or savings account. Oftentimes, Seth has insufficient funds in these accounts, and he has been forced to pay overdraft fees. Unfortunately, he has a habit of keeping secrets from Deborah about his nonessential expenditures and fees, as well as his undisclosed checking account. Deborah and Seth have frequent arguments about finances and have discussed divorce.

According to the latest 2024 Fidelity Investments Couples and Money Survey, one in four couples consider money the biggest challenge in their marriage, and this can lead to frequent disagreements.[3] Unfortunately, this friction can also lead to financial infidelity, such as hiding purchases or debt from a partner.

In 2021, the National Endowment for Financial Education (NEFE) found that 43 percent of US adults who ever combined resources, confess to having committed some act of financial deception, and 85 percent of those people said it affected their relationship in some way.[4]

Often, people who commit financial infidelity fear that their partner will be disapproving of their actions or financial decisions, so they intentionally keep secrets.

Currently, there's a lack of research on financial infidelity due to many reasons. First, it's hard to study since it frequently goes undercover and is a challenge to observe. Next, ethical aspects of research designs make it difficult to conduct studies with random assignment on such a taboo topic. Also, there isn't a lot of agreement on the definition of financial infidelity. For instance, does the term encompass just hiding money, or does it include gambling and small acts of omission such as concealing the purchase of a new item of clothing? Because financial infidelity is hard to define, it's difficult to write an operational definition, which is necessary if researchers want to test out a hypothesis. Finally, we don't currently have a valid measurement tool at our disposal to capture and test out a hypothesis about financial infidelity.

Infidelity is fairly common in romantic relationships and one of the main causes of divorce. Up until recently, the focus of most research on infidelity has been on sexual or physical betrayal, and there have been few studies that have documented the harmful impact that financial infidelity has on a relationship. Physical infidelity shatters trust and forces the person who was betrayed to ask many questions— such as "How well do I know my partner?" It also creates insecurity and questions about the future of the relationship. However, a recent study by Garbinsky et al. has shown that financial infidelity can take the same emotional toll as physical or sexual infidelity.[5] In addition to the questions commonly raised by a partner who was betrayed and has broken trust, it can leave a family without financial resources.

In recent years, the popular press and research studies have acknowledged that failure to disclose debt is one of the main secrets couples keep from each other. Research by Garbinsky et al. discovered that financial deceit has a destructive impact on intimate relationships that's perpetual and the issues are less likely to be resolved than nonmonetary ones.[6] It can be frustrating for couples when they argue about financial infidelity over and over again. It's hard to feel like our partner doesn't hear or understand us or the way we see things. Given these facts, it's not a surprise that financial infidelity has become a leading cause of divorce.

The Reasons Why Financial Infidelity Happens

Often financial infidelity can be a symptom of deeper issues in a marriage. As with Deborah and Seth, it can have roots in feelings of insecurity and a need for protection or control. Like many couples, they rarely spoke about money and have had separate checking and savings accounts for a few years due to Deborah's mistrust of Seth when it comes to finances. As a result, it was easy for Seth to feel entitled to stash away funds in a secret account and to feel it was unnecessary to tell Deborah because he earned the money and it was his personal checking account. When she asked him questions about his spending, he would get defensive, and it often escalated into an attack-defense mode (see Chapter 2), with both of them digging their heels in during an argument.

One of the main reasons that many people commit financial infidelity is that they feel uncomfortable sharing how much money they have in the bank, how much they get paid, who they've lent money to or borrowed from, and how much credit card debt they owe.[7] Money is a taboo topic for many people, and this might give them a reason to keep secrets or to lack transparency. I've seen these propensities in my couples therapy sessions over and over again.

Another reason is that they feel fear and shame related to the financial decisions they've made. According to financial advisor, Spencer Sherman, MBA, "Couples conceal bank accounts or credit cards with one another, thus living separate and secret lives and fostering a kind of lie — while living together. Trust is eroded, communication deteriorates. If you don't know your partner's sense of values, style of dealing with money, definition of abundance, vision of the financial future, can you honestly say you know your partner?"[8]

The consequences of financial infidelity can be devastating to a couple on many levels, including emotional and financial. An unwillingness to be transparent about money with your partner, such as credit card debt, can backfire. It can increase your debt because credit cards are designed to encourage people to spend money they don't have, especially if they're not held accountable for overspending.

Deborah puts it like this,

> I felt quite betrayed and ashamed. Mainly because Seth tried to make me believe I was an awful person for questioning why he was starting a new business when he knew we were strapped financially. I also felt so angry when I found out he had been skimming money from his paycheck and hiding it in a secret account, and all along we've been struggling to pay monthly bills. Seth often calls me a "control freak" with money, but I don't know how to cope with our problems or talk to him about our finances.

Control Is a Key Issue in Financial Infidelity

Why is control such a compelling characteristic in situations where there is financial infidelity? First, control issues can be either direct or indirect. In his book *The New Rules of Marriage*, author Terrence Real, explains how manipulation can be a form of indirect control.[9] When Deborah and Seth fell in love, she was unaware that he had a lot of baggage from his family relationships that had not healed. His father became disabled when he was ten years old, and his family's income dropped significantly. Because he didn't feel valued and supported in his large, low-income family, he learned to use indirect control and tried to manipulate situations because he felt overlooked. In his marriage to Deborah (and at work), he attempted to gain leverage by intentionally keeping secrets about money. In addition, his money status script developed because he didn't have access to resources growing up. Seth learned to manipulate people and situations to try to control outcomes that would be favorable to him and elevate his status with other people.

When Seth calls Deborah a "control freak," he's projecting his undesirable traits onto her to lessen his anxiety about his financial infidelity. By not taking responsibility for his harmful behavior and blaming Deborah, he was not helping to solve their financial problems. In fact, his credit card debt has increased to over $25,000 over the last few years, and he has been unable to contribute to paying their monthly expenses. This couple's inability to pay for essential bills such as rent (to Seth's mother), groceries, and utilities created a lot of stress until they sought help from a financial planner and started meeting with me for couples therapy.

In cases of direct control, some people pride themselves on being good with money, and they take direct control of finances in marriage or committed relationships, not allowing their partner to have a say or to give him or her much input. This can leave the spouse who doesn't have control feeling resentful. In some cases, they might even act out by committing financial infidelity to gain some sense of autonomy and control. This was true during the early stages of Lillian and Brian's marriage. Because Lillian has a money vigilance script, when she became aware of Brian's high credit card debt, she kept him on a tight leash (checking their accounts often), and this caused him to feel anger and resentment.

Financial Infidelity Often Goes Unnoticed

Sometimes, financial infidelity goes unnoticed for years, while in other cases, a partner may suspect it's happening but use rationalization or denial because they have trouble believing that their loved one would be deceitful (see Chapter 2). This is especially true during an early period of marriage or cohabitation when couples tend to wear rose-colored glasses and want to see the best in each other. This can cause people to overlook mistakes or flaws in their partner's character. Then when they do realize financial infidelity is happening, a spouse might feel ashamed to acknowledge it and then sweep it under the rug. And because it isn't dealt with directly, denial might magnify the issues and extend the time it occurs.

However, secrets have a tendency to grow more burdensome the longer they have been kept. It's understandable that you wouldn't want to use full disclosure about your finances on your first date. Still, by the time things have gotten serious with a person you're dating, this is the time to be transparent about your financial situation, including debts, assets, loans, and credit scores.

In my research for my book *The Remarriage Manual*, I found that 40 percent of the couples I interviewed experienced financial infidelity, but most of the partners who were betrayed were unaware of it for many years.[10] Susan, forty-eight, a graphic designer, and Jeremy, forty-six, a physical therapist, blended their families six years ago and raised four children together. Like many couples, Susan and Jeremy rarely spoke about their finances, so it was easy for Susan to feel entitled to stash away funds in a secret account from a trust fund she inherited from her family prior to their marriage. In fact, she receives a large sum of $3,000.00 a month from her trust fund, and she has been hiding this money. Jeremy found out about it when he noticed a statement from a bank that he didn't recognize, and he asked Susan questions about it, and she told him the truth. When we discussed her secret during our interview, Susan stated that she used to feel it was her right to keep this secret account private. I explained to her that privacy isn't the same as secrecy and that her behavior crossed the line into secrecy because of her motivation to hide a large sum of income that could potentially benefit her family and their well-being. I also mentioned that because her intentions and actions were deceitful, they had the potential to destroy her marriage.

When a couple has poor communication skills and baggage from the past, it can be problematic because it destroys trust and intimacy. Likewise, when couples are dishonest and one or both partners try to gain control or achieve security by withholding important financial information, the fabric of a marriage or committed relationship could be damaged if it goes unchecked. In Susan's case, she rationalized concealing her trust fund because her mother advised her not to tell Jeremy, and she had trust issues from her first marriage. But after several years, the weight of her secret became hard to bear, and she felt guilty long before she was candid with Jeremy.

Susan reflects,

> I was mostly disgusted with myself and embarrassed when Jeremy found out about my secret account. How could I rationalize doing to my second husband what my ex had done to me? I know this is an excuse, but I just felt so insecure about money and I felt like I had to hide some in case Jeremy decided to take off suddenly like Sam did. I'm not sure that I will ever recover from the fact that Sam took off with my life savings and all the cash I had.

Fortunately, Susan was able to heal from the betrayal of her first husband when she realized that Jeremy didn't resemble Sam at all in terms of his personality or behavior. In fact, Jeremy is reliable, honest, and trustworthy. During our two Zoom interviews for this book, Jeremy was also able to take responsibility for his actions, including shutting down and avoiding talking about finances at times because it triggered his anxiety. Jeremy developed a money avoidance script because he had disdain for money and believed "money is the root of all evil" (see Chapter 1).

The Difference Between Privacy Versus Money Secrets

It's important to keep in mind that we all need some sense of privacy and that it's not a common practice for couples to account for every penny they spend. Most reasonable people wouldn't want to micromanage their partner's financial behavior, and they wouldn't want this censure inflicted upon them regarding small purchases. In order to better differentiate between privacy and secrecy, it's important to consider a person's intentions, motivations, and the amount of money involved. For instance, secretly saving for a special night out with your partner is very different from loaning $500.00 to a friend and not telling your partner about it.

According to Debra Kaplan, MA, MBA, and Rick Kahlar, MS, CFP, it's helpful to differentiate between privacy and secrecy when discussing the topic of financial infidelity.[11] In *Coupleship, Inc.*, they write, "Privacy is not the same as secrecy. Privacy crosses the line into secret keeping and infidelity when one partner is not transparent with money and takes steps to avoid the consequences of their financial behavior."

In the case of Susan and Jeremy, Susan was keeping a large inheritance secret even though she knew Jeremy would be upset when he found out and that the money would be beneficial for the family since she had struggled with job layoffs as a graphic designer. In this example, Susan was aware that she was keeping a secret from Jeremy and that it was financial infidelity because she was intentionally hiding financial information from him and purposefully withholding it, even though it could have negative consequences for their relationship.

One of the first steps in healing from financial infidelity is gaining awareness by recognizing the warning signs so you and your partner can effectively deal with it. In other words, awareness is the first step in changing human behavior. What are the warning signs that you're dealing with financial infidelity? I discovered these "red flags" while researching my book *The Remarriage Manual*.[12]

Eight Red Flags of Financial Infidelity

When you read through the list of red flags, keep in mind that it's not an all-or-nothing list.[13] Even if you or your partner can check off two of these items, for instance, you probably have an issue with financial infidelity. The good news is that the sooner you recognize the signs in your partner's behavior or your own, the better you will be able to stop them in their tracks or address them.

1. You find secret credit card or bank statements for accounts (paper or online). You notice paperwork for an account you know nothing about. The spending was disguised or kept secret from you and typically has a significant balance. This might mean your partner is hiding cash, has a secret credit card account, or is keeping a separate bank account, or made an investment that they're hiding from you. Ultimately, your partner may try to gain control over accounts and passwords for all of your accounts.

2. Your name has been removed from a joint checking, savings, or credit card account. You probably don't find out about this right away, and your spouse probably has a reasonable explanation to cover up the real reasons he or she is making this move without telling you.

3. Your partner becomes overly concerned about collecting the mail. They might even leave work early to make sure that they collect the mail before you do.

4. Your partner has new possessions that he or she attempts to hide from you, and when you ask a question about them, they seem too busy to talk or change the topic.

5. Cash or money in your savings or checking account goes missing. Your mate doesn't really have a good explanation for this, and they brush it off as a mistake by the bank or minimize the loss.

6. Your partner becomes overly emotional or defensive when you want to discuss money. He or she may yell, accuse you of being insensitive, and/or start crying when you bring up finances.

7. Your partner lies about expenses, and when you confront them, they get defensive. They use denial as a defense mechanism and refuse to admit that they have a problem.

8. Your partner seems very worried about money and overly interested in budgeting. While this can be a good thing in the long run, it may be a sign that they're being deceptive, siphoning money into a secret account, or have a hidden spending problem.

If you identify that your partner is currently (or has in the past) committed financial infidelity, read ahead to the section titled "How Couples Can Heal from Financial Infidelity." However, before you do this, read the next section about Financial PTSD to discern if you're suffering from this condition as a result of your partner's betrayal. The most recent statistics state that approximately 23 percent of Americans and 36 percent of millennials experience financial stress at levels that qualify them for a diagnosis of Financial PTSD.[14]

What Is Financial PTSD?

Although it's a challenge to get a definitive definition for Financial PTSD, most psychologists define it as an intense and enduring emotional response to past or current financial distress.[15] Currently, Financial

PTSD doesn't have an official diagnosis in the DSM-5 (the American Psychiatric Association's manual used to diagnose people). However, there's a growing body of evidence indicating that Financial PTSD warrants attention and more research from mental health professionals.

Psychologist Alex Melkumian, founder of the Financial Psychology Center in Los Angeles, describes symptoms of Financial PTSD as negative reoccurring thoughts and flashbacks.[16] It's characterized by physical, emotional, and cognitive deficits which developed over at least a three-month period, which include:

- insomnia or sleeplessness,
- nervous energy or restlessness,
- irritability,
- sudden outbursts of anger (especially toward loved ones),
- hyper-reactivity to triggers that remind them of financial loss (such as a phone ringing from a bill collector),
- difficulty enjoying things you once enjoyed,
- persistent negative thoughts (ruminating),
- predicting negative outcomes in life situations, and
- trouble concentrating and/or distractibility.

Given this long list of symptoms, it's no surprise that individuals who experience Financial PTSD also find that their intimate and romantic relationships suffer. Experiencing even a couple of the symptoms from the above list would cause a person to feel less of a desire to be close and open with their partner.

Kayla, age fifty, shared her difficulty coping with the job insecurity and financial infidelity that triggered her Financial PTSD during our recent interview on Zoom. Kayla worked as a yoga instructor for many years until her studio closed due to lack of participation and increased rent in an affluent suburb. Meanwhile, her husband, Curt, age fifty-four, was laid off temporarily due to a change in ownership of the software firm where he worked. During this time, they had two children in college and a mortgage to pay. As a result, they used up their emergency fund and lived off credit cards for six months.

Kayla explains,

> I started keeping secrets from Curt because I didn't want him to feel embarrassed about his layoff at work. I also felt I could have done more to keep my yoga studio strong enough to prevent closure. This caused me a lot of stress which affected my sleep and mood; and my intimacy with Curt hit rock bottom. I just didn't enjoy life, and my marriage suffered.

During a six-month period, until Curt was called back to work and she found a new job, Kayla told me that she used credit cards like cash and unfortunately still dined out in restaurants and didn't tell Curt that her credit card debt had climbed to over $15,000. Her PTSD symptoms were also triggered when she got a text from one of her children requesting money due to a car accident while at college. This made her nervous and irritable for several weeks afterward.

In other cases, where Financial PTSD is present and there have been reoccurring acts of financial infidelity, couples may avoid discussions about money because they feel poorly equipped to deal with conflict or fear loss of love and acceptance. For example, Lilliam and Brian have struggles due to Brian's withholding information intentionally about credit card debt (about $35,000) and student loans that he has defaulted on due to lack of disposable income.

Lillian reflects,

> I didn't know the amount of Brian's credit card debt or his student loans until we got married, and I felt betrayed. If I knew about them, we could have tried harder to pay them off, and they wouldn't have destroyed our credit score. It made me suspicious of him, and I asked him what else he was hiding from me. We're renting, and at this point, I wonder if our credit score will ever rise enough so we can buy a home. I was frustrated when I found out about his debt by reading his credit card statements left on our desk. I also know he's buried in late fees for not making payments on time.

How to Have Courageous, Transparent, and Honest Conversations with Money

In most families, parents don't prepare their children to discuss the touchy and taboo topic of money. What we do learn from our parents is usually dysfunctional ways to deal with these conversations which involve blame, accusations, dishonesty, defensiveness, and personal attacks. As you learned in Chapter 2, defensiveness is, at its roots a way to avoid unpleasant feelings such as anxiety, but it makes it impossible to deal with the real issues.

However, when financial infidelity is present in a marriage or committed relationship, it's imperative that couples be willing to address their shortcomings. First, taking responsibility for the behavior that causes the financial infidelity (hiding debt, overuse of credit cards, overspending, and loaning others money, etc.) is a necessity. Then the partner who was betrayed must stay open to listening to their partner's side of the story, use kind words such as "I care about you," and be patient with the process of full disclosure.

In Lillian and Brian's case, it took a few years for them to pay off most of Brian's debts and student loans and to elevate his credit scores so they could apply for a loan for a starter home. By adopting a growth mindset versus a fixed one, this couple was able to gradually crawl out of debt and move from a scarcity mindset toward an abundance mentality. In her renowned book *Mindset*, psychologist Carol S. Dweck, posits that people who believe that abilities are fixed are less likely to flourish than those who adopt a growth mindset — those who believe that abilities can be developed.[17] Fortunately, Lillian and Brian's conversations became a lot more honest and transparent during couples therapy. Most importantly, Brian was able to own his error in judgment of withholding important financial information from Lillian. He acknowledged that he had grown up in a family where money was scarce and he felt insecure about the fact that Lillian came from a middle-class home. Talking about their family backgrounds openly helped both of them blame their backgrounds rather than blaming each other.

Once Lillian was able to accept Brian for his flaws and forgive him for keeping secrets, their communication and loving feelings improved. During our last couples therapy session, they had paid down enough debt to enjoy a one-week vacation at a desirable location without ditching their budget plan or going into debt. By saving money (through automatic transfer) in a separate savings account, they had a healthy vacation budget of $1,500.00 to pay for a small rental (near the beach) and food for five days. Their new abundance mentality caused them to grow from believing "We don't have enough" to "We have money flowing in our lives."

How Couples Can Heal from Financial Infidelity

The first step in healing from financial infidelity is acknowledging that there's a problem and cultivating a willingness to get professional help. Both people need to be honest about their present and past financial mistakes so that they can truly repair the damage done. That means bringing out every statement, credit card receipt, bill, app, checking or savings account statement, loan, or other evidence of spending. For some people, full disclosure can evoke shame, and it may trigger their insecurities.

Kayla puts it like this,

> I've never felt the kind of shame I felt after Curt found out that I had been hiding my credit card debt from him. He really lost trust in me, and I had to earn it back by not using my credit cards. So, I slashed the plastic and came to terms with being more accountable and dealing with my shopping addiction. I never want to pay high interest or late fees on my credit cards again.

One of the most important steps in overcoming the detrimental impact of financial infidelity is for a couple to make a commitment to work through issues together. The person who was betrayed needs time to adjust to the details of the breach of trust, and this doesn't happen overnight. In most cases, it's not an easy ride. Likewise, the perpetrator of the financial infidelity needs to be completely transparent and willing to admit their betrayal and make a promise to stop the destructive behavior. They must change their daily habits of spending and/or hiding money, lending money to others, or even gambling. That means bringing out every statement (bank and credit card), app, loan, or evidence of spending.

If someone has a gambling addiction, they will need to seek specialized treatment for this problem before couples therapy can be effective. In any case, feelings of anger, betrayal, and grief need to be dealt with if a couple is going to regain trust. Keep in mind that it takes time to do this, and couples therapy can be effective in the process.

When Lillian and Brian were able to openly discuss financial infidelity in their therapy sessions and make a commitment to work on their difficulties together, they could begin to heal. Fortunately, Brian made a promise to stop hiding credit card debt and to stop using his cards like cash. In therapy, they worked hard on changing their daily habits (like frequent takeout) and they worked out a feasible budget with a savings plan. Over time, they began to argue less and their attack-defensive style of arguing became a lot less frequent. As a result, Lillian was able to build trust in Brian, and they celebrated their sixth wedding anniversary in their home with family and friends.

Given the important role that finances play in the well-being of couples, they can benefit from being aware of the negative consequences of financial infidelity. It can greatly impede a couple's ability to achieve financial health and goals like buying a home, saving for retirement, and enjoying vacations. Financial planners and therapists can do well to explain what financial infidelity encompasses and to encourage them to share joint checking and/or savings accounts and to have greater transparency.

Recently, Financial Therapy, which aims to help people reach their financial goals, is more accessible to couples who experience financial infidelity. Couples who want to preserve their marriage or relationship and need support to overcome financial infidelity can often benefit from reaching out for help. They can ask their physician or insurance company for a referral to a professional who specializes in counseling couples with financial issues. There's no need to suffer needlessly and silently. Developing financial literacy can empower couples to become better fiscal partners and attain a life of abundance.

Four Steps to Dealing with Financial Infidelity in Your Marriage or Committed Relationship (adapted from my book The Remarriage Manual[18]*):*

1. Understand that your partner may need time to process your disclosure if you have been keeping secrets. When you first tell them about your secrecy, they may be in shock and feel deeply hurt and betrayed. Don't expect it to be a smooth ride, especially if your partner stumbles upon the financial infidelity and you don't disclose your secret to them.

2. Share details about your past and current debts, secrets, and spending habits. Keep in mind that you'll be discussing emotions as well as numbers. For instance, Deborah said to Seth, "I felt so hurt when I found out about your secret bank account. We have not taken a vacation in years. I need you to be transparent with me."

3. Promise to stop doing behavior that is toxic regarding finances. Offer your partner reassurance that you've made a commitment to change. You may need to do this by showing them bank, loan, and credit card statements, and having weekly check-ins with full disclosure. If your partner uses apps for financial transactions, such as Venmo or PayPal, be sure to check these.

4. Commit yourself to doing whatever is necessary to restore trust with your partner and to rid yourself of debt and spending habits that are contributing to any financial problems in your marriage. Consider therapy sessions as a couple to gain support and a neutral party's feedback for at least several months or until you see improvement.

While it takes incredible courage to deal effectively with financial infidelity, take comfort in the fact that you and your partner will be building trust and loving conversations about money. The first two steps are usually the hardest, so be patient with yourself and your partner. Imagine yourself sitting at a nice restaurant on a Saturday night discussing finances without feelings of tension, shame, or regret. By tackling the challenges of financial infidelity, you're on your way to reaching your goal of financial health, honesty, and authenticity.

Chapter 10
Remarriage Finances
How to Adopt an "Us Against the Problem" Mindset

Money is a delicate topic for all couples, but the financial considerations of a remarriage are more complex than those of a first marriage, often involving alimony and child support payments and leftover debt from a former marriage. Other concerns involve who will pay for children's clothing, medical bills, weddings, and school or college expenses—yours, mine, and ours. Some remarried couples, especially those with high assets, might want to consider a prenuptial agreement, particularly if they have survived financial infidelity, have unequal assets, or feel that they want to protect their children should their marriage fail.

While second marriages can offer couples a second chance at happiness, they come with their own challenges, including financial tension. Couples who remarry often bring financial baggage with them, including obligations, responsibilities, and stressors—especially if they have children from their first marriage. According to the Pew Research Center, four in ten American adults have at least one step-relative in their family.[1] When you add the 11.6 million stepchildren in the United States (16 percent of all kids), the total is an estimated 113.6 million Americans who have a step relationship. The financial pressure couples experience living in a stepfamily can be compounded by the economic strain of having one or more "mutual children" who are born to the couple after they remarry.

Some remarried couples bring debt from a previous marriage into the partnership that needs to be addressed during the early phase of blending two families. It won't get easier as time passes; it will only get worse if financial information is hidden or not discussed. Since the average age of remarried couples is older than first-time married ones, saving for retirement can become a concern for many couples who marry a second time around. For instance, in 2019, the National Center for Family and Marriage Research reported that the median age at remarriage for men was forty-eight and forty-four for women (compared to forty-six for men and forty-three for women in 2013).[2]

On the other hand, in 2023, the age of men getting married for the first time was thirty, and for women twenty-eight years of age, according to Anna Fleck reporting on Statista.com.[3] It makes sense that remarriage becomes more common with advancing age, since it takes time to enter into marriage, divorce, and then enter into a subsequent one.

Unsurprisingly, remarriage brings with it many complex issues, according to Christopher Yalanis, MBA, who is a CFP working with couples.[4] During a recent interview, he said,

> Remarriage is the intersection of competing interests. On the one hand, we have the well-developed interests of each individual (versus, say, twenty-five-year-olds whose lives are still actively developing and aren't giving up as much by going from "me to we"), versus the interests of a new couple. We add this to the complexities and interests of the children from the prior marriages. Further, there are federal and state estate and income tax rules (such as IRA distributions and inheritance rules, which follow set guidelines).

While navigating all of these issues can be a challenge, Kristin and Rick have been in a successful second marriage for over fifteen years.

Kristin, age sixty, a physical therapist, considers her second marriage a success because she believes she learned many lessons from her first marriage and that her husband Rick, sixty-three, is a good match for her. When Kristin married Rick, a small business owner, they each had two teenagers from their former marriages. When we met for an interview in their comfortable ranch-style home, they both described their first marriages as problematic due to clashes in personalities, interests, and parenting styles with their ex-spouses. Even though this couple both told me that they're happy in their remarriage, Kristin complained about how Rick's permissive parenting style almost destroyed their second marriage. Until recently, he was loaning and giving large sums of money to help support his two adult daughters, and he wasn't receptive to feedback from Kristin about how this behavior was jeopardizing their retirement.

Kristin explains,

> I love Rick and his daughters, but finances were always tight with four kids, and my two sons are still attending college. Rick feels that he needs to help out his daughters because one is a single parent, with a two-year-old, and the other one has difficulty managing her finances. Once I got wind of the large sums that were coming out of our savings to help them, I had to make sure Rick stopped. It took a while to sink in, but he understands why it can't continue.

Rick puts it like this,

> I had a lot of guilt because I had a bad divorce from my first wife, and she never helped finance our daughter's college costs, so they have big student loans. My guilt only went away when I started helping them out financially. It's still really hard for me to talk to Kristin about our finances, but she's right to put a lid on money pouring out of our savings. I knew she'd probably leave me if I kept it up, so I stopped covering my daughter's expenses.

Many people are fearful of destroying their second marriage if their new spouse discovers debts or obligations from their past or present that they have concealed. Therefore, it's crucial for you to be transparent about money if you want your remarriage to succeed (see Chapter 2). If you make a "Communication Pledge" to have regular money talks, this will protect your relationship against miscommunication and breakup, and you can build a strong financial future.

By both of their accounts, Kristin and Rick have a stronger remarriage now that their goals are in alignment. Since they are both moderate savers, they're able to discuss a vision for their future and plan for a comfortable retirement. They seem to have worked through their issues with money and received help from a couples therapist and a financial planner. Rick has come to terms with the fact that not setting boundaries on his two daughters' requests for financial support was putting a strain on his marriage to Kristin, and he doesn't want their marriage to fail.

However, it's important to keep in mind that building trust in a second marriage takes time and tolerance. Like most remarried couples, if you tied the knot a second (or third) time, you probably didn't have the luxury of getting to know each other over an extended period of time. Your courtship might have been sped up due to your age, loneliness, and a desire to create a new family—without the time to adjust to the ups and downs of living in a stepfamily. Love can be sweeter the second (or third) time around but once the bliss wears off, the reality of joining two distinct worlds sets in. It's crucial to take off your rose-colored glasses and realize that marriage can be hard work. And no one can make you happy all of the time, especially when dealing with real-life issues such as ex-spouses, stepparenting, and the pressures of keeping everyone afloat financially.

Regardless of how madly in love you are with your partner, you need to keep in mind that second marriages don't run on automatic and you will be asked to accept your partner's shortcomings. After all, we are all flawed. Gaining tolerance and showing love and compassion about financial issues is critical to building a successful marriage the second time around. If you expect your partner to love and honor you despite all the baggage you bring, you need to show the same latitude toward him or her.

Remarried Couples Have More Economic Challenges

In *Money Advice for Your Successful Remarriage*, financial expert Patricia Schiff Estess explains that remarried families with children are worse off economically, relative to other married people.[5] She posits that they may experience ongoing money worries because they simply have more financial obligations than first-time married couples. For instance, Diana and Mike, a remarried couple, raised five children with very little financial support from their ex-spouses.

During an interview, Diana, age fifty-five, a stepmother to three children and mother of two biological daughters, explains her financial issues with her two stepsons who are now grown but still present with economic needs. She's a moderate saver with a money vigilance script, and Mike is a moderate saver with a money avoidance script. Essentially, they both know how to save money, but their communication is negatively impacted by Mike's tendency to shut down and avoid discussing money because he believes that "money is the root of all evil" and he doesn't want to spend it. It's essential that Diana and Mike have more productive, low-conflict conversations about money so they don't have misunderstandings or build up resentment.

Diana explains,

If we didn't have so many children, we'd be fine financially. My husband Mike is fifty-six and has three kids from his first marriage, and I have two from mine. Most of our financial problems have had to do with who is paying for all five children's college tuition and other expenses as young adults. It's really daunting because our two parenting styles collide, and we argue about how much we should each contribute to college expenses and other requests. Whereas I believe we're responsible for helping out all of our kids, Mike disagrees because he thinks we're enabling them. To make matters even more complicated, my ex told my two girls that they wouldn't have to take out student loans for college, so that set a precedent. It wasn't a surprise when they complained when we asked them to take out student loans.

Diana pauses and continues,

Paying for weddings is another struggle. Mike's daughter, Andrea, is getting married next summer, and her mom is currently unemployed, so has limited ability to help fund her daughter's wedding. It scares me that we might be expected to pay for most of Andrea's wedding costs. I don't want to be seen as a "tightwad," but we just don't have a huge bundle in savings, so we'd have to charge a lot of it or take funds out of our retirement.

Throughout their growing up years, the ongoing expected and unexpected expenses of children are often the responsibility of biological parents and stepparents. In spite of the fact that stepparents are not legally responsible for their spouse's children, life is not exactly simple, and the vast majority of stepparents take on some financial responsibility for their stepchildren. This is primarily due to caring about their well-being and because their lives intermingle over time. However, according to the Pew Research Center, most adults who have step relatives report a stronger obligation (financially and in other forms of support) to their biological family members than they do to step kin (i.e., stepchildren, spouse's parents, etc.).[6] This loyalty conflict can surface when biological children and stepchildren are residing together in a stepfamily, and it can create tension between the remarried couple.

Diana speaks,

> Mike's daughter, Andrea, is engaged to be married soon and is deep in debt. She got laid off from her job as an athletic trainer for not meeting her sales goals several months in a row, and she is only working part-time. I feel that we need to help Andrea and loan her enough to get back on her feet, but Mike thinks we're enabling her to be dependent on us. Mike also scoffs when I buy one of my daughters a new outfit or give them money for tickets to a concert. There's no easy solution to any of this, and that's why we're seeking couples therapy. Mike and I are both frugal and savers, but we have a lot of stress about finances and often disagree.

Finances Are a Major Stress in Stepfamilies

Despite the fact that financial issues and money problems are the number one subject couples argue about and a leading cause of divorce, there are very few studies of stepfamilies' financial preparations. One study by Ganong and Coleman discovered that only 25 percent of remarried couples had discussed their finances prior to marrying.[7] Even though remarried couples may have more assets than first-time married partners, they often have independent financial goals and resentment about paying for the expenses of their spouse's biological children. It's no wonder, since money matters trigger intense emotions for many people and are a major cause of stress in marriage.

In my case, I was a single parent raising two elementary-age children when I met my second husband, Craig, through a mutual friend. We fell in love and got married two years later. Since I operate from a scarcity mindset (see Chapter 1), I tend to worry about never having enough money. This created problems in my second marriage because I became easily annoyed at many of the purchases Craig would make (even supplies for home improvement), and we started arguing more often about the expenses of raising three children in a stepfamily after our mutual child was born.

It took me a few years to trust that Craig had my best interests at heart, so I kept secrets about some aspects of my two older children's college expenses. But after much turmoil and self-reflection, I realized that if I was transparent and shared my worries with him, we could adopt a "us against the problem" mindset and creatively solve financial problems together. After I started practicing full disclosure, we started facing our financial challenges together instead of "us against each other." As a result, we began saving money several years ago, and our debts decreased dramatically.

If remarried couples have not established a bedrock of trust and vulnerability together, they might be more prone to committing financial infidelity. If you consistently feel uneasy because you can't trust your partner, even minor mistakes or errors in judgment can make you feel mistrustful, in spite of your partner offering a good explanation for their actions. In other words, by keeping secrets or lying to your partner, you put your relationship in jeopardy because he or she may have lost a sense of trust and security that couples need to thrive and grow resilient together. I discovered that financial infidelity was more common in the remarried couples in my study than in those who were in first marriages due to trust issues and baggage from their first marriage that weighed them down.

Building Financial Trust in Stages

Considering the following stages can help you gain insight, build trust, and have realistic expectations about finances when you get married a second time around. Remember that there are degrees of financial betrayal (if it exists), and one size doesn't fit all remarried couples.

The following stages about building financial trust in your remarriage were adapted from my book *The Remarriage Manual*.[8]

1. The Romantic Stage. Couples typically wear rose-colored glasses while dating and when first married. They are so happy to have found love the second time around that they might be reluctant to disclose debts and financial obligations. Be aware of this and seek to be more open and honest with your partner, since keeping secrets can breed mistrust.

2. The Keep the Peace Stage. Once a couple has lived together for a while and struggles emerge, it's normal for partners not to want to rock the boat. During this phase, it's crucial to sit down with your partner away from your children to discuss your income, financial responsibilities, debts, and budget. You should also discuss your financial history and realize that this conversation can have emotional overtones. Meet in a private space, unplug electronic devices, and let other family members know that you don't want to be disturbed.

3. Reality Sets In Stage. Once you have been remarried for several years, you'll be forced to confront many money issues, including prior debt you and your spouse brought to the marriage, the expenses of your biological and stepchildren, spending styles, budgeting issues, and a myriad of other related topics. Now is not the time to be coy or beat around the bush. Keeping secrets or concealing debt or financial responsibility usually backfires and won't engender trust and good communication with your partner over time.

4. Acceptance Stage. Remarried couples who stay together for over a decade usually reach a stage where they are tired of arguing about money, so they accept and surrender. This means that they have reached a point where compassion and compromise have come into the marriage, and couples find ways to pay off debts, finance college, and plan for retirement. Unfortunately, couples who have been keeping debts secret, overspending, or experiencing a decline in income due to job loss or poor investments may feel a sense of panic at this stage. Wise couples seek financial help when this happens,

and they approach their money troubles with a "united we stand" mindset rather than allowing financial strain to divide them and lead to a breakup.

With time and patience, you will be able to identify your fears and concerns about finances. Remember there's no "right" or "wrong" way to deal with issues such as unequal assets, child support and alimony payments, and private school and college expenses. Remember that feelings are not "good" or "bad"; they are just real emotions that need to be identified, processed, and shared effectively without blaming your partner. If you don't feel that you have been able to reach the "Acceptance Stage" in a timely fashion, it's a good idea to seek couples therapy. and the help of a financial planner. Make sure that the financial planner you select has the designation of CFP and that they have experience working with couples.

How to Compromise About Finances in a Stepfamily

When Teresa, forty-two, and Christopher, forty-four, met at a mutual friend's holiday party six years ago, Christopher swept Teresa off her feet. She had two children from her first marriage who were in elementary school, and she was looking for a partner who could give her the love and security she lacked in her first marriage. Her first husband betrayed her physically and financially, and she was left with few resources after the divorce. Soon after getting married to Christopher, they rushed to get pregnant (due to her age) and found that the dynamics in their loving relationship changed. Teresa realized that having a third child, Mark, was joyous at times but added a lot of stress to her marriage. Since Christopher was a vice principal at a high school who worked long hours, they rarely discussed finances. When they did, Teresa and Christopher had difficulty understanding each other's perspective since Teresa is a super saver with a money vigilance script and Christopher is a super spender with a money status script (see Chapter 1).

Teresa reflects,

I became more worried about money after Mark was born and came to terms with the fact that Christopher was rarely available to talk to me and our finances were tight. I often felt like a single parent, and I was struggling to make ends meet. Since I'm an elementary school counselor, I get overwhelmed with my own kids sometimes, and I don't like to ask for help. Christopher also had a habit of shopping online at expensive stores and buying unnecessary items that shimmer like a new car every couple of years. He's more of a spender and wants to impress people with what we own, and I'm more of a saver who keeps track of expenses and focuses on saving for our future.

Christopher responds,

You knew when we got married that I was a busy vice principal at a high school with a lot of after-school responsibilities. I love your two kids like my own, and Mark is the light of my life. But when you complain that I'm too busy and spend too much money, it aggravates me because I work hard to make extra income so we can afford to buy the things we need. Sometimes you underestimate the costs of raising three kids on our salaries and maintaining our lifestyle.

This couple, like many of the remarried couples I interviewed for *The Remarriage Manual*, were looking for love to be sweeter the second time around, and they were blindsided by the stress of raising three children in a stepfamily.[9] Teresa believed that Christopher was her soul mate and would erase all the anguish and hurt left over from her ex-spouse. She sized up Christopher to be a great stepdad to her two children from her first marriage because he has a responsible job and enjoys being around children.

On the other hand, Teresa underestimated the impact that Christopher working long hours would have on her and their three kids. The demands of raising two school-age children and a toddler made her feel overwhelmed at times, and she often felt like giving up on her marriage. Only recently, after starting couples therapy, did Christopher and Teresa gain awareness about the "occupational hazards" of working in school systems all day and parenting 24/7. Teresa also realized that her money vigilance script and trust issues from her former marriage caused her to have financial baggage. When she felt mistrustful of Christopher, Teresa would criticize him rather than express her needs in a productive way, pushing him further away from her and their children.

When I explained to this couple that a strong couple relationship acts like a positive model for children during their formative years and later on when they form their own romantic relationships, they perked up. I also suggested that they take the Financial Styles Quiz and Money Script Inventory (see Chapter 1) so we could discuss their different attitudes about money.[10] Teresa admitted to some postpartum depression after giving birth to Mark (that made her irritable) and Christopher disclosed that he joined a pickleball league at his school (which kept him out three nights a week) to elevate his status and avoid arguments with Teresa.

The compromise that this couple reached was that they would hire a babysitter one night a week so Teresa could go to a dance class and Christopher would reduce playing pickleball to two nights, giving him more time with the children and Teresa. They also asked Teresa's mom to babysit on a Saturday, and they sat down together to discuss their views on finances, including where they clashed and where they agreed. This conversation paved the way for developing a budget plan which helped them to decide how much money they could save after setting aside an agreed-upon amount for an emergency fund.

Fortunately, Christopher and Teresa also agreed to go out on a money date night one evening a month to discuss their finances and their vision for their future. Christopher had some resistance in the beginning, but after a few months, he saw the benefits of money dates. During these talks, and with the support of our therapy sessions, they recommitted to their marriage and stopped issuing ultimatums during arguments about finances and other issues.

Teresa explains,

> Once we stopped talking about divorce and started focusing on building intimacy and trust, we both felt happier and back to seeing the good in each other. We were able to create a budget and a savings plan. It would allow us to take one vacation a year with our kids and another one with just us (with my mom babysitting).

This couple saw their compromise as a win-win and believes that it will help their marriage thrive.

Why Is the Divorce Rate So High for Remarried Couples?

Since many divorced people remarry and at least 42 percent of them bring one or more children to the union, the number of stepfamilies and blended families in America is significant.[11] Despite the best of intentions, statistics show that second or third marriages are much more likely to end in divorce than first marriages. A lot of couples enter into a remarriage with baggage from their former marriage and unrealistic expectations. They're often unprepared to deal with the stress of blending children, stepchildren, and the financial pressures of living in a stepfamily.

According to Forbes Advisor contributor, Christy Bieber, JD, the divorce rate for second marriages hovers around 60 percent, compared to 43 percent for first-time married couples.[12] Unfortunately, the divorce rate for third marriages is a striking 73 percent. Why doesn't practice make for a perfect union the second time around? Truth be told, most second marriages break up because there are more elements to balance, and the stress of commingling families and financial pressures can weaken the remarriage couples' bond to the breaking point.

In *For Better or for Worse: Divorce Reconsidered*, psychologist and researcher E. Mavis Hetherington, PhD, explains that the reasons the divorce rate is so much higher for remarried couples compared to first-time married partners are multifaceted.[13] She posits that they usually involve the stress of combining people from two different worlds. She also suggests that remarried couples don't always make a full commitment to stay married after problems arise, and they view divorce as an option for dealing with adversity. Arguing about finances is at the top of the list of the perpetual things couples argue about, and most couples don't know where to turn for support.

Money Management: Yours, Mine, and Ours

Coming up with a money management system that you both agree on can be a challenge. This may bring up the issues of unequal assets, debts, and differences in your philosophies about spending, saving, and so on. Stepfamily researcher Barbara Fishman interviewed many middle-class stepfamilies and found that most tend to adopt a one-pot (common-pot), a two-pot economic system, or a three-pot system.[14] In the common-pot system, economic resources are pooled and distributed according to need regardless of biological relatedness, whereas in the two-pot system, economic resources are divided and distributed mostly according to biological lines. The three-pot system is really a mixture of the common and two-pot systems, but the focus is on partners being responsible for their own biological children and not commingling finances. Her findings suggest that concern for the common good underlies the one-pot economic system, whereas the two-pot encourages economic independence and personal autonomy. These are the most common money systems for remarried couples, which are described in Chapter 3 in depth. The following description pertains to stepfamilies or blended families.

One-pot: In this model, also referred to as a common-pot system, all of a couple's money is combined into one checking and one savings account. This includes both partners' incomes and any alimony or child support. Couples literally pool their financial resources together. All expenses and debts, including child support payments, are paid out of these accounts. Resources of time, services, goods, and cash are distributed according to an individual and family member's needs, regardless of their biological relatedness. As a result, there is no distinction between biological children and stepchildren when it comes to expenses such as college tuition.

Two-pot: In this model, resources are distributed to family members mostly according to biological identity and only secondarily according to expressed or perceived need. Couples keep their incomes, payments, bills, and debts in two separate checking and savings accounts and handle all child-rearing and household expenses on a fifty-fifty basis. With this system, partners tend to share the costs of joint household expenses, but otherwise divide their spending for children along biological lines. For instance, a stepparent might contribute to his or her stepchild's college tuition, but it would be voluntary (and deposited in a joint checking account), rather than expected.

Three-pot: Each partner handles personal expenses of themselves and the children they brought to the marriage separately, and funds are not commingled. Often couples use apps like PayPal or Venmo to reimburse each other. However, they both might contribute to a third account that is used for the upkeep of the entire family (mortgage, rent, household repairs, vacations, etc.), but it's not necessarily on a fifty-fifty basis. In other words, parents would pay for expenses of their biological children from a prior relationship (clothes, college tuition, etc.) through their own separate account.

Overall, studies show that higher functioning remarried families pool finances and have higher levels of commitment, trust, and family cohesion using the one-pot system compared to families who keep their money separate. Chelsea L. Garneau et al., and family researchers at the University of Missouri, investigated remarried couples' belief systems about finances and found that couples who simply endorsed the belief that their money should be pooled had more positive interactions and higher marital quality than those who don't.[15] These findings support the premise that discussing beliefs about financial management, coming to an agreement, and sharing resources is associated with marital well-being in recoupled families.

Paying for day care, private school, and college tuition are common issues that can cause financial stress for remarried couples. Many couples feel comfortable with the three-pot system in order to make things somewhat fair for partners who don't have children or who might resent paying for the educational expenses of their stepchildren. You might recall reading about Grace and Neil in Chapter 3 and their reasons for choosing the three-pot model. Since Neil had two sons when they met and Grace didn't have children, they believed this system allowed Grace to have personal autonomy. On the other hand, many couples who don't have firm boundaries regarding educational expenses are agreeable to funding their partner's children's college expenses.

In our family, the common-pot system has worked well for over two decades because it prompts us to have full disclosure about finances and to rely on each other for financial and emotional support. When my husband, Craig, first suggested that we adopt this method, I resisted it due to my former pattern of being overly watchful about our spending habits and very independent. But in the long run, using this method has brought us closer together through regular communication about money and sharing resources. In my life, the things that I resist often are just those things that allow me to learn the most valuable lessons, and adopting the one-pot system of money management is one of those things.

Other couples may find that the two-pot or three-pot system works well for their relationship, according to stepfamily researcher Kay Pasley and her colleagues.[16] The key to success is being able to discuss your options openly and to come to an agreement or compromise that suits your personal and family objectives. Overall, the common-pot system promotes more transparency in stepfamilies. The beauty of open disclosure of finances is that you're allowing each other to be vulnerable about one of the touchiest topics for all couples. It's quite a hurdle to jump over if you can come to an agreement about a money system. It's cause for celebration together with your favorite meal, beverage, or snuggle on the couch. Choosing a money management system that is a good fit for your stepfamily is a worthwhile goal and achievement.

For better or worse, our relationship with money starts during childhood and is a blend of family background and our unique take on the role it plays in our happiness. In terms of remarried couples, we also have the histories from our former marriages to consider. This includes our divorce settlement and how we feel about child support payments and custody issues.

"Us Against the Problem" Mindset

What I came to realize about remarriage and stepfamily life, over the past two decades, is that remarriage is complex and financial matters can drive a wedge between couples if they lack awareness and skills. For many couples, coming out of an unhappy first or second marriage makes them better prepared for a successful remarriage. Hopefully, they've taken the time to deal with baggage such as trust issues and finding ways to deal with perpetual challenges such as parenting differences. This was the case for Barbara, fifty-nine, and Nick, sixty-four, who met through mutual friends while line dancing.

Barbara and Nick, who you met in Chapter 3, blended four children twenty years ago (two kids each) and have sought couples therapy to work through the complications of unequal finances. Nick is a successful attorney, and Barbara is an occupational therapist who works in a clinic. Barbara admits that she wanted to be more generous than her husband by paying for all of their children's college costs, whereas Nick believed that all four kids should pay half of their costs. After in-depth discussions, they came up with a compromise and agreed to pay 75 percent of their children's tuition, room, and board.

Barbara put it like this,

> We don't agree on all money issues, and Nick makes more money than I do. But when I give him a good reason to spend money, such as loaning one of our kids money, he'll usually agree. Since I've never received child support payments, and we have a joint checking account, I've relied heavily on Nick's income to support my children, and I'm grateful for this support.

For remarried couples, like Barbara and Nick, key topics related to money management include how to share everyday financial chores like paying bills, who pays for expenses and college tuition for children (yours, mine, and ours); as well as estate planning, inheritance, and heirlooms. Other issues include paying for the weddings of yours, mine, and ours. In their case, they found it beneficial to have a joint checking account to pay for most household expenses, but they agreed to keep separate checking accounts to cover expenses for their children. They also have separate savings and retirement accounts. Essentially, they adopted the three-pot system, and they are transparent about their income, expenses, and how much they can save for retirement.

Remarried couples need to find ways they can adopt an "us against the problem" rather than an "us against each other" approach to finances, which means working as a team to face the challenges that arise together. Sharing financial issues in a way that honors love and does not put couples at odds with one another is crucial to building attachment in a second marriage. As a result, there's a lot of meaning around money in marriage, and it affects a couple's emotions and sense of well-being. This is especially true for remarriage, compared to first-time marriages, because they are merging two distinct worlds and often have one or more children when they marry. However, over time, remarried couples can learn to compromise and manage day-to-day conflict over money successfully, rather than be at odds with one another.

One of the oldest couples in my study, Paula, seventy-five, and Tim, seventy-seven, were also one of the wisest couples that I interviewed. Paula, a retired nurse, and Tim, a retired engineer, used full disclosure from the beginning of their forty-year remarriage, and both agreed on the "one-pot" system, which allowed them to combine finances into joint checking and savings accounts.

After taking the Financial Styles Quiz and the Money Script Inventory, Paula and Tim became aware that they both had money vigilance scripts and were moderate savers.[17] Since both sets of parents had endured the Great Depression and taught them the value of being fiscally conservative, they embraced these values. Sharing similar beliefs about money helped them avoid arguments throughout their long marriage. However, taking time to get a closer look at their financial styles and money beliefs was meaningful because they were able to feel gratitude for their similarities and understand a few of their differences.

Paula explains, "We remarried in our early thirties with three children each, and so we really grew up together. In the early days, I would get angry at Tim's ex for not paying her share of their children's expenses. But we both had good incomes, worked hard, and paid the bills together. We learned to focus on the big picture, not to sweat the small stuff, and to compromise, so everyone got their needs met most of the time."

As Paula shared her words of wisdom about having a happy second marriage, it became apparent that she shared a view of finances with Tim that was about abundance rather than scarcity. She explained, "We don't disagree much about money because we have common goals in life. We wanted to create a home where our children could feel secure, loved, supported, and safe. We kept this shared commitment and money flowed fairly easily in our lives."

Five Tips for a Loving and Open Discussion About Finances in a Remarriage:

1. **Don't issue ultimatums or threaten to end the marriage.** Remember that discussions about money can trigger intense feelings and fears in one or both partners, so focus on building trust and intimacy.

2. **Turn toward your partner and use active listening skills.**[18] Really listen to what your partner is saying (turn toward each other

with good eye contact) rather than turning away (screen time) or against (walking away or changing the topic). Say things like "I'm interested in what you have to say" rather than "I'm too busy to pay attention to you."

3. Be transparent about your financial history, feelings about money, assets, and debts. As mentioned previously, this usually means sharing bank, loan, and credit card statements, as well as apps.

4. Don't keep score. On most financial issues, there is more than one option. Ditch the emotional scoreboard and work toward a solution that both of you can live with.

5. Consider meeting with a mediator or couples therapist if needed to improve communication. Your medical doctor or insurance company should be able to give you a referral.

Learning how to have productive, low-conflict discussions about money is the first step to handling remarried finances in a healthy way. The skills needed to ensure that these discussions take place will serve you well since the financial considerations of a second marriage are more complicated than those of a first marriage. Reading Chapter 11 will give you and your partner the tools to effectively manage conflicts about money so that your remarriage can thrive.

Chapter 11
Manage Conflict About Money and Get Back on Track After a Dispute

What can you do to improve your marriage or committed relationship when your conversations about money are mostly negative and conflictual? While this is a common problem, the solutions are far from ordinary. While conflict may appear to be a destructive force in relationships, it can enhance intimacy if you learn the skills needed to communicate effectively and to get back on track after an argument. In a strong partnership, both people must take turns compromising and become transparent about finances. It's comforting to know we can survive conflict about money and even repair from it. Many couples, however, get stuck in endless rounds of arguing and blaming that they don't know how to get out of. When fights go unchecked and unrepaired, they can eventually erode love, respect, and friendship, which are the bedrock of any successful relationship.

For example, Robin, forty-two, and Erik, forty-three, struggle mightily to get what they want from their marriage, and finances are a big source of tension. They've been married for ten years and have two young children. During a recent couples therapy session in my office, their dialogue demonstrated the tendency they both have to be "right" and to start a discussion by attacking each other, causing their partner to become defensive and either fight or shut down. During the following conversation, they were discussing whether they should continue to rent or take the plunge and try to buy their first home.

Erik puts it like this, "Listen to me, Robin. You need to stop spending money on things you don't need. We're never going to get ahead and own our own house. You don't respect my opinion about where we should live, and you always need to be right, just like your mother. You don't understand finances like I do."

Robin responds,

> You don't get it. I'm listening to you but you don't make sense. You want to use up all of our savings to buy a house in an undesirable area where the prices are lower, but there's more crime. I don't feel safe there, and that doesn't seem to matter to you. I have expressed this point many times. Then you went ahead and called a realtor and have been looking for houses. You also loaned money to your brother John, who is irresponsible.

Cutting Robin off in mid-sentence and leaning toward her, Erik says, "I hate it when you talk down to me. You say I don't think about you, and I've devoted the last decade of my life to you and our kids. My brother will pay us back. You're just too uptight about it."

Robin says, "Forget it (as she walks out of my office). You never listen to me and there's no point in talking to you since you're just a bully who always has to get his way."

Since I wasn't interested in letting this argument continue, I asked Erik to text Robin and invite her to come back to my office and finish the session. When she returned five minutes later, she seemed a little calmer and sat on the couch next to Erik. I explained to this couple the principle that I learned from Terrence Real which is "Do you want to be right or do you want to be married?"[1] We discussed the advantages of learning to manage conflict about money without blaming each other and creating bad feelings such as shame (which leads to not feeling good enough). I also told Robin and Erik that the process of creating an "us against the problem" approach to dealing with finances begins with having more positive interactions and making repair attempts when they argue.

Stop Trying to Prove You're Right and Make Repair Attempts

What Robin and Erik need is a way to stop blaming each other and to eliminate their pattern of trying to prove they're right, which is a toxic relationship strategy. It's similar to keeping an emotional scoreboard or falling into a "Right Trap," a term coined by therapist and author Andrew W. Marshall, to denote a self-righteous approach.[2] Marshall explains, "When a couple is in conflict, and the arguments get nasty, both partners are quick to cloak themselves in righteousness." However, "being right" is a trap because it casts your partner as "wrong," part of the problem, and therefore "deserving" of your anger, bitterness, and frustration. Worse still, your partner is defending his or her unpleasant behavior by using just the same defense of being "right."

Letting go of needing to be "right" and keeping score is empowering to both partners. The first step toward changing this dysfunctional pattern of relating is awareness. This couple can benefit from developing a collaborative approach to dealing with conflict about money—realizing that working together is more important than being right. When each partner asserts his or her position and differences are addressed, a compromise is possible, and a partnership is formed. What matters is preserving love and attachment and getting back on track after a dispute.

In *The Seven Principles for Making Marriage Work*, Dr. John Gottman describes repair attempts as the secret weapon that emotionally intelligent couples employ that allows their marriage to flourish rather than flounder.[3] A repair attempt is any statement or action—verbal, physical, or otherwise—intended to diffuse negativity and keep a conflict from escalating. In over forty years of research in his classic "Love Lab" studies, Dr. Gottman discovered that the number one solution to marital problems is to get good at repair skills after an argument. He explains that repair attempts allow a couple to feel heard, and they're an important way to avoid resentment.

During our therapy sessions, I also encouraged Robin and Erik to use a "softened start up" when discussing their needs during conflict, which is another way to curb defensiveness.[4] With this approach, a person names their emotions, states why they feel this way, and asks for what they need even if their partner has indicated that they are unwilling to accommodate those needs. For example, Robin might say to Erik, "I feel hurt when you don't consider my feelings because living in a safe neighborhood is important to me. I really need you to listen to my viewpoint and consider my needs."

Another way to diffuse defensiveness during arguments is to take responsibility for your behavior, and we will cover this later in the chapter. For instance, whenever Erik was unwilling to take responsibility for his controlling behavior regarding searching for a home in neighborhoods where Robin doesn't want to live, Robin felt hurt and unappreciated. This behavior triggered Robin's insecurities and resentment.

Emotional Baggage Can Cause Us to Overreact to Triggers

During their couples therapy sessions, Robin and Erik had a low-conflict conversation which allowed them to process their earlier disagreement, each person owning their part in it and expressing their views on how to search for a home. At this point, they were ready for a compromise that would meet both of their needs for a moderately priced home in a safe neighborhood. Rather than rupturing the bond in their relationship, their repair attempt helped bring them closer. They were both able to talk about their feelings without getting defensive, using a "softened start up," and taking responsibility for their actions.[5]

In the beginning of their relationship, Robin and Erik were so elated to have discovered each other that they focused more on their similarities than their differences. They fell wildly in love, got married quickly, and never discussed their family backgrounds, beliefs about money, or ways to handle conflict. After a while, emotional baggage from past relationships was causing them to overreact to triggers (such as Erik loaning his brother money), and they started becoming more critical and defensive with each other. They lost sight of the loving feelings that brought them together in the first place.

Robin put it like this, "We tend to get irrational and dig our heels in when we fight—like we're kids. When Erik says, "You're always right,

Robin, you know you're always right," this makes me rage even more, and I feel like getting back at him."

Erik explains, "Usually one of us will say, 'I love you and I want to make up.' But we're not always able to do this. I used to think arguing was a bad thing, but I'm learning to fight fair. I hope this will help us have better finances and stop keeping score."

During one of our couples therapy sessions, Robin and Erik took my Financial Styles Quiz and The Money Script Inventory and talked about their family backgrounds.[6] Robin shared how she was adopted and never really felt good enough, so tended to spend money on herself to lift her mood. She also said that her super spender financial style and money worship script influenced her decisions to buy expensive nonessential items (like multiple pairs of leather shoes) with little regard for the impact on their financial health. When Erik showed empathy while Robin talked about her background and vulnerabilities, she felt loved, understood, and validated.

On the other hand, Erik was raised in a middle-class family with strong family values, and he is a moderate saver with a money vigilance script. As a result, he was able to save money fairly easily after he began his career as a high school math teacher. Since he was able to show Robin understanding about her reasons for being a super spender, she sat quietly and listened to him talk about his abundance mentality and vision for their financial future. During our next session the following week, this couple completed a budget and a savings plan that they could both live with. They had also made a list of potential homes in areas that they could possibly afford that were safe enough for their children. With their new way of managing conflict and teamwork, they were on their way to a more prosperous and happy future.

What Robin and Erik learned is that every relationship has its inevitable difficulties, and conflict goes with the territory. Sometimes couples avoid conflict because it has led to bitter disputes that never got resolved in their family of origin. Avoiding conflict about finances backfires in intimate relationships. Bottling up negative thoughts and feelings doesn't give your partner a chance to change their behavior. However, one of the characteristics of a good intimate relationship is learning to choose battles wisely and to distinguish between petty issues and truly important ones. With this approach, you will find yourself bickering less often and feeling happier. However, when a couple has perpetual arguments that never seem to resolve, it's worth exploring whether they've developed a "pursuer-distancer" dynamic.

The Pursuer-Distancer Dynamic and Finances

During a recent therapy session, Lillian and Brian, whom you met previously, talked about their tendency to have the same disagreements about money over and over again. Lillian describes how they both blame each other, have different needs for communication, and a pursuer-distancer dance follows—which intensifies the pattern. She feels rejected when Brian withdraws, and he often feels criticized when Lillian approaches him to discuss their financial problems, which include high credit card debt and financial infidelity. On the other hand, Brian has expressed frustration about Lillian wanting more conversations about money than he's comfortable with. In Chapter 1, you learned that Lillian is a super saver and has a money vigilance script, while Brian is a super spender and has a money status script. They often clash when they have conflict, and their pursuer-distancer dynamic has accelerated lately.

While all couples need autonomy and closeness, many couples struggle with the pursuer-distancer dance and feel chronically dissatisfied with their degree of intimacy. When one partner becomes critical or upset and intensely pursues their partner, the other might become distant or defensive. This negative dynamic can cause couples to have the same fights repeatedly. In many cases, the distancer retreats and seeks alone time when they feel stressed, and this intensifies their partner's quest for closeness and desire to pursue. But the more they move toward their partner for intimacy or communication, the more the distancer pushes them away.

A problem exists when the pattern of pursuing and distancing becomes ingrained because the behavior of one partner provokes and maintains the behavior of the other, according to marriage expert Harriet Lerner, PhD.[7] She writes, "Keep in mind that it's the pattern not the person that's the problem in the relationship. Understanding the pattern and your part in it is the first step toward breaking out of it."

While pursuing and distancing are common ways that couples relate to one another when they're under financial stress, this pattern can become dysfunctional. If they go unnoticed and persist for a long time, they can even lead to the demise of a relationship or marriage. But with self-awareness and a willingness to change, couples can break their negative cycle of relating and build love, trust, and intimacy.

Why is the pursuer-distancer dance so damaging to an intimate relationship? One partner becomes increasingly unhappy with his or her partner—feeling that their needs for intimacy aren't being met. Although the pursuer may have made ongoing attempts to get their partner (who is a distancer) to open up, they're left feeling their efforts to bring him or her closer have failed. In fact, many of the clients I've met with in my clinical practice admit that they've resorted to nagging and didn't feel good about its impact on their relationship. The problem is that if this pattern becomes deeply entrenched, couples can become resentful and chronically unhappy with the role they're playing. However, sometimes a distancer realizes too late that their partner is so distressed that she or he is making plans to end their relationship.

So, let's see how the pursuer-distancer dynamic usually works in a typical scenario with Lillian and Brian. Lillian sees her hyper-vigilance as a way to motivate Brian to open up. But in this case, the ways that Lillian and Brian respond to each other backfires—going from bad to worse.

"Let's talk about why we're not able to get ahead financially," Lillian complains as her husband Brian reads the newspaper. "How can we save money if you don't talk to me?"

"I'm not sure what you're talking about," Brian says. "We're doing OK," as he walks out of the room.

Lillian feels increasingly frustrated with her attempts to draw Brian out. Meanwhile, he resorts to his classic distancer strategy—perhaps stonewalling her attempts to communicate. As Lillian continues to express more disappointment in Brian, he further withdraws. If this pattern isn't reversed, it's easy to see how they can both begin to feel criticized and contempt for each other—two of the major warning signs that their relationship is doomed to fail, according to Dr. John Gottman.[8] In fact, Dr. Gottman's extensive research showed that the pursuer-distancer dynamic is extremely common, and if it persists, it can lead to marital breakdown. He also warns us that if couples get stuck in this pattern in the first few years of marriage, they have more than an 80 percent chance of divorcing in the first four or five years.

It's no wonder that many of the interactions between couples about finances become deadlocked into the pursuer-distancer pattern and end up in a stalemate or with partners feeling bitter and disillusioned about their relationship. Repair work begins with expressing your intent in a positive way and taking responsibility for your part in it rather than pointing the finger at your partner. That said, both people need to make a commitment to work on improving their communication so they can get rid of the pursuer-distancer pattern and restore harmony.

Here Are Some Ways to Have a Dialogue When Your Intent Is to Become More Loving and Intimate:

When I feel like distancing myself from Craig, these are comments I've found helpful to say to him:

- "I feel worried about our finances right now. I'm fearful that I will say something I regret, so I need to take some space. Can we talk later?"
- "I feel frustrated with our interaction right now and would like to take a break. I hope we can get back together later."

The following are comments that the pursuer can say to break the pursuer-distancer dynamic:

- "I feel left out when you don't talk to me about what's going on in your head about our finances, and I'd like to know what you're thinking, but I can wait."
- "I feel hurt when you don't include me in plans about spending. I'd like to be kept posted, even if you prefer to order items on your own."

Rather than expressing criticism or contempt, this type of dialogue will hopefully foster positive communication since the intent is to get information rather than to criticize or nag. In addition, I always tell couples that if they want to strengthen emotional intimacy and deepen their love, they need to remember to turn toward each other.[9] This means responding to bids for connection by having good eye contact and making positive comments. In contrast, turning away from your partner promotes disconnection. Examples might be looking at your phone or laptop rather than at your mate. Lastly, turning against your partner could mean shutting down by walking away, getting defensive, or making a critical or negative comment when he or she makes a bid for connection. The following is an example of turning toward your partner.

Turning toward Lillian, Brian says, "I know I avoid dealing with conversations about money because I've made so many bad decisions that have hurt you, Lillian. When you speak to me in a loving way and hear my side of the story, I don't feel like disappearing."

The irony of the pursuer-distancer pattern is that it's reinforced by popular self-help books and websites to save your marriage. While most of these articles encourage couples to open up and communicate more, they don't explain that this can fail unless couples understand that a plea to get closer by one spouse can be perceived as a criticism or nagging by the other. It's likely that the person at the other end of a "sharing feelings" conversation will feel blamed and attacked if their underlying message is "You are doing something wrong that needs to be fixed."

Four Ways to Break the Pursuer-Distancer Pattern:

1. Work on changing your reactions to your partner and take responsibility for your part in interactions with him/her about finances. Stop being the pursuer or distancer and think of other ways to get your needs met.
2. Write in a journal or dialogue with a close friend or trusted therapist—this can be extremely helpful.
3. Make peace by stopping the blame game. If you can actually embrace this concept, you and your partner will feel an almost immediate sense of relief.
4. If your partner seems flooded, walk away but not in anger or blame. Disengage as a way to restore your composure—not to punish your partner. Let your partner know that you will return when calm. If you're the pursuer, give your partner time and space to come closer to you. If you're the distancer, say something positive to your partner and let them know you care

about their feelings. If you need to pause in order to break the pursuer-distancer dynamic, do so for at least twenty minutes.

Lillian reflects: "We bicker a lot about money. After a while, we're no longer addressing the issue at hand, and it creates a vicious cycle of negative feelings that never get resolved. The more I approach Brian and try to talk, the more he distances himself and withdraws. We understand more about our histories and issues, but we still argue too much. Brian withdraws when he feels I'm being too critical, especially about his credit card debt."

Has this ever happened to you? It's been so long since you've had a neutral or pleasant talk with your partner about finances that you don't know where to start. Or do you often find yourself getting defensive, which only escalates the conflict? Couples like Lillian and Brian need to find positive ways of getting their points across without being too critical, withdrawing, or escalating an argument.

How to Avoid Criticizing Your Partner and Get Your Needs Met

In the heat of a dispute, Teresa, who you met in Chapter 10, says things to her husband Christopher that she later regrets, such as, "You're selfish and you don't care about me and our kids." Notice how her words come across as critical, rather than asking for what she wants in a positive way, such as, "I'd love to talk about how we can finance a family vacation so we can spend time together." Couples who bicker about money often say more about what they don't want than what they do want or need.

Stan Tatkin, author of *Saying Yes to a Relationship of Depth, True Connection, and Enduring Love,* believes that couples are often geared toward a one-person orientation versus a two-person orientation when they communicate their requests.[10] He writes, "In a two-person model, the needs of the relationship come first, where neither partner will agree on a solution at the expense of the other. Secure-functioning relationships are two-person psychological systems where both partners feel respected, heard, and safe. The partners' wagons are hitched together." Putting a finer point on Tatkin's observation, Teresa might say to Christopher, "I'd like to plan a time to work on our budget for a family vacation," instead of, "You never consider my needs." While the first statement expresses empathy and a willingness to collaborate, the second one might cause Christopher to get defensive and retaliate.

Truth be told, what we often think of as constructive criticism or feedback often feels like downright criticism to the person on the receiving end. And criticism triggers a person to become defensive and protect themselves from an attack, which prohibits the resolution of a conflict. For instance, when Teresa calls Christopher selfish, it comes across as a criticism, not feedback. On the other hand, if she said something like, "I'd love for you to spend more time with me and the kids; we miss you. Can we plan an outing together?" he might be receptive to Teresa stating her needs in a positive way without blaming him.

So, as with so many crucial tools you can employ in the pursuit of happiness with your partner, the bottom line is to use effective and empathetic communication. To a great extent, where you start dictates where you end up in terms of conflict resolution. When you feel criticized, even in a loving and trusting relationship, there's a strong likelihood that you'll take your partner's comments as a personal attack and become defensive.

Taking this sort of active approach to managing conflict is brave, and it requires openness and vulnerability. But the aspects of relationships that are courageous are also the things most likely to lead to lasting love. By being honest and exposing your vulnerabilities, we're fostering deeper trust and intimacy. Once a couple has established a loving and open dialogue, working on compromise is possible.

Compromise Can Help Couples to Manage Conflict

Compromise is an essential tool needed to preserve a marriage. Discussing financial concerns that arise with your partner in a timely and respectful way will help you become better at repair skills. If you embrace the notion that conflict is an inevitable part of an intimate relationship and learn the skills to compromise and repair from conflict, you'll bounce back from disagreements about money faster and build a successful, long-lasting partnership.

What is the meaning of the word compromise? It's a settlement by which each side makes concessions. And while this doesn't sound romantic, if you decide you want to have a happy relationship, you have to learn to negotiate—which is the essence of compromise. Negotiation is about diplomacy and is a tool that will help you and your partner get on the same side and become intimately connected. Over time, productive arguments can actually help you stay together. You can learn ways to have fruitful disagreements—more like discussions than arguments—so you won't hold onto recycled anger or feelings of resentment.

In order to successfully navigate financial issues, you need to employ a deliberate approach to communication that begins with a "pre-compromise warm-up." During this time, offer observations on each other's positive qualities and behaviors. Showing love through gestures, including words and affection, can facilitate warm feelings. The goal is to remind each other "that you are fighting for each other, not against each other."

Next, agree on an "area of tension" between you and your partner that will remain the focus of the conversation until both of you have had a chance to offer your perspective and unpack your feelings. This exercise is as much about listening as it is about articulating one's own point of view. This kind of measured, structured, compassionate mode of communication allows both partners to be heard and facilitates a solution to the problem in that week's meeting. The aim is to help you understand each other and arrive at a compromise.

For instance, if Teresa wants to come to a compromise about saving more money with her husband Christopher, they could talk about what is going well with their budget, such as they're eating out less often. They can also negotiate who is cooking dinner or cleaning up after family meals. Then they could talk calmly about their area of tension which is not enough money to pay for a vacation to a family resort. When both Teresa and Christopher use a gentler approach to expressing their feelings, say why they feel this way, and state their needs, it's also important for them to listen without interrupting or criticizing one another. Then, hopefully, they can come to a compromise about saving money for a family vacation. One solution might be a long weekend camping (low cost and fun for their kids). Another option might be a weekend at a hotel that has a swimming pool and is close to an amusement park and shopping, meeting most of their recreational needs.

But solving the problem at hand through compromise can only be achieved when you openly identify your core needs. In some cases, core needs might clash badly, such as one partner wanting to retire early and the other wanting to work until their mid-seventies. Indeed, the problem-solving process might also fail when partners are not open to being influenced by each other, or when one partner gives up too much. While it's not possible to solve all relationship conflict, you can still achieve happiness if you adjust your expectations and appreciate the issues you can compromise on.

Following the suggestions below will help you build empathy for your partner, manage conflicts, reach compromises, and achieve positive engagement. Try these tips for a period of two weeks and then discuss progress with your partner over coffee or while eating lunch at your favorite restaurant to avoid rushing.

Couples Activity: Seven Ways to Compromise with Your Partner

Before you practice the exercise below, you and your partner need to write down issues that you believe are important to work on. Then, identify the ones both of you can be flexible about and those that are a challenge to consider worthy of compromise. For instance, a core need for you might be having an emergency fund, and your partner might want to achieve a zero balance on all credit cards. Discuss the issues you are willing to be flexible about and those that are nonnegotiable deal-breakers, or the ones you're unwilling to be flexible about. Make sure that you don't come across as "right" and listen to your partner with interest and respectful questions.

Seven Steps to Reach a Compromise:

1. Establish common goals that you and your mate can agree on. Be sure to discuss any feelings you share on the issues you're discussing and identify your "core needs."

2. Use the "pre-compromise warm-up." Start by saying something to your partner about their positive qualities, such as "I appreciate your willingness to listen."

3. Practice empathy by trying to imagine yourself walking in your partner's shoes. Show willingness to help your partner meet one of their personal goals or dreams by asking how you can help them.

4. Listen actively without making evaluative comments. When your partner identifies an inflexible area of a need, ask for more clarification about why it's important to him or her and include their feelings, beliefs, and values on this issue.

5. Determine your deal-breakers—those nonnegotiable items that are crucial to your happiness. For instance, your partner might want to go on more vacations, but you might want to save more money for retirement.

6. Use compromise to achieve a "us against the problem" solution. Draw two boxes—one for negotiable issues and one for nonnegotiable ones—and compromise on the negotiable issues. List aspects of your positions that are negotiable. These are your flexible areas that you're open to compromising on, such as timing, place, or ways to achieve your goal.

7. Write down one compromise that honors both of your needs, wishes, and dreams. Save it in a place where you can reflect upon it often and celebrate with a special dinner or dessert.

In the end, the fruits of learning to compromise can create not only open but productive dialogue between you and your mate, and can bring solutions into focus that previously seemed unclear or impossible. Compromise is about accepting differences and accommodating each other's needs and desires. It's about finding common ground. This method can be successful when you're dedicated to improving your relationship and ready to do the hard work to make a more fulfilling future together.

Even happy couples have disagreements about money at times. Discussing concerns that arise in a timely and respectful way will help you become better at repair skills. Accept the reality that you'll face stresses in your relationship; you'll have disputes, frustrations, and anger. However, you don't have to let anger over finances build into resentment. Learning to repair from regrettable arguments will help you stay rock solid as a couple.

Managing Conflict by Repairing After Regrettable Incidents

While dealing with financial decisions can be fraught with psychological and logistical challenges for all couples, it's even more of a struggle if you have differences in family backgrounds about finances or you have a tendency to blame each other for setbacks. Increased financial pressure from issues such as funding college tuitions, job layoffs, loaning others money, the birth of a child, and financial infidelity can strain a relationship to the breaking point.

It makes sense that you and your partner might have different lists of financial priorities, and this can increase conflict. As a result, it's important to find ways to repair from regrettable comments that are made to each other. Developing shared goals and building a sense of trust around saving for the future will spare you from the strain that comes from arguing over managing money in a marriage or committed relationship.

How to Repair from Regrettable Incidents

The key to having productive arguments that can be seen as an opportunity to learn about each other is to find ways to clear up misunderstandings and to repair hurt feelings after regrettable incidents. Happy couples learn ways to manage conflicts about money in ways that are more like discussions than fights. Differences of opinion about finances can be complementary if you learn to discuss and validate each other's perspectives. For instance, if you're a spender and your partner is a saver, you can learn to save for desired goals, and your partner can learn to enjoy spending a little more on nonessential items such as vacations. Repair attempts after a regrettable incident are advantageous to both people and can create a positive outcome.

A good rule of thumb is to make repair attempts after an argument or regrettable incident about money by processing what happened without reigniting the argument. The first step is listening to your partner's viewpoint and communicating that you understand it, even if it differs from your own. The focus needs to be on accepting each other's realities and perceptions without blaming each other. Next, both partners need to validate each other's perspectives. This includes making comments such as "I didn't realize how my words affected you." The last step is bringing something positive into the dialogue with your partner.

For example, after Robin and Erik had their initial argument in my office, I advised them to process their recent disagreement about shopping for a new home. While they were talking about a regrettable incident, I encouraged Erik to tell Robin something like, "I care about your feelings and want to hear your point of view about where we live." I also advised them to use "I" statements rather than "You" statements to diffuse some of their defensiveness.[11] For example, Robin could say, "I feel left out when you don't consider my feelings about where we live," rather than "You don't get it; my needs don't matter to you."

Finally, by taking responsibility for their part in the argument, Robin and Erik were able to recover from hurt feelings and regain the loving feelings they wanted to experience. The following are details of ways to repair from regrettable incidents or comments.

Six Ways to Repair Effectively from Conflict About Finances:

1. Practice having a recovery conversation after an argument. Make an effort to actively listen to your partner's perspective and validate it, even if you don't agree with it. Take turns listening and talking. A recovery conversation can reveal information about your relationship, lead to a resolution of the fight, and restore intimacy, according to psychologist Daniel B. Wile.[12] Be careful not to rekindle the argument by dismissing your partner's feelings.

2. Accept responsibility for your part in a regrettable incident and identify your triggers. It's a good idea to identify triggers if you're aware of them. For instance, "I've been very stressed and worrying about money lately and I know I've been irritable. I regret what I said to you and I'm sorry that I hurt your feelings. I will try not to do this again." Take a risk and deal with hurt feelings—especially if it's an important issue rather than stonewalling or shutting down. If you or your partner

feel an apology is appropriate, give one that reflects taking responsibility and genuine concern for the effect your behavior had on your partner.

3. Avoid blaming, criticizing, or putting down your partner. Talking about specific concerns is different from a criticism. For instance, a complaint is: "I'm upset because you didn't tell me about spending money on new clothes. We agreed to be open with each other, and money is tight right now." Versus a criticism: "You never tell me the truth. How can I trust you?" Avoid showing contempt for your partner (rolling your eyes, ridicule, name-calling, sarcasm, etc.). Starting conversations with a soft and curious tone such as, "I feel confused about our financial goals right now; can we talk soon so we can get on the same page?" will lessen your partner's defensiveness.

4. State your needs in a positive way. Listen to your partner's requests and ask for clarification on issues that are unclear. Approach your partner with a positive request such as "I would appreciate you sharing your plan to purchase something big with me in advance." State your feelings as neutrally as possible and transform any complaint about your partner into a positive need. Stay in the moment and resist the urge to touch on your partner's raw spots, such as a financial infidelity in the past.

5. Take time to reset if you feel overwhelmed (approximately twenty minutes). This will give you time to calm down and collect your thoughts so you can have a more meaningful dialogue with your partner. Be sure to get back together within twenty-four hours so you don't avoid dealing with the issue.

6. Remember to focus on repair rather than who's right or who's wrong. Recovering after conflict is about restoring trust and intimacy by making sure you and your partner both feel heard and validated.

Once you've learned to manage conflicts about finances effectively, it becomes much easier to repair disputes and to get back on track. If you find yourself struggling, tell your partner what's on your mind. For instance, say something like "Can you hold me or tell me you love me? I feel like attacking you but I don't want to do that." Most of the time, you'll restore intimacy by being honest and open with your partner during times of high conflict or distress.

It takes time and practice to develop good repair skills, so be patient with yourself and your partner. Adopting an "us against the problem" rather than a "us against each other" approach to discussing money-related topics will help you protect your relationship and become more successful partners. It's my hope that your strong connection with each other, along with learning the communication skills needed to achieve a collaborative approach, will set the stage for having low-conflict conversations about money in the years to come.

Acknowledgments

There are many people who made writing this book possible. First, I want to express appreciation to my husband, Craig, who was in my corner throughout the book-writing process and showed me total backing. He believed in my skill to draft the manuscript, even on days when I was fatigued from my visits to our local library, where I spent countless hours.

I am forever grateful to all of the individuals and couples who generously shared their financial pressures and successes with me. Their experiences and wisdom gave me the courage to persist in crafting this book.

Let's Talk About Money would never have been written without the unwavering support of my agent Joelle Delbourgo, owner of Delbourgo Associates, and my former agent Jacqueline Flynn, now an executive editor at Bloomsbury Publishing. They both believed in my ability to draft a book to help couples have lower conflict about money and achieve prosperity.

Most importantly, I am grateful for the love and support of my family. Thanks again to Craig for cooking many meals and cheering me on during the days when I would return home from the library famished and in need of a hug. And thanks to my three wonderful and loving children, Sean, Tracy, and Catherine, for being steadfast in your support and encouragement.

Notes

Introduction

1. Spencer Sherman, *The Cure for Money Madness: Break Your Bad Money Habits, Live Without Financial Stress—and Make More Money* (New York: Broadway Books, 2009), 85–115.
2. Bradley Klontz, Sonya L. Britt, and Jennifer Mentzer, "Money Beliefs and Financial Behaviors: Development of the Klontz Money Script Inventory," *Journal of Financial Therapy* 2, no. 1 (2011): 3–21.

Chapter 1

1. Emily N. Garbinsky et al., "Love, Lies, Money: Financial Infidelity in Romantic Relationships," *Journal of Consumer Research* 47, no. 1 (June 2020): 1–24.
2. Nirajana Mishra, Emily N. Garbinsky, and Suzanne B. Shu, "Discussing Money with the One You Love: How Financial Stress influences Couples' Financial Communication," *Journal of Consumer Psychology, Wiley Online*, June 15, 2024, https://myscp.onlinelibrary.wiley.com/doi/abs/10.1002/jcpy.1430 (July 8, 2024).
3. Brad Klontz and Ted Klontz, *Mind Over Money: Overcoming the Money Disorders That Threaten Our Financial Health* (New York: Crown Business, 2009), 9–11.
4. Klontz and Klontz, *Mind Over Money* 9–11.
5. Bradley Klontz, Sonya L. Britt, and Jennifer Mentzer, "Money Beliefs and Financial Behaviors: Development of the Klontz Money Script Inventory," *Journal of Financial Therapy* 2, no. 1 (2011): 3–21.
6. Klontz, Britt, and Mentzer, "Money Beliefs and Financial Behaviors," 3–21.
7. Klontz, Britt, and Mentzer, "Money Beliefs and Financial Behaviors," 3–21.

8. Klontz, Klontz, *Mind Over Money,* 20–32.
9. Deborah Kaplan and Rick Kahler, *Coupleship, Inc.: From Financial Freedom to Financial Intimacy* (Rapid City: Coupleship Publications LLC, 2023), 28–33.
10. Klontz and Klontz, *Mind Over Money,* 31.
11. Klontz, Britt, and Mentzer, "Money Beliefs and Financial Behaviors," 3–21.
12. Klontz, Britt, and Mentzer, "Money Beliefs and Financial Behaviors," 3–21.
13. Klontz, Britt, and Mentzer, "Money Beliefs and Financial Behaviors," 3–21.
14. "2024 Fidelity Investments Couples and Money Survey," *Fidelity Investments*, February 1, 2024, https://preview.thenewsmarket.com/Previews/FINP/DocumentAssets/660835_v4.pdf (July 5, 2024).
15. Klontz and Klontz, *Mind Over Money,* 1–62.
16. Klontz, Britt, and Mentzer, "Money Beliefs and Financial Behaviors," 3–21.
17. Klontz, Britt, and Mentzer, "Money Beliefs and Financial Behaviors," 3–21.

Chapter 2

1. Nirajana Mishra, Emily N. Garbinsky, and Suzanne B. Shu, "Discussing Money with the One You Love: How Financial Stress Influences Couples' Financial Communication," *Journal of Consumer Psychology, Wiley Online,* June 15, 2024, https://myscp.onlinelibrary.wiley.com/doi/10.1002/jcpy.1430 (July 27, 2024).
2. Brad Klontz and Ted Klontz, *Mind Over Money: Overcoming the Money Disorders That Threaten Our Financial Health* (New York: Crown Business, January 1, 2009), 9–11.
3. Shanti Feldhahn and Jeff Feldhahn, *Thriving in Love and Money: 5 Game-Changing Insights About Your Relationship, Your Money, and Yourself* (Boston: Bethany House, 2020), 29–47.
4. Feldhahn and Feldhahn, *Thriving in Love and Money,* 43–7.
5. "Money, Marriage, and Communication," *Ramsey Solutions*, September 27, 2021, https://www.ramseysolutions.com/relationships/money-marriage-communication-research (July 27, 2024).
6. "Stress in America 2023: A Nation Recovering from Collective Trauma," *American Psychological Association*, November 2023, https://www.apa.org/news/press/releases/stress/2023/collective-trauma-recovery (July 27, 2024).
7. E. N. Garbinsky and J. J. Gladstone, "The Consumption Consequences of Couples Pooling Resources," *Journal of Consumer Psychology* 29, no. 3 (2019): 353–69.

8. Daniel B. Wile, *After the Fight: Using Disagreements to Build a Stronger Relationship* (New York: Guilford Press, September 1995), 117–26.
9. John Gottman and Nan Silver, *Why Marriages Succeed or Fail: and How You Can Make Yours Last* (New York: A Fireside Book published by Simon and Schuster, 1994), 84–95.
10. Terrence Real, *The New Rules of Marriage: What You Need to Know to Let Love Work* (New York: Ballentine, 2008), 40–4.
11. Dr. John Gottman and Nan Silver, *The Seven Principles for Making Marriage Work: A Practical Guide From the Countries Foremost Relationship the Seven Principles Expert* (New York: Three Rivers Press, 2015), 164–5.
12. Gottman and Silver, *The Seven Principles for Making Marriage Work*, 164–5.
13. Cheryl Fraser, *Buddha's Bedroom: The Mindful Loving Path to Sexual Passion and Lifelong Intimacy* (Oakland: Reveal, 2019), 94–101.
14. Fraser, *Buddha's Bedroom*, 94–101.
15. Gottman and Silver, *The Seven Principles for Making Marriage Work*, 164–5.
16. Spencer Sherman, *The Cure for Money Madness: Break Your Bad Money Habits, Live Without Financial Stress—and Make More Money* (New York: Broadway Books, 2009), 85–115.
17. Sherman, *The Cure for Money Madness*, 108–9.
18. Sherman, *The Cure for Money Madness*, 108–9, 35–9.
19. John Gottman and Julie Schwartz Gottman, *The Love Prescription: Seven Days to More Intimacy, Connection, and Joy* (New York: Penguin Books, 2022), 35–9.
20. Gottman and Gottman, *The Love Prescription*, 35–9.
21. Gottman and Gottman, *The Love Prescription*, 5–10.

Chapter 3

1. John M. Gottman and Julie Swartz Gottman, *The Science of Couples and Family Therapy: Behind the Scenes of the Love Lab* (New York: W. W. Norton & Company, 2018), 144–59.
2. J. J. Gladstone, E. N. Garbinsky, and C. Mogilner, "Pooling Finances and Relationship Satisfaction," *Journal of Personality and Social Psychology* 123, no. 6 (2022): 1293–314.

3 Jeff Motske, *The Couples Guide to Financial Compatibility: Avoid Fights About Saving and Spending and Build a Happy and Secure Future Together* (Boston: DeCapo Press, 2015), 8–9.
4 Barbara Fishman, "The Economic Behavior of Stepfamilies," *Family Relations* 32, no. 3 (July 1983): 359–66.
5 Alice Holbrook, "Does Marriage Have to Mean Merging Money?" *Nerd Wallet*, October 29, 2020. Nerdwallet.com/article/banking/marrying-how-to-join-your-finances-after-marriage (August 12, 2023).
6 Kay Pasley, Eric Sandras, and Mary Ellen Edmonson, "The Effects of Financial Management Strategies on the Quality of Family Life in Remarriage," *Journal of Family and Economic Issues* 15, no. 1 (Spring 1994): 53–70.
7 Debra Kaplan and Rick Kahler, *Coupleship Inc: From Financial Conflict to Financial Intimacy* (Rapid City: Coupleship Publications, LLC, 2022), 113.

Chapter 4

1 Kathryn Vassel, "The Secrets to Managing Money as a Couple," *CNN Business*, March 23, 2022, https://www.cnn.com/2022/03/23/success/budgeting-tips-couples-feseries/index.html (July 28, 2024).
2 Kelsey Waddill, "More Employers Offer Employer-Sponsored Same-Sex Coverage," *Tech Target Health Payer Intelligence*, December 2, 2020, https://www.techtarget.com/healthcarepayers/news/366604545/More-Employers-Offer-Employer-Sponsored-Same-Sex-Spousal-Coverage (September 7, 2023).
3 Christine Matthieu (Certified Wealth Coach), Note Advisors LCC, Buffalo, NY. In discussion with author, May 5, 2024, on Zoom.
4 Shanti Feldhahn and Jeff Feldhahn, *Thriving in Love and Money: 5 Game-Changing Insights About Your Relationship, Your Money, and Yourself* (Boston: Bethany House, 2020), 53.
5 Dr. John Gottman and Nan Silver, *The Seven Principles for Making Marriage Work: A Practical Guide from the Countries Foremost Relationship Expert* (New York: Three Rivers Press, 2015), 25–46, 99–116.
6 Nora Graves, *Budgeting for Couples 101: Improve Your Money Management Skills to Grow Wealth for You and Your Partner* (North Haven: Nora Graves Publishing, 2020), 77.
7 Elizabeth Warren and Amelia Warren Tyagi, *All Your Worth: The Ultimate Lifetime Money Plan, a Guide to Personal Finances* (New York: Free Press, 2005), 24–9.

8. Warren and Warren Tyagi, *All Your Worth*, 24–9.
9. Warren and Warren Tyagi, *All Your Worth*, 24–9.
10. "America Retains Rent Burdened Status, How Insurance Premiums Could Eventually Intensify the Strain," *Moody Analytics*, November 27, 2023, https://www.moodys.com/web/en/us/about/insights/data-stories/q3-2023-rental-affordability.html (July 8, 2023).
11. "Freddie Mac: New Survey Shows Gen Z Apprehensive About the Path to Home Ownership," *Freddie Mac Home Media Room*, November 16, 2022, https://freddiemac.gcs-web.com/news-releases/news-release-details/freddie-mac-new-survey-shows-gen-z-apprehensive-about-path (July 7, 2024).
12. Michael Finke in Martha C. White, "Why a 60/30/10 Budget Could Be a New 50/30/20," *Time Magazine*, March 15, 2024, 77, https://time.com/6916834/how-to-budget-60-30-10/ (July 7, 2024).
13. White, "Why a 60/30/10 Budget Could Be a New 50/30/20."
14. Feldhahn and Feldhahn, *Thriving in Love and Money*, 63.
15. Graves, *Budgeting for Couples 101*, 77.

Chapter 5

1. "Money, Marriage, and Communication," *Ramsey Solutions*, September 27, 2021, https://www.ramseysolutions.com/relationships/money-marriage-communication-research (July 29, 2024).
2. Alana Semuels, "Why We Overspend," *Time Magazine* 203, nos. 9–10 (March 28, 2024): 40.
3. Emily N. Garbinsky et al., "Love, Lies, Money: Financial Infidelity in Romantic Relationships," *Journal of Consumer Research* 47, no. 1 (June 2020): 1–24.
4. Chelsea Brennen, "Good Debt vs Bad Debt," *Forbes Advisor*, March 29, 2021, https://www.forbes.com/advisor/credit-score/good-debt-vs-bad-debt/ (August 2, 2024).
5. Brennen, "Good Debt vs Bad Debt."
6. Christopher Yalanis, MBA, CFP (Financial Advisor), in discussion with the author, May 13, 2024, Wells Fargo Advisors, Newport, RI.
7. "The Massachusetts Attorney General's Guide to Consumer Credit," *Office of The Massachusetts Attorney General*, February 2018, https://www.mass.gov/doc/ago-guide-to-consumer-credit/download (August 1, 2024).

8 Becky Pokora and Harlan Vaughn, "Credit Card Statistics and Trends in 2024," *Forbes Advisor*, March 28, 2024, https://www.forbes.com/advisor/credit-cards/credit-card-statistics/ (August 1, 2024).

9 Jeff Motske, *The Couples Guide to Financial Compatibility: Avoid Fights About Saving and Spending and Build a Happy and Secure Future Together* (Boston: DeCapo Press, 2015), 29–30.

10 Garbinsky et al., "Love, Lies, Money," 1–24.

11 Yuqian XU in Semuels, "Why We Overspend," 40.

12 McKinsey Survey in Semuels, "Why We Overspend," 41.

13 Pokora and Vaughn, "Credit Card Statistics and Trends in 2024."

14 Yuqian XU in Semuels, "Why We Overspend," 41.

15 Semuels, "Why We Overspend," 41.

16 M. McCall and H. J. Belmont, "Credit Card Insignia and Restaurant Tipping: Evidence for an Associative Link," *Journal of Applied Psychology* 81, no. 5 (1996): 609–13, https://doi.org/10.1037/0021-9010.81.5.609 (May 15, 2024).

17 Jeffrey Dew, Sonja Britt, and Sandra Huston, "Examining the Relationship Between Family Issues and Divorce," *Family Relations* 61, no. 4 (2012): 615–28.

18 "American Psychological Association Survey Shows Money Stress Weighing on Americans' Health Nationwide," *American Psychological Association*, 2015, https://www.apa.org/news/press/releases/2015/02/money-stress (May 15, 2024).

19 "Stress in America 2023: A Nation Recovering from Collective Trauma," *American Psychological Association*, November 2023, https://www.apa.org/news/press/releases/stress/2023/collective-trauma-recovery (July 27, 2024).

20 Mary Hunt, *Debt Proof Your Marriage: How to Manage Your Money Together* (Grand Rapids: Revell, 2010), 108.

21 Hunt, *Debt Proof Your Marriage*, 21.

22 Elle Martinez, *Jumpstart Your Marriage and Your Money* (Dublin: Coventry House, 2017), 99–100.

23 Dave Ramsey, *The Total Money Makeover, a Proven Plan for Financial Fitness* (Nashville: Thomas Nelson, May 14, 2024), 105–23.

24 Ramsey, *The Total Money Makeover*, 105–23.

25 Ramsey, *The Total Money Makeover* 105–23.

26 Martinez, *Jumpstart Your Marriage and Your Money*, 99–100.

27 E. N. Garbinsky and J. J. Gladstone, "The Consumption Consequences of Couple Pooling Resources," *Journal of Consumer Psychology* 29, no. 3 (2019): 353–69.

Chapter 6

1. Jamela Adam, "American Savings by Generation: How Balances and Goals Vary by Age," *Forbes Advisor*, August 15, 2024, https://www.forbes.com/advisor/banking/savings/average-american-savings/ (August 20, 2024).
2. Dave Ramsey, *The Total Money Makeover: A Proven Plan for Financial Fitness* (Nashville: Thomas Nelson, May 14, 2024), 124–39.
3. "Northwestern Mutual Study Americans Now Believe They Will Need $1.25 Million for a Comfortable Retirement," *Northwestern Mutual*, October 25, 2022, https://news.northwesternmutual.com/2022-10-25-Northwestern-Mutual-Study-Finds-Americans-Now-Believe-They-Will-Need-1-25-Million-for-Comfortable-Retirement (September 20, 2024).
4. Tanza Loudenback, "How Much of My Paycheck Should I Save?" *Buy Side from WSJ*, September 13, 2024, https://www.wsj.com/buyside/personal-finance/financial-tips/how-much-of-my-paycheck-should-i-save (September 20, 2024).
5. Loudenback, "How Much of My Paycheck Should I Save?"
6. Ramsey, *The Total Money Makeover*, 140–51.
7. Beth Braverman, David Schiff, and Amanda Gengler, "99 Great Ways to Save 2023 Beat Inflation Special Edition," *AARP*, July 2023, https://www.aarp.org/money/budgeting-saving/info-2023/99-great-ways-to-save.html (January 10, 2024).
8. Braverman, Schiff, and Gengler, "99 Great Ways to Save, 2023 Beat Inflation Special Edition."
9. Consumer Price Index, *U.S. Bureau of Labor Statistics* 2024, https://www.bls.gov/cpi/ (November 14, 2024).
10. Lane Gillespie, "Bankrate 2024 Annual Emergency Savings Report," *Bankrate*, June 20, 2024, https://www.bankrate.com/banking/savings/emergency-savings-report/ (January 12, 2024).
11. Jeff Motske, *The Couples Guide to Financial Compatibility: Avoid Fights About Saving and Spending and Build a Happy and Secure Future Together* (Boston: DeCapo Press, 2015), 9–10.

12. Christopher Yalanis, MBA, CFP (Financial Advisor), in discussion with the author, May 13, 2024, Wells Fargo Advisors, Newport, RI.
13. Yalanis, discussion.

Chapter 7

1. Linda J. Ravdin, "Pondering a Prenup," *Family Advocate* 42, no. 1 (Summer 2019): 31, 34.
2. Karen Covy (Lawyer, Divorce Coach), in discussion with the author, April 30, 2024, Zoom.
3. Covy, discussion.
4. Allen Gabe, "American Academy of Matrimonial Lawyers (Surveyed)," *Allen Gabe Law, P.C.*, October 18, 2021, https://www.allengabelaw.com/prenuptial-agreements-usa-increasing/ (May 1, 2024).
5. Covy, discussion.
6. Covy, discussion.
7. *Off the Fence*, "Katy Mickelson: Can Pre and Post Nups Make Stronger Marriages?" Podcast, Karen Covy interviews Katy Mickelson, episode 71, 39 minutes, interview aired May 29, 2024. https://podcasts.apple.com/gb/podcast/katy-mickelson-can-pre-and-post-nups-make-stronger/id1678017149?i=1000657169384
8. Jennifer Bell, "The Pros and Cons of Prenups," *movingpastdivorce.com*, September 24, 2020, https://movingpastdivorce.com/2021/09/the-pros-and-cons-of-prenups/ (May 2, 2024).
9. Karen Covy, "The Ultimate Guide to Prenups: The Pros, the Cons, and How Prenups Work," *KarenCovy.com*, June 7, 2019, https://karencovy.com/the-ultimate-guide-to-prenups/ (May 3, 2024).
10. John Gottman and Julie Schwartz Gottman, *The Love Prescription: Seven Days to More Intimacy, Connection, and Joy* (New York: Penguin, 2020), 96–7.
11. Gottman and Gottman, *The Love Prescription*, 96–7.
12. Gottman and Gottman, *The Love Prescription*, 83–103.
13. Bell, "The Pros and Cons of Prenups."
14. Gottman and Gottman, *The Love Prescription*, 83–103.
15. Covy, discussion.
16. Ravdin, "Pondering a Prenup," 31, 34.
17. Covy, "The Ultimate Guide to Prenups."

18. Covy, "The Ultimate Guide to Prenups."
19. Ravdin, "Pondering a Prenup," 31, 34.
20. Covy, "The Ultimate Guide to Prenups."
21. Bell, "The Pros and Cons of Prenups."
22. Covy, discussion.
23. Covy, discussion.
24. Bell, "The Pros and Cons of Prenups."
25. *Off the Fence,* "Katy Mickelson: Can Pre and Post Nups Make Stronger Marriages?"
26. Tim Grant, Pittsburgh Post-Gazette, "Postnuptial Agreements Gaining Traction with Couples," *Working Woman Report,* September 9, 2014, https://workingwomanreport.com/postnuptial-agreements-gaining-traction-with-couples/ (August 24, 2024).
27. Covy, "The Ultimate Guide to Prenups."
28. Emily Garbinsky et al., "Love, Lies, Money: Financial Infidelity in Romantic Relationships," *Journal of Consumer Research* 47, no. 1 (June 2020): 1–24.
29. Ray Prather, Dan Ebner, and Landon Wilson, "What Every Couple Should Know About Postmarital Agreements," *Prather/Ebner/Wilson,* July 25, 2013, https://pewlaw.com/2023/07/25/what-every-couple-should-know-about-postmarital-agreements/ (August 24, 2024).
30. *Off the Fence,* "Katy Mickelson: Can Pre and Post Nups Make Marriages Stronger?"

Chapter 8

1. "Estate Planning Statistics to Read Before Writing Your Will," *Legal Zoom* June 30, 2024, https://www.legalzoom.com/articles/estate-planning-statistics (September 9, 2024).
2. David N. Bazar (Attorney, Bazar & Associates), in discussion with the author, May 7, 2024, Zoom.
3. Jeff Motske, *The Couples Guide to Financial Compatibility: Avoid Fights About Saving and Spending and Build a Happy and Secure Future Together* (Boston: DeCapo Press, 2015), 150.
4. "Estate Planning Statistics to Read Before Writing Your Will," *Legal Zoom.*
5. Bazar, discussion.
6. "A Blended Family," *AARP Magazine,* April/May 2024.

7 Bazar, discussion.
8 Sara Hostelley, "EstatePlanning Checklist: a Step by Step Guide for Peace of Mind" (June 2, 2025).
9 Pitman Law Office, *Basics of Estate Planning,* Youtube video, 10:14 minutes, aired August 24, 2023, Basics of Estate Planning—YouTube. https://video.search.yahoo.com/search/video?fr=mcafee&p=you+tube+videos+of+estate+planning+pittman+law+firm&type=E210US752G91946#id=2&vid=714018779334e5c60008de142ad947f0&action=click
10 Bazar, discussion.
11 Bazar, discussion.
12 Nicholas N. Lambros (Attorney, Lambros Law Office, LLC) in discussion with the author, August 15, 2024, Zoom.
13 Christy Bieber, "Revocable vs. Irrevocable Trusts: Differences, Pros and Cons," *Forbes Advisor,* April 22, 2024, https://www.forbes.com/advisor/legal/estate-law/revocable-vs-irrevocable-trust/ (October 14, 2024).
14 Bieber, "Revocable Vs. Irrevocable Trusts."
15 Pittman Law Office, *Basics of Estate Planning.*
16 Lambros, discussion.
17 Lambros, discussion.
18 Lambros, discussion.
19 Lambros, discussion.
20 Michelle Kaminsky, Esq. "Do I Need a Living Trust?" *Legal Zoom,* August 4, 2025. https://www.legalzoom.com/articles/do-i-need-a-living-trust
21 Lambros, discussion.
22 Kaminsky, "Do I Need a Living Trust?"
23 Bazar, discussion.
24 Tiffany Lam-Belfour, "Living Trust: Definition, How Living Trusts Work," *Nerd Wallet,* June 19, 2024. https://www.nerdwallet.com/article/investing/estate-planning/revocable-living-trust?trk_channel=web&trk_copy=Living%20Trust%3A%20Definition%2C%20How%20Living%20Trusts%20Work&trk_element=hyperlink&trk_elementPosition=5&trk_location=PostList&trk_subLocation=tiles (September 14, 2024).
25 Lambros, discussion.
26 Lambros, discussion.
27 Lambros, discussion.
28 Lambros, discussion.
29 Kaminsky, "Do I Need a Living Trust?"

30. Kaminsky, "Do I Need a Living Trust?"
31. Lam-Belfour, "Living Trusts: Definition, How Living Trusts Work."
32. Lam-Belfour, "Living Trusts: Definition, How Living Trusts Work."
33. Lambros, discussion.
34. Lam-Belfour, "Living Trusts: Definition, How Living Trusts Work."
35. Motske, *The Couples Guide to Financial Compatibility*, 154.
36. Bazar, discussion.
37. Bazar, discussion.
38. Lambros, discussion.
39. Lambros, discussion.
40. "Estate Planning Statistics to Read Before Writing Your Will," *Legal Zoom*.
41. Lambros, discussion.
42. Motske, *The Couples Guide to Financial Compatibility*, 151.

Chapter 9

1. "2 in 5 Americans Admit to Financial Infidelity Against Their Partner," *National Endowment for Financial Education (NEFE)*, November 18, 2021, https://www.nefe.org/news/2021/11/2-in-5-americans-admit-to-financial-infidelity-against-their-partner.aspx (January 6, 2024).
2. D. Bruce Ross III and Ed Coambs, "Narrative Financial Therapy Considerations in Exploring Complex Trauma and Impaired Financial Decision Making," *Journal of Financial Therapy* 9, no. 2 (2018): 36–53.
3. "2024 Fidelity Investments Couples and Money Survey," *Fidelity Investments*, February 1, 2024, https://preview.thenewsmarket.com/Previews/FINP/DocumentAssets/660835_v4.pdf (January 7, 2024).
4. "2 in 5 Americans Admit to Financial Infidelity Against Their Partner," *National Endowment for Financial Education (NEFE)*.
5. Emily N. Garbinsky et al., "Love, Lies, Money: Financial Infidelity in Romantic Relationships," *Journal of Consumer Research* 47, no. 1 (June 2020): 1–24.
6. Garbinsky et al., "Love, Lies, Money: Financial Infidelity in Romantic Relationships," 1–24.
7. Garbinsky et al., "Love, Lies, Money: Financial Infidelity in Romantic Relationships," 1–24.

8   Spencer Sherman, *The Cure for Money Madness: Break Your Bad Money Habits, Live Without Financial Stress—and Make More Money* (New York: Broadway Books, 2009), 15.

9   Terrence Real, *The New Rules of Marriage: What You Need to Know to Let Love Work* (New York: Ballentine, 2008), 47.

10 Terry Gaspard, *The Remarriage Manual: How to Make Everything Work Better the Second Time Around* (Boulder: Sounds True, 2020), 73–96.

11 Debra Kaplan and Rick Kahler, *Coupleship Inc: From Financial Conflict to Financial Intimacy* (Rapid City: Coupleship Publications, LLC, 2022), 92–6.

12 Gaspard, *The Remarriage Manual*, 73–96.

13 Gaspard, *The Remarriage Manual*, 73–96.

14 Galen Buckwater, "Are You Struggling with Financial PTSD?," *Goop*, April 26, 2018, https://goop.com/wellness/career-money/are-you-struggling-with-financial-ptsd/ (January 8, 2024).

15 Ross and Coambs, "Narrative Financial Therapy Considerations in Exploring Complex Trauma and Impaired Financial Decision Making."

16 Alex Melkumian in Julie Frago, "How to Deal with Financial Trauma," *New York Times,* July 5, 2023, https://www.nytimes.com/2023/07/05/business/financial-trauma-spending-debt.html (January 9, 2024).

17 Carol S. Dweck, *Mindset: The New Psychology of Success* (New York: Ballentine Books, 2013), 6–9.

18 Gaspard, *The Remarriage Manual*, 76–9.

Chapter 10

1   "A Portrait of Stepfamilies," *Pew Research Center*, January 13, 2011, https://www.pewresearch.org/social-trends/2011/01/13/a-portrait-of-stepfamilies/ (July 20, 2024).

2   Leslie Renyolds, "Remarriage Rate in U.S.: Geographic Variation, 2019," *Bowling Green State University, National Center for Family and Marriage Research (NCFMR)*, 2021, https://www.bgsu.edu/ncfmr/resources/data/family-profiles/reynolds-remarriaage-US-geographic-variation-2019-fp-21-18.html?fbclid=IwY2xjawGu5iVleHRuA2FlbQlxMQABHZTQQ9C271fxiuTU4mouvK8m62bh3_SbzZ2icWuWm15ULg0DhKa-IdeMyA_aem_8xV5d2i9MN1M3CN4Hnjytw (November 23, 2024).

3   Anna Fleck, "Americans Are Getting Married Older Than Ever," *Statista.com*, December 15, 2023, https://www.statista.com/chart/7031/americans-are-tying-the-knot-older-than-ever/ (November 22, 2024).

4   Christopher Yalanis, MBA, CFP (Financial Advisor), in discussion with the author, May 13, 2024, Wells Fargo Advisors, Newport, RI.

5. Patricia Schiff Estess, *Money Advice for Successful Remarriage* (Lincoln: ASJA Press, 2001), 95–117.
6. "A Portrait of Stepfamilies," *Pew Research Center*.
7. Lawerence H. Gagnon and Marilyn Coleman, "Preparing for Remarriage, Anticipating the Issues, Seeking Solutions," *Family Relationships-Interdisciplinary Journal of Applied Family Science* 38, no. 1 (January 1989): 28–33.
8. Terry Gaspard, *The Remarriage Manual: How to Make Everything Work Better the Second Time Around* (Boulder: Sounds True, 2020), 80–1.
9. Gaspard, *The Remarriage Manual*, 7–15.
10. Bradley Klontz, Sonya L. Britt, and Jennifer Mentzer, "Money Beliefs and Financial Behaviors: Development of the Klontz Money Script Inventory," *Journal of Financial Therapy* 2, no. 1 (2011): 3–21.
11. "A Portrait of Stepfamilies," *Pew Research Center*.
12. Christy Bieber, "Revealing Divorce Statistics in 2024," *Forbes Advisor*, May 30, 2024, https://www.forbes.com/advisor/legal/divorce/divorce-statistics/ (July 21, 2024).
13. E. Mavis Hetherington and John Kelly, *For Better or for Worse: Divorce Reconsidered* (New York: W. W. Norton & Company, 2002), 1–16.
14. Barbara Fishman, "The Economic Behavior of Stepfamilies," *Family Relations* 32, no. 3 (July 1983): 359–66.
15. Chelsea L. Garneau, Brian Higginbottom, and Francesca Adler, "Remarriage Beliefs as Predictors of Marital Quality and Positive Interaction in Stepcouples: An Actor-Partner Interdependence Model," *Family Process* 54, no. 4 (December 2015): 730–45.
16. Kay Pasley, Eric Sandras, and Mary Ellen Edmondson, "The Effects of Financial Management Strategies on the Quality of Family Life in Remarriage," *Journal of Family and Economic Issues* 15, no. 1 (Spring 1994): 53–70.
17. Klontz, Britt, and Mentzer, "Money Beliefs and Financial Behaviors," 3–21.
18. John Gottman and Julie Schwartz Gottman, *The Love Prescription: Seven Days to More Intimacy, Connection, and Joy* (New York: Penguin, 2020), 3–11.

Chapter 11

1. Terrence Real, *The New Rules of Marriage: What You Need to Know to Let Love Work* (New York: Ballentine, 2008), 40–1.

2. Andrew G. Marshall, *The Happy Couples Handbook—Powerful Life Hacks for a Successful Relationship* (London: Marshall Publishing, April 30, 2019), 107.

3. Dr. John Gottman and Nan Silver, *The Seven Principles for Making Marriage Work: A Practical Guide From The Countries Foremost Relationship Expert* (New York: Three Rivers Press, 2015), 22–3.

4. John Gottman and Julie Schwartz Gottman, *The Love Prescription: Seven Days to More Intimacy, Connection, and Joy* (New York: Penguin, 2020), 96–7.

5. Gottman and Gottman, *The Love Prescription*, 96–7.

6. Bradley Klontz, Sonya L. Britt, and Jennifer Mentzer, "Money Beliefs and Financial Behaviors: Development of the Klontz Money Script Inventory," *Journal of Financial Therapy* 2, no. 1 (2011): 3–21.

7. Harriet Lerner, *Marriage Rules, A Manuel for the Married and the Coupled Up* (New York: Gotham Books, 2012), 75.

8. John M. Gottman and Julie Swartz Gottman, *The Science of Couples and Family Therapy: Behind the Scenes of the Love Lab* (New York: W. W. Norton & Company, 2018), 144–59.

9. Gottman and Gottman, *The Love Prescription*, 3–11.

10. Stan Tatkin, *We Do: Saying Yes to a Relationship of Depth, True Connection, and Enduring Love* (Boulder: Sounds True, 2018), 210.

11. Gottman and Silver, *The Seven Principles for Making Marriage Work*, 164–5.

12. Daniel B. Wile, *After the Fight: Using Disagreements to Build a Stronger Relationship* (New York: Guilford Press, September 1995), 167–98.

Bibliography

Adam, Jamela. "American Savings by Generation: How Balances and Goals Vary by Age." *Forbes Advisor*, August 15, 2024. https://www.forbes.com/advisor/banking/savings/average-american-savings/.

Bell, Jennifer. "The Pros and Cons of Prenups." *Moving Past Divorce*, September 24, 2020. https://movingpastdivorce.com/2021/09/the-pros-and-cons-of-prenups/.

Bieber, Christy. "Revocable vs. Irrevocable Trusts: Differences, Pros and Cons." *Forbes Advisor*, April 22, 2024. https://www.forbes.com/advisor/legal/estate-law/revocable-vs-irrevocable-trust/.

Brennan, Chelsea. "Good Debt vs. Bad Debt." *Forbes Advisor*, January 28, 2019. https://www.forbes.com/advisor/credit-score/good-debt-vs-bad-debt/.

Covy, Karen. "Katy Mickelson: Can Pre and Post Nups Make Stronger Marriages?" Off the Fence, https://karencovy.com/podcast-katy-mickelson-pre-nuptial/.

Dew, Jeffrey, Sonya Britt, and Sandra Huston. "Examining the Relationship Between Financial Issues and Divorce." *Family Relations* 61, no. 4 (October 2012): 615–28. https://doi.org/10.1111/j.1741-3729.2012.00715.x.

Dweck, Carol S. *Mindset: The New Psychology of Success*. New York: Ballantine Books, 2007.

Fargo, Julie. "How to Deal With Financial Trauma." *New York Times*, July 5, 2023. https://www.nytimes.com/2023/07/05/business/financial-trauma-spending-debt.html.

Feldhahn, Shaunti, and Jeff Feldhahn. *Thriving in Love and Money: 5 Game-Changing Insights about Your Relationship, Your Money, and Yourself*. Minneapolis: BethanyHouse, a division of Baker Publishing Group, 2020.

Fidelity Investments. "2024 Fidelity Investments Couples and Money Survey," February 1, 2024. https://preview.thenewsmarket.com/Previews/FINP/DocumentAssets/660835_v4.pdf.

Fishman, Barbara. "The Economic Behavior of Stepfamilies." *Family Relations* 32, no. 3 (July 1983): 359–66.

Fraser, Cheryl. *Buddha's Bedroom: The Mindful Loving Path to Sexual Passion & Lifelong Intimacy*. Oakland: Reveal Press, 2018.

Ganong, Lawrence H., and Marilyn Coleman. "Preparing for Remarriage: Anticipating the Issues, Seeking Solutions." *Family Relations* 38, no. 1 (January 1989): 28–33. https://doi.org/10.2307/583606.

Garbinsky, Emily N., and Joe J. Gladstone. "The Consumption Consequences of Couples Pooling Finances." *Journal of Consumer Psychology* 29, no. 3 (July 2019): 353–69. https://doi.org/10.1002/jcpy.1083.

Garbinsky, Emily N., et al. "Love, Lies, Money: Financial Infidelity in Romantic Relationships." *Journal of Consumer Research* 47, no. 1 (June 2020): 1–24. https://doi.org/10.1093/jcr/ucz052.

Garneau, Chelsea L., Brian Higginbotham, and Francesca Adler-Baeder. "Remarriage Beliefs as Predictors of Marital Quality and Positive Interaction in Stepcouples: An Actor–Partner Interdependence Model." *Family Process* 54, no. 4 (December 2015): 730–45. https://doi.org/10.1111/famp.12153.

Gaspard, Terry. *The Remarriage Manual: How to Make Everything Work Better the Second Time Around*. Boulder: Sounds True, 2020.

Gladstone, Joe J., Emily N. Garbinsky, and Cassie Mogilner. "Pooling Finances and Relationship Satisfaction." *Journal of Personality and Social Psychology* 123, no. 6 (December 2022): 1293–314. https://doi.org/10.1037/pspi0000388.

Gottman, John, and Julie Schwartz Gottman. *The Love Prescription: Seven Days to More Intimacy, Connection, and Joy*. The Seven Days Ser, v. 1. New York: Penguin Books, 2022.

Gottman, John, and Nan Silver. *What Makes Love Last? How to Build Trust and Avoid Betrayal*. New York: Simon & Schuster, 2012.

Gottman, John, and Nan Silver. *Why Marriages Succeed or Fail: And How You Can Make Yours Last*. Riverside: Simon & Schuster, 1995.

Gottman, John Mordechai, and Julie Schwartz Gottman. *The Science of Couples and Family Therapy*. New York: W. W. Norton & Company, 2018.

Gottman, John Mordechai, and Nan Silver. *The Seven Principles for Making Marriage Work*. New York: Crown Publ, 1999.

Hetherington, Eileen Mavis, and John Kelly. *For Better or For Worse: Divorce Reconsidered*. 1st ed. New York: W. W. Norton & Company, 2002.

Hunt, Mary. *Debt-Proof Your Marriage: How to Manage Your Money Together*. Grand Rapids: Revell, a division of Baker Publishing Group, 2016.

Kaplan, Deborah, and Rick Kahler. *Coupleship, Inc.: From Financial Freedom to Financial Intimacy*. Rapid City: Coupleship Publications, LLC, 2023.

Klontz, Bradley, Sonya L. Britt, Jennifer Mentzer, and Ted Klontz. "Money Beliefs and Financial Behaviors: Development of the Klontz Money Script Inventory." *Journal of Financial Therapy* 2, no. 1 (January 1, 2011). https://doi.org/10.4148/jft.v2i1.451.

Klontz, Brad, and Ted Klontz. *Mind over Money: Overcoming the Money Disorders That Threaten Our Financial Health*. 1st ed. New York: Broadway Books, 2009.

Loudenback, Tanza. "How Much of My Paycheck Should I Save?" WSJ Buyside, September 13, 2024. https://www.wsj.com/buyside/personal-finance/financial-tips/how-much-of-my-paycheck-should-i-save.

Marshall, Andrew G. *The Happy Couples Handbook—Powerful Life Hacks for a Successful Relationship*. London: Marshall Publishing, 2019.

Martinez, Elle. *Jumpstart Your Marriage and Your Money*. Dublin: Coventry House, 2017.

McCall, Michael, and Heather J. Belmont. "Credit Card Insignia and Restaurant Tipping: Evidence for an Associative Link." *Journal of Applied Psychology* 81, no. 5 (October 1996): 609–13. https://doi.org/10.1037/0021-9010.81.5.609.

Mishra, Nirajana, Emily N. Garbinsky, and Suzanne B. Shu. "Discussing Money with the One You Love: How Financial Stress Influences Couples' Financial Communication." *Journal of Consumer Psychology*, June 15, 2024, jcpy.1430. https://doi.org/10.1002/jcpy.1430.

Motske, Jeff. *The Couple's Guide to Financial Compatibility: Avoid Fights About Spending and Saving & Build a Happy and Secure Future Together*. First edition. Boston: Da Capo Lifelong Books, 2015.

National Endowment for Financial Education (NEFE). "2 in 5 Americans Admit to Financial Infidelity Against Their Partner," November 18, 2021. https://www.nefe.org/news/2021/11/2-in-5-americans-admit-to-financial-infidelity-against-their-partner.aspx.

Pasley, Kay, Eric Sandras, and Mary Ellen Edmondson. "The Effects of Financial Management Strategies on Quality of Family Life in Remarriage." *Journal of Family and Economic Issues* 15, no. 1 (March 1994): 53–70. https://doi.org/10.1007/BF02353724.

Pew Research Center. "A Portrait of Stepfamilies," January 13, 2011. https://www.pewresearch.org/social-trends/2011/01/13/a-portrait-of-stepfamilies/.

Pokora, Becky. "Credit Card Statistics and Trends 2024." *Forbes Advisor*, March 9, 2023. https://www.forbes.com/advisor/credit-cards/credit-card-statistics/.

Ramsey, Dave. *The Total Money Makeover: A Proven Plan for Financial Fitness*. Nashville: Thomas Nelson, 2024.

Real, Terrence. *The New Rules of Marriage: What You Need to Know to Make Love Work*. Ballantine books Trade pbk. ed. New York: Ballantine Books, 2008.

Reynolds, Leslie. "Remarriage Rate in the U.S.: Geographic Variation, 2019." Bowling Green State University, 2019. https://www.bgsu.edu/ncfmr/resources/data/family-profiles/reynolds-remarriaage-US-geographic-variation-2019-fp-21-18.html.

Ross, D. Bruce, and Ed Coambs. "The Impact of Psychological Trauma on Finance: Narrative Financial Therapy Considerations in Exploring Complex Trauma and Impaired Financial Decision Making." *Journal of Financial Therapy* 9, no. 2 (2018). https://doi.org/10.4148/1944-9771.1174.

Schiff Estess, Patricia. *Money Advice for Successful Remarriage*. Lincoln: ASJA Press, 2001.
Semuels, Alana. "Why We Overspend." *Time*, March 28, 2024.
Sherman, Spencer D. *The Cure for Money Madness: Break Your Bad Money Habits, Live without Financial Stress-and Make More Money!* New York: Broadway Books, 2009.
Tatkin, Stan. *We Do: Saying Yes to a Relationship of Depth, True Connection, and Enduring Love*. Boulder: Sounds True, 2018.
Warren, Elizabeth, and Amelia Warren Tyagi. *All Your Worth: The Ultimate Lifetime Money Plan*. Riverside: Free Press, 2005.
White, Martha C. "Why a 60/30/10 Budget Could Be the New 50/30/20." *Time*, March 15, 2024. https://time.com/6916834/how-to-budget-60-30-10/.
Wile, Daniel B. *After the Fight: Using Your Disagreements to Build a Stronger Relationship*. New York: Guilford Press, 1993.

Index

50/30/20 budgeting method 90–4
   categories 90–1
   ways to troubleshoot issues
      with 92–4
60/30/10 budget plan 91–2

abundance 174
abundance mindset 2, 12
adverse financial events 77
Alipay 102
All Your Worth: The Ultimate Lifetime Money Plan (Warren) 90
American Academy of Matrimonial Lawyers 135
American College of Financial Services 91
American Psychological Association 41–2, 105
Apple Pay 102
attorney hiring, estate planning 156–7
auto loans with high interest 98

bad debt 95–111
   characterization 98
   credit card debt 96, 104–10
   examples of 98
   financial technology and 102–3
   good debt vs. 97–101
   shopping addiction and 103–4
   smart ways to get out of 108–10
Bazar, David 153–7, 166

Bell, Jennifer 137
Bieber, Christy 164, 198
big purchases, savings plan for 123
Braverman, Beth 117, 121
Brennan, Chelsea 97–8
Britt, Sonja L. 19
budget, couples 72–3
   50/30/20 90–4
   money to save in 93
   money values and 72–90
   realistic 77
   relationship with money and 78
   sticking to 77
   understanding of money dynamics for 78
   value-based 84–90
   ways to troubleshoot issues with 92–4
Budgeting for Couples 101 (Graves) 93

certified financial planner (CFP) 65
code word 50
Coleman, Marilyn 192
common-pot system 199–201
communication
   about money 61–2
   financial 3–5
   tool 50

Communication Pledge 71, 81, 112
compromise
    about remarriage
        finances 195–7
    to manage conflict 215–18
    steps to reach 217–18
conflict about money
        management 205–22
    avoid criticizing partner 214–15
    compromise 215–18
    emotions in 208–10
    pursuer-distancer dynamic and finances 210–14
    repair attempts 207–8
    repair from regrettable incidents 219–22
    by repairing after regrettable incidents 219
constructive money 3
contempt 80
control freak 175
The Couple's Guide to Financial Compatibility (Motske) 99
Coupleship, Inc. (Kaplan and Kahler) 70, 178
Covid-19 pandemic 102
Covy, Karen 132, 145, 147
credit cards 24, 31, 45, 64, 100–1, 103, 108, 114, 174
    abusing 1, 6–7, 19
    as cash 99, 103, 106, 119, 172, 181–4, 217
    debt 96, 104–10
        due to overspending with 96–7
        financial stress and 104–5
        personal stress and 105
        reasons to get rid of 104–6
        surviving lean times and 105
        way to eliminate 106–10

    interest on 108
    rewards 65
criticism 80
The Cure for Money Madness (Sherman) 52

debt 98
    credit cards 96, 104–10
    good *vs.* bad 97–101
    six ways to talk to partner about 99–101
Debt Avalanche method 106–8
debt-proof living 105–6
Debt-Proof Your Marriage (Hunt) 105
Debt Snowball method 106–8
defensiveness
    about money, stop being 48–52
    dynamics of 48
    financial harmony in marriage, impact on 45–6
    five tips to curb 50–1
    mechanisms impact finances 45–6
        denial 45
        identification 46–7
        intellectualization 46
        projection 46
        rationalization 45–6
    during money talks 47–52
    pattern of 48
    self-protection and 48
denial, defense mechanism 45
disagreements about finances 11
divorce 80, 173
documents for estate planning 157–60
driving-related expenses, savings plan for 120–1
Dweck, Carol S. 183

emergency fund 38–9, 114–15
emotions, money and 37

Employer Health Benefits Survey (Kaiser Family Foundation) 77–8
entertainment, savings plan on 121–2
estate planning 151–70
  about 153–5
  attorney hiring 156–7
  Bazar, David on 153–7, 166
  beyond formal 165
  guardianship issues 166
  irrevocable trusts 164–5
  Kaminsky, Michelle on 160–1, 163
  key documents for 157–60
  Lambros, Nicholas A. on 157–63
  Motske, Jeff on 153
  process of 155–60
  to provide safeguards for future 153–5
  provisions 154
  revocable trusts 157–8, 164
  things that can go wrong with 167–70
  troubleshooting tips for smoother 169–70
  for unexpected 151–70
  will-centered plan vs. trust-centered plan 160–3
Estess, Patricia Schiff 190–1

family backgrounds 16–17
  communication, impacts on 17
  financial style, impacts on 17, 42–3
  money script, impacts on 17
feedback loop 48
Feldhahn, Jeff 40–1, 79
Feldhahn, Shaunti 40–1, 79
finances
  disclosure about 39–42
  with partner, advantages of merging 60–1

financial closeness 52–4
financial communication 3–5
financial conflicts 39
financial disparities 37
financial harmony in marriage, defense mechanisms impact 45–6
financial health
  achieve 13, 25, 29, 35–6, 41, 52, 60
  adverse financial events and 77
  bad debt and 95–111
  budget for 72, 77–94
  essentials of 7
  with joint accounts 61
  power of money scripts on 19
  savings plan for 111–28
financial infidelity 5, 38, 62, 97, 101, 111, 171–86
  consequences of 174
  control issues in 175–6
  courageous, transparent, and honest conversations with money 183–4
  healing from 184–6
  in marriage/committed relationship 183–4
  privacy vs. money secrets 178–9
  reasons 174–5
  red flags of 179–80
  unnoticed 176–8
financial intimacy 5, 39, 52
  ask open-ended questions for 54
  financial closeness for 52–4
  financial communication, ask open-ended questions 54–5
  low-conflict conversations lead to 52–7
  tips to boost 55–7
financial issues 1, 5–6

financial literacy   14
financial obligations   42, 71, 190, 194
financial plan   111–28; see also savings
financial post traumatic stress disorder (PTSD)   171–2, 180–2
financial safety net   111
financial security   20
financial stress   5, 36, 41–2, 98–9, 103–5, 180, 200, 211
financial style   2, 6, 11–16, 28–33, 39–40.
   family backgrounds impacts on   16–17, 39–43
   incompatibility, deal with   33–6
   quiz   29–33
   scoring procedures   33
Financial Style Quiz   29–33, 53, 112, 197, 203, 209
financial technology   102–3
Financial Therapy   185
financial transparency   70
financial well-being   12
   of LGBTQ+ American couples   78
Finke, Michael   91
Fishman, Barbara   63, 199
flashfood app   117
Fleck, Anna   188
For Better or for Worse: Divorce Reconsidered (Hetherington)   198
Fraser, Cheryl   50
frictionless payments   102–3

gambling addiction   185
Ganong, Lawrence H.   192
Garbinsky, Emily N.   42, 97, 173
Garneau, Chelsea L.   200
gasoline, savings plan for   120–1
Gengler, Amanda   117, 121

Gladstone, Joe J.   42, 60
good debt
   vs. bad debt   97–101
   forms   97
Google Pay   102
Gottman, John   48, 54, 56, 60, 80, 142, 207, 211
   on causes of divorce   80
   The Love Prescription   142
   on money talk   60
Gottman, Julie Schwartz   56, 60
   The Love Prescription   142
Gottman, Julie Swartz   142
Graves, Nora   93
groceries shopping
   at discount   117
   lists   117
   loyalty card   118
   money saving on   117–20
   new store brands to buy   117–18
   rewards for purchasing   118
   self-checkout at stores   118
   shop at different stores   118
   store's app   118
   tips to help grocery shoppers save money   117–19
   use coupons   118
guardianship issues, estate planning   166

healthcare directive   158–9
health insurance plan   78
Hetherington, E. Mavis   198
Holbrook, Alice   64
holographic wills   156
house poor   97
Hunt, Mary   105–6

imbalance in relationship   39, 40
intellectualization, defense mechanism   46
irrevocable trusts   164–5

joint accounts 70–2; see also
money management
systems (used by
couples)
essential steps to set up 70–1
Generation Z and 71
marriage and 61
millennial couples and 71
tips for developing a
sustainable 72
"us against the problem"
mindset and 62
Jumpstart Your Marriage and Your Money (Martinez) 106–7

Kahler, Rick 70, 178
Kaiser Family Foundation 77–8
Kaminsky, Michelle 160–1, 163
Kaplan, Debra 70, 178
Klontz, Brad 18–27, 40
Klontz, Ted 18–27, 40
Klontz Money Script Inventory-
Revised (KMSI-R) 20–7
scale interpretation 23–7
scoring procedures 22
KMSI-R; see Klontz Money Script
Inventory-Revised

Lam-Balfour, Tiffany 161–2, 164
Lambros, Nicholas A. 157–63, 166
Lerner, Harriet 210–11
LGBTQ+ American couples,
financial well-being
of 78
lifestyle changes 93–4
living trust; see revocable trust
loans
auto 98
marriage 15–16
payday 98
Loudenback, Tanza 115
The Love Prescription (Gottman
and Gottman) 142
low-conflict money talks 42–5

Mack, Freddie 91
mad money 93
for nonessential items 71
marriage 131
financial harmony in,
defensiveness
impact 45–6
financial infidelity in 173,
183–4
joint accounts and 61
loan 15–16
money and 15–16, 59–73
money script in 27–8
postnuptial agreement
and 131, 148–50
prenuptial agreement
and 131–48
savings plan improve
relationship in 124–7
second 187–204
steps to dealing with financial
infidelity in 186
Marshall, Andrew W. 207
Martinez, Elle 106–7
Massachusetts Office of
Consumer Affairs 98
Mathieu, Christine 78
Melkumian, Alex 180
Mentzer, Jennifer 19
Mickelson, Katy 136–7, 148
Mind Over Money (Klontz and
Klontz) 18
Mindset (Dweck, Carol S.) 183
Mishra, Nirajana et al. 12, 40
mistrust 62, 143, 174, 194
mobile payment apps 102
money
attitude about 2
avoidance 19, 23
beliefs 12–16
constructive 3
courageous, transparent, and
honest conversations
with 183–4

emotions and   37
family backgrounds awareness
    and   16–17
histories   11–16
issues with   1, 5–6
KMSI-R   20–7
in long-term relationships/
    marriages   1
marriage and   15–16
mindsets about   12, 16–17
relationship with   12
saving   2
as sign of success   12
spending   1–2
status   19–20, 23, 43
talks (see money talks)
values   13, 72–90
vigilance   18–20, 24, 26–9,
    35, 37–40, 43–4, 65–6,
    68, 77, 80, 82, 103, 124,
    168, 172, 176, 191, 195,
    197, 203, 209–11
worship   19, 23, 38
*Money Advice for Your
    Successful Remarriage*
    (Estess)   190–1
money laundering   93
money leak   92
Money Madness (Sherman)   5
money management systems
    (used by couples)   59–73
finances with partner,
    advantages of
    merging   60–1
one-pot model   63
selection of   61–2
three-pot model   63–70
tips for developing
    sustainable   72–3
two-pot model   63
money script   12–16, 18–20
awareness about   27–8
categories of   19

family backgrounds impacts
    on   16–17
identification of   18–20
incompatibility, deal with   33–6
KMSI-R   20–7
in marriage/relationship   27–8
money avoidance   19
money status   19–20, 43
money vigilance   18–20, 24,
    26–9, 35, 37–40, 43–4,
    65–6, 68, 77, 80, 82,
    103, 124, 168, 172, 176,
    191, 195, 197, 203,
    209–11
money worship   19
Money Script Inventory   197,
    203, 209
money talks   39–44
defensiveness during   47–52
for financial intimacy   39, 52–7
ask open-ended
    questions   54
financial closeness   52–4
financial communication,
    ask open-ended
    questions   54–5
low-conflict conversations
    about money   55–7
tips to boost   55–7
five tips to curb defensiveness
    for constructive   50–1
low-conflict   42–5
to strengthen couple's
    intimacy   52
ways to achieve financial
    goals   39–41
money value differences   82–4
money values   72–90
Moody's Analytics   91
mortgage   97
payment   97
refinance   97
Motske, Jeff   61, 99, 153, 165,
    167

National Center for Family and Marriage Research 188
National Endowment for Financial Education (NEFE) 171–2
The New Rules of Marriage (Real) 49, 175
Northwestern Mutual study 115

one-pot money management system 63, 199
   disadvantages of 65
online money management 61
oral wills 156
overspending 38, 111–12

Pasley, Kay 68
payday loans 98
payoff method 106–8
PayPal 64, 102, 119
personal stress 105
Pew Research Center 187
physical infidelity 173
Pittman, Amy 156, 158
plant edible perennials 119
Pokora, Becky 98
postnuptial agreement 148–50
   definition 131
   Mickelson, Katy on 136–7, 148
   vs. prenuptial agreement 148–50
   reasons for 148–50
pour-over will 162–3
power of attorney 159
prenuptial agreement 131–48
   advantages of 138–40
   attorney hiring for 147
   Bell, Jennifer on 137
   common questions about 145–8
   conversation, way to initiate 141–3
   coverage 136
   Covy, Karen on 132, 145, 147
   custody/child support and 146
   definition of 145
   disadvantages of 140–1
   discuss reasons to partner about 143–4, 145–6
   fair 137–8
   legal advice on 147
   need for 132–7, 145
   vs. postnuptial agreement 148–50
   process 147
   recent increase in 135–6
   "softened start up" approach for 142–3
   step-relative and 146
   voluntary 137–8, 146
   for wealthy people 146
   what to do if your partner wants 144
privacy vs. money secrets 178–9
projection, defense mechanism 46
pursuer-distancer dynamic 210–14

QuickBooks, online money management 61

Ramsey, Dave 41, 95, 107, 114, 116
   on emergency fund 114
   on retirement planning 115–16
Ramsey Solutions 41
rationalization, defense mechanism 45–6
Real, Terrence 49, 175
red flags of financial infidelity 179–80
remarriage finances 187–204
   building financial trust in stages 193–5
   compromise about 195–7

economic challenges 190–2
loving and open discussion about, tips for 203–4
as major stress in stepfamilies 192–3
The Remarriage Manual 177, 179
remarried couples 155
building financial trust in stages 193–5
divorce rate 198
economic challenges for 190–2
money management 198–201
"us against the problem" mindset in 201–4
retirement
definition 116
savings plan for 115–17
tips for planning 115–16
revocable trusts 157–8, 164
Right Trap 207
Rocket Money app, online money management 61

saving habit 2
savings 111–28
Americans 111
for big purchases 123
for couples, suggestions to boost 125–7
for driving-related expenses 120–1
emergency fund 114–15
on entertainment 121–2
for gasoline 120–1
for groceries 117–20
improve marriage/committed relationship 124–7
for low-cost/free 122–3
overview 111–14
for retirement 115–17
spending less 127–8
on traveling 121–2

Saying Yes to a Relationship of Depth, True Connection, and Enduring Love (Tatkin) 214
scarcity mindset 1–2, 11–12
Schiff, David 117, 121
second marriages 187–204; *see also* remarriage finances
self-defeating money behaviors 19
self-protection, defensiveness and 48
self-righteous approach 207
Semuels, Alana 95, 102–3
The Seven Principles for Making Marriage Work (Gottman) 207
Sherman, Spencer 5, 52, 174
shopping addiction 103–4
"softened start up" approach 142–3
spending habit 2
spending less 112, 127–8
"Stress in America 2023" (APA) 41–2

Tatkin, Stan 214
three-pot money management system 63–70, 199–200
practical option for couples 66
in stepfamilies and blended families 64–8
vs. two-pot money management system 64–9
Thriving in Love and Money (Feldhahn and Feldhahn) 40, 79
traveling
off season 121–2
savings plan on 121–2
trusts 39, 70

centered plan   160–3
document   164
irrevocable   164–5
marriage and   172
remarriage financial   193–5
revocable   157–8, 164
romantic relationships
   and   172
two-pot money management
   system   63, 199
   challenges of   66
   encourages both cooperation
      and personal
      autonomy   68
   practical option for
      couples   66
   in stepfamilies and blended
      families   64–8
   vs. three-pot systems   64–9

unnoticed financial infidelity   176–8
"us against each other"
   mindset   11, 193
"us against the problem"
   mindset   6, 11, 41

adoption   193
joint accounts and   62
in remarried couples   201–4
to save money   113

value-based budget   84–90
values about money   72–90
Vasel, Kathryn   77
Vaughn, Harlan   98
Venmo   64, 102, 119

Warren, Elizabeth   90, 91
   50/30/20 budgeting
      method   90–4
   *All Your Worth: The Ultimate
      Lifetime Money
      Plan*   90
White, Martha C.   91
Wile, Daniel B.   48
will   158
will-centered plan vs. trust-
      centered estate
      plan   160–3

Yalanis, Christopher   98, 188
Yuqian XU   102

About the Author

Terry Gaspard, MSW, LICSW is a licensed therapist with over thirty years of clinical experience specializing in children, individuals, families, marriage, remarriage, and divorce. She's also an author, nonfiction writer, and college instructor. Terry is a popular speaker and blogger who often offers commentary on relationship issues, marriage, remarriage, and divorce. Two of her research studies on the long-term impact of divorce have been published in the *Journal of Divorce and Remarriage*. Her book *The Remarriage Manual: How to Make Everything Work Better the Second Time Around* was published in 2020. Terry's other book, *Daughters of Divorce: Overcome the Legacy of Your Parents' Breakup and Enjoy a Happy, Long-lasting Relationship*, was published in 2016. She's the owner of movingpastdivorce.com and is a regular contributor to *The Gottman Institute Blog*, Patheos.com, marriage.com, and the goodmenproject.com.